FROM RAGS TO RICHES

BOOKS BY JOHN TEBBEL

Biography

From Rags to Riches: Horatio Alger, Jr., and The American Dream
The Inheritors
An American Dynasty
George Horace Lorimer and The Saturday Evening Post
The Marshall Fields
The Life and Good Times of William Randolph Hearst

History

The American Indian Wars (with Keith Jennison)
George Washington's America
The Battle for North America (editor)

Novels

The Conqueror
Touched with Fire
A Voice in the Streets

Medical

The Magic of Balanced Living
Your Body: How to Keep It Healthy

Anthology

The Epicure's Companion (with Ann Seranne)

Textbook

Makers of Modern Journalism (with Kenneth N. Stewart)

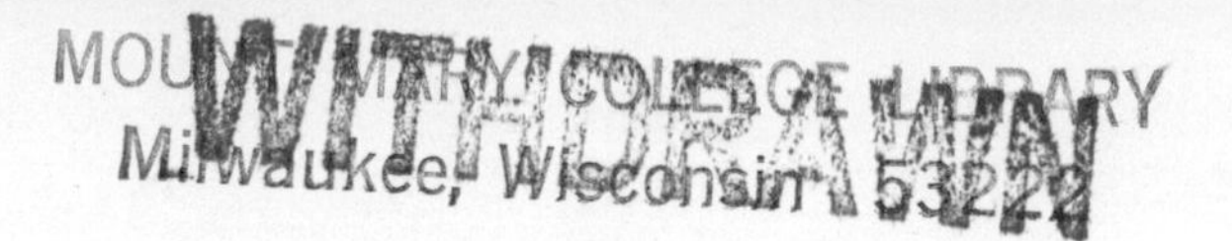

JOHN TEBBEL

FROM RAGS TO RICHES

Horatio Alger, Jr., and The American Dream

The Macmillan Company, New York

First Printing

Printed in the United States of America

The Macmillan Company, New York
Collier-Macmillan Canada, Ltd., Toronto, Ontario

Library of Congress catalog card number: 63-16134

DESIGN BY R. A. KASELER

AUTHOR'S NOTE

Thirty-five years ago a young editor named Herbert R. Mayes wrote a book called *Alger, a Biography Without a Hero*. It was the first biography of Horatio Alger, Jr., and until the present volume has remained the only one. Mr. Mayes, of course, went on to become one of the best and most distinguished editors in magazine history and today is president of the McCall Corporation.

It is a tribute to the research he did at twenty-eight to note that it can hardly be improved upon nearly four decades later. The primary sources of Alger material are meager, indeed, but Mr. Mayes appears to have examined all of them, and no new original material has turned up in the intervening decades. In preparing his book Mr. Mayes also had access to the memories of Alger's family and friends alive at the time, and now dead.

In respect to these materials, Mr. Mayes's research was definitive and I have drawn upon it freely for the biographical section of this book, supplementing it with the secondary source material, also extremely sparse, which is available. The interpretations of these materials are, naturally, my own. For the further study of Alger I have relied upon the scanty critical work which has been published, but primarily on a reading and examination of some fifty Alger books.

I am grateful to the staff members of the New York Public Library and The New York Historical Society who were so helpful to me in the research for this volume, and to the critics and other literary figures who have so generously discussed with me the place of Horatio Alger, Jr., in the stream of American literature.

JOHN TEBBEL

New York, March 4, 1963

CONTENTS

PART ONE

THE RISE AND FALL OF THE AMERICAN DREAM

CHAPTER 1

TO LOOK back on Horatio Alger, Jr., from the vantage point of the twentieth century is to contemplate not only one of the curiosities of American publishing but to view, from a truer perspective, that phenomenon we have come to know as "the American Dream."

What *is* this American Dream that has served so well in our language as to be a household phrase? Obviously it has a variety of meanings, and it has been further obscured by its usefulness as a political catch phrase. The annals of campaign oratory, and of afterdinner speechmaking, are replete with its usage. Like an enormous umbrella, "the American Dream" shelters everything in American life that typifies the rise of the United States from British colony to world power.

In contemporary terms the dream is often regarded as our "image," the aspect we present, or believe we present, to the people of other countries, and endless controversy surrounds it. The fallacy in this concept is that it does not take into account the radically different "images" held by differing groups of Americans. To span the extremes, an elder member of the John Birch Society in California has an entirely different idea of the American image than a New York City intellectual. A far more important difference is the popular vision of the nation, nurtured by the stereotypes that pass for American history in our educational system, and the general view held by those who have made a professional study of that history. Certainly it can be said, in any case, that there is no collective view of America which would constitute a commonly held image, an agreed-upon "American Dream."

To many people the phrase is a synonym for the democratic vista itself, for the ideas and principles embodied in the Declaration of Independence and the Constitution. It is widely believed by millions of Americans that until the Founding Fathers set forth these documents, the human race had never attempted to govern itself in a democratic society, and our dream has been to demonstrate to mankind that it could be done. Others go even further. They are convinced that democracy began as soon as the "searchers for religious freedom," as they are termed, landed on our shores.

These are dreams, indeed, but even as dreams they lack the nearly universal acceptance which attends the one idea dominant in American life for a hundred and fifty years or longer—that the United States is a place where anyone, no matter what his origins, no matter how poor and obscure he may be, can rise to fame and fortune. It is possible to contemplate the American baby in his swaddling clothes and envision him as President of the nation. It is possible in other countries, too, but to the average American the rise from obscurity to fame is peculiarly the special virtue of his country.

It was the tremendous nineteenth-century expansion of the United States which gave birth to this idea and made it secure in our folklore. In the eighteenth century we had been a nation guided and directed by an intellectual aristocracy of comparatively rich landowners. Then, as Jefferson's vision of an agrarian society began to crumble before the swift and formidable growth of an industrial economy, the era of the common man truly began. To every fresh immigrant from Ireland, Germany or elsewhere the promise shone bright and true: this was a country where the rigid social and economic structures of older societies did not prevail, and a humble immigrant could rise from the streets of New York, Boston or Philadelphia to the splendid mansions which were beginning to line the avenues of those cities.

They were the mansions of businessmen, from Fifth Avenue and eventually westward to Prairie Avenue and Nob Hill. Thus the dream was not political, but commercial. The power of money was the generally desired end, not the power of political influence. Let the politicians grub about City Hall, said the smart young men on the way up. Their petty corruptions were as nothing compared with the fortunes to be made in supplying a new nation with goods, or developing its natural resources. The politicians were overshadowed by the titans of business, and were in their power, by and large. No man could foresee the day in another century when a great corporation could boast that it owned the United States Senate, but the way for this mockery was being prepared by the politicians in state legislatures and in Congress who owed their status to the powerful businessmen who put them there.

The protesters against the system were already at work early in the century. Publishers like Horace Greeley were embracing mild Socialist philosophies exported from Europe. Greeley and others were encouraging the farmers to continue exerting the kind of power that had put Andrew Jackson in the White House. Labor unions were beginning to organize and slowly gather strength for the bloody wars of the century's last three decades. The reformers in government had begun to throw up legislative breastworks against the assault of the trusts. The sins of the rich were attacked in the newspapers from the day James Gordon Bennett's New York *Herald* appeared on the streets, and there were a few, but lamentably few, men in influential pulpits who measured the men of money against the needle's eye and found them wanting.

Protest was far from absent, and it led in time to great struggles in our national life, but through it all the original dream remained oddly undiminished. At the beginning of the century there had been virtually no tarnish on it. To be successful in business, and if possible to be rich, was the honorable path which led straight ahead for every young man entering the business world. Only the queer and dedicated became preachers and teachers; doctors and lawyers were already on a higher level than these underprivileged classes.

By the time the century ended, and the rich and privileged were reeling under the assaults of powerful unions, liberal ministers, crusading publishers like Pulitzer and Hearst, and the growing corps of muckrakers, the dream shone forth as brightly as it had at the beginning. It survived nearly intact into the next century, and soon, during the boom years of the twenties, it became almost a religion in America, with high priests in Wall Street and its litanies recited every month in mass circulation magazines like *The Saturday Evening Post* and the *American.*

The dream ended with the Crash—or so it seemed. The high priests leaped from their own temples; the litanies were dropped from the magazines and new formulas replaced them. For nearly a decade young men entering business, with few exceptions, did not think much about rising to fame and fortune; they considered themselves fortunate to have jobs. The literature of protest, which had been gathering force since the turn of the century, depicted America as a nation built on false values. For a time the American Dream appeared almost unfashionable.

It was restored by the great leap forward which followed the Second World War, but the restoration was not the original, nor was it likely ever again to resemble the free and unfettered vision of the nineteenth century. The reasons were numerous and complicated, but they had to do chiefly with the sheer bigness of America. Giant corporations were simply too large to be under the control of a single man. The committee, the "team," was the mainspring of business, as it was in government, in mass communications (which had replaced that plain girl, journalism), and even in labor unions. If there was a fading image in American life, it was the disappearing figure of the rugged, driving entrepreneur, the epitome of the nineteenth century, now replaced by the organization man.

The American Dream has not disappeared from our national life, but the vehicle has been changed, the road upward is cluttered with traffic signals, and the terminal at the end of it is no longer designed for single occupancy but more nearly resembles a parking lot.

When the propagandists of Big Business talk about the validity of the American Dream today, and insist that America is still a nation where an obscure young man can start at the bottom and end as chairman of the board, they are telling the truth. It *is* still possible, and it is accomplished over and over. But the difference between the means employed and the ends accomplished today, as compared with the means and ends of the last century, are as different as life itself is different in the Space Age.

We have been told often enough about the road from rags to riches in contemporary society, and it is strikingly different from the nineteenth-century road. For one thing, it no longer begins with rags. The moguls of the last century were almost entirely, with few exceptions, poor boys who began at the absolute bottom of the ladder; most of them had only a perfunctory education. Today a slum child without schooling could rise to the top only if he were an authentic genius, or if he had the quick and sensational success which comes to some figures in show business. But there is little resemblance between the cretinous young man, yesterday's busboy, who becomes a teen-age idol overnight by means of a million-record sale and the traditional Alger hero. Both, one may add, are equally unreal.

The road from bottom to top is as well marked now, in its own way, as it was for the Alger heroes who dreamed the American Dream. There is, first of all, the good school, or in any case the college degree. The good school, with its resulting friendships and alumni connections, may make the road smoother and more certain in some occupations. It is not essential, however. The boy who is graduated from an unsocial, unglamorous Middle Western campus, without visible status, may nevertheless be tapped by the eager industry recruiters. The young scientists go quickly into their own world. The others are locked neatly into the organizational system, with its well charted route from trainee to junior executive. Whether at that point the junior becomes a senior, aimed at the highest chair of all, depends on a number of considerations which are becoming so familiar as to be an accepted way of life, despite their sometimes horrifying implications.

This system is deplored by intellectuals, and quite naturally defended by everyone with a vested interest in it. Whether or not it is essentially corrosive, any major change in it, supposing such an unlikely event, would certainly not be in the direction of the past. In spite of the Old Guard's occasional nostalgia for the laissez faire of yesterday, they would not really want to return to it, even if it were possible. Things are a good deal more secure at the top than they were in the nineteenth century, just as they are at the bottom and on the rungs in between, and the organization of modern business is a vast improvement in every respect over the disorganized, cutthroat practices of the robber barons.

Indeed, there is substantial reason to believe that the American Dream was in itself a chimera, without real substance, a delusion so strongly held that no one dared question it, and so beloved for itself that no one wanted to doubt it. Even now, in the minds of some conservatives, it is vaguely un-American to deny its validity. To them it is like saying that America is not really the land of opportunity, with the implication that there is something wrong with the operation of people's capitalism. But it is no denigration of America's unequaled role in history as a developing country, inexhaustibly abundant with opportunity, to argue that the concept embodied in the American Dream was false to the core.

What was, in fact, the essence of this dream? Henry Steele Commager has stated it succinctly in *The American Mind*. The stories Alger told of poor boys who made good, he says, were alike in "preaching the same moral in language so simple that even the most immature mind could not fail to grasp it: opportunities lie all about you; success is material and is the reward of virtue and of work." Millions of Americans read and believed this thesis, because they wanted so desperately to believe it.

In the twentieth century, the dream as expounded by Alger was no longer the belief of millions but the transmuted property of a conservative bloc in Big Business, with an auxiliary in the advertising industry. The propaganda and practices of this coalition, as Commager says, "exalted the worst manifestations of individualism, pandered to the worst instincts of jealousy, snobbery, and fear, and reduced competition to its most primitive form."

Thus the rise and fall of the American Dream. How it became so firmly implanted in the nation's consciousness, and Alger's implausible role as its chief prophet, deserve a closer examination which may serve to demonstrate why it was doomed from the beginning.

II

Horatio Alger, Jr., had been writing for a dozen years when, in 1868, he began to produce the books which still make his name a household word nearly a century later. His first book, *Bertha's Christmas Vision,* in 1856, had been a modest collection of sentimental stories and poetry. A year later appeared the narrative poem, *Nothing to Do*, generally attributed to Alger but published anonymously and not positively identified as his own. It was heavy-handed social satire, in the vein of the popular magazines. During the later years of the war Alger could be seen groping toward his true métier with the publication of two boys' books, drawn from life and designed quite frankly to be inspirational literature for the home front. As propaganda these books were primitive, but as heralds of an emerging writer for the masses they were impressive.

After the war, Alger made two curious detours on his own road from rags to riches. In 1866 he produced *Helen Ford*, the only book he ever wrote with a girl as principal character. It is a strange book in many respects, and merits the more extended examination it will be given in a later chapter, but again it was an attempt to establish a formula, although Alger probably did not do so consciously. If he failed, it was because poor little Helen could not follow the still unblazed trail to fame and fortune in an antifeminist society. By the use of his usual outrageous plot devices, however, Alger was able to elevate her from penniless obscurity as a child to a prosperous young girlhood. There he left her. He could not deal with the problems of adults, fictional or real.

Yet it was the adults for whom he yearned to write—the old story of the comedian who aspires to play Hamlet. Alger wanted to be known as a serious novelist, and his first attempt at it was his second detour, in 1866, with the publication of *Timothy Crump's Ward*. It was entirely typical of Alger's weak character that he did not have the courage to sign his name; the book was published anonymously. As an adult novel it was a failure, even by the popular standards of the day. The characters were incredible caricatures of real people, and the plot so unbelievable that it surpassed most of Alger's efforts in this respect. When the book appeared later, slightly rewritten as *Jack's Ward*, a boys' book, the rewrite appeared to have been hardly necessary.

All these false starts were only preliminaries to the flood of books which began in 1868 with *Ragged Dick*, and continued to flow with posthumous material, forgeries and imitations long after Alger died in 1899. The last Alger book of undoubted authenticity did not appear until 1908.

Of the 117 bona fide Alger titles which reached print between hard covers, and of which only 106 were actually written by Alger, nearly all are derived directly or indirectly from the author's involvement with the Newsboys' Lodging House, where he found an endless source of material and a psychological satisfaction which could well be the subject of psychoanalytic theorizing. Alger loved these boys, spent most of his later years with them, and through their confidences learned in detail about the lives of street urchins, both before and after they came to New York. These facts, which he used freely in his fiction with little alteration, comprise a valuable social documentation which is often reminiscent of Dickens. Unfortunately, Alger had no compulsion to explore and probe, nor did he have the intellect to make his books the major reform novels they might have been. He could do no more than cast his stories into a single mold, and repeat the pattern endlessly because it was so wildly successful and the public clamored for more.

Why did they clamor? The answer is as complicated as the dimensions of the clamor itself, which was not as broadly based as many people suppose. Frank Luther Mott has pointed out that Alger was not a best-selling author in his lifetime, with a single exception. At the time of his death, his total sales were not more than 800,000, a respectable figure but hardly to be compared with those of real best-selling writers whose sales were more than a million copies for a single title. Alger's only best-seller was *Ragged Dick*, and that appeared at a time when a book had to sell only 300,000 to qualify, under the sensible ground rules which Dr. Mott has laid down.

The big Alger sales did not come until the paperback publishers began to take him up after his death, first in twenty-five-cent editions and finally in the dime novel format. Alger enthusiasts have departed so far from reality as to estimate his total sales as high as three hundred million, a figure not to be taken seriously. One hundred million has been accepted as the correct number by some literary historians, but this is only slightly less exaggerated. Mott estimates the total at no more than sixteen or seventeen million, an estimate in which other experts concur. Single titles often sold between one hundred and two hundred thousand copies each, but others did not reach six figures.

Of course sales figures do not accurately reflect the number of people who read Horatio Alger's books. From the beginning they were passed from boy to boy, read assiduously by whole families of children, and handed down from one generation to another. Many a boy reading Alger in the twenties was turning the pages of a volume printed in the 1880's and passed on to him through that nearly vanished institution, the family library. Consequently it is possible to estimate that between 1868 and the present there may have been as many as fifty million Americans, possibly more, who read an Alger book. Since they were mostly young Americans in their teens, Alger's influence is inestimable.

If we attempt to assess it, however, we come back once more to the riddle of his popularity. Did growing boys in an expanding America love the rags-to-riches formula because it excited their ambition and moved them to emulate it? That is the popular belief, but a closer reading and analysis of the Alger volumes leads to the suspicion that this was not the case. For beneath the stilted prose, the ponderous moralizing and the melodramatic plotting of Horatio Alger's books lurks the astonishing implication that the author himself did not believe in the American Dream and distrusted his own formula. He may have been selling something quite different to his young audience, whose members recognized it and whose elders were too obtuse to see beyond "Holy Horatio's" moral preachments.

Consider the stuff of which these books are made, and the kind of audience which was reading them so avidly. Fundamentally Alger's stories were about life in New York, except for those whose locales were California, Australia, the world of the traveling circus or some other equally strange and exciting environment. What could have been more fascinating to the millions of boys in the villages, towns and cities of America, earthbound by the lack of airplanes and automobiles? As late as the end of the first quarter of this century, there remained those millions in the small towns and on the farms who thought of New York City as their fathers and grandfathers had envisioned it—as the great, wicked metropolis, full of forbidden pleasures, the eyrie of the rich and powerful, the center of the universe. The ubiquitous automobile, commercial air travel and the Second World War shattered that image, although tradition is still strong enough to draw more tourists annually to New York than to any other American city.

For his eager provincial readers, Alger wrote about New York with something of the same wonder he had brought to the city from his native Massachusetts. It *was* a great and wicked city in those days, whereas it is now merely great, and more sin to the square inch can be found in the provincial's own hometown than in any comparable area of Manhattan. There was little of the real New York in Alger's books, but there was enough of it to titillate his young and unsophisticated readers. He gave them the sordid details as long as relations between men and women were not concerned; the prudery of his tales approaches the pathological. His descriptions of life in the city are parochial and almost wholly lacking in insight, with a few exceptions, but since his readers had nothing on which to base a comparison, they accepted uncritically and avidly what he *did* give them.

Against this background of myriad fascinations, Alger spun stories ideally suited to the fantasies of boys growing up in that time and place. How many millions of them must have dreamed of being in the Great City, poor but honest, hungry but talented, with the whole metropolitan oyster waiting to be opened. Another and much later generation identified similarly with Thomas Wolfe–Eugene Gant, afloat in New York and ready to experience everything it offered. To Eugene, riding the wave of twentieth-century freedom, experience meant primarily sex; to the Alger hero, it meant getting ahead in the world and possibly amassing a fortune, in the authentic nineteenth-century manner. Cannily, Alger never carried the fantasy to the point of realization, except for a page or two of summary at the end. His young readers could understand and appreciate the agonies of the rise, because they were relatively poor and struggling upward themselves, wherever they might be in their commonplace environments, but they could no more comprehend the world of fulfillment than Alger himself, who had not the slightest understanding of the rich and successful.

To his devoted readers, then, Alger gave a combination of

exotic background and simple wish fulfillment related in terms anyone with no more than an eighth-grade education could understand. This was the real secret of his success. When he had exhausted New York, he turned to far places which boys would find as intriguing. Australia was as far away as the moon to most of them, and to read of it was like reading science fiction in another generation. As for California, it had been the place since 1849 where a man could go to seek his fortune. To "go West" was another boyhood dream on which Alger shrewdly capitalized.

It is clear, then, that Alger's books did embody the essence of the American Dream in its purest form. What he came to be celebrated for, however, was precisely what he did not do. He constantly preached that success was to be won through virtue and hard work, but his stories tell us just as constantly that success is actually the result of fortuitous circumstance. His heroes are virtuous beyond belief, and they are compelled to work hard by reason of the sweatshop practices of that era, but it is not virtue and hard work which make the ultimate difference. It is almost always an incident which brings them to the attention of a successful businessman, who gives them the job which makes the difference between mere struggle and opportunity. After that, there are no further problems. The rest is easy.

In some stories Alger violates the dream even more grossly by thrusting fortune upon his hero through the revelation that he is a long-lost heir to a fortune, or that he has been unjustly deprived of his rightful wealth by some other means. Money, Alger seems to be saying, should be the natural reward for honesty and hard work, but it makes a better story if the boy gets it by saving a rich man's son from drowning or proving to be that same man's son, kidnaped in childhood by a scheming relative.

But if money, material success, is the pinnacle of human accomplishment, as Alger and nineteenth-century society believed, the author's attitude toward those who have achieved it is difficult to understand. With the exception of those rich and successful men who befriend poor boys, exuding platitudes in an unctuous and sententious stream as they do so, the rich do not come off well in Alger's books. They are often shown as grasping and mean, conniving and not above any unscrupulous measure to acquire more wealth. Nor are their progeny much better. Rich boys in Alger novels are often cast as villains. Their idle ways and arrogance are contrasted with the straightforward, honest simplicity of the poor boys.

Alger frequently tries to find an excuse for such behavior. The sneering, ill-mannered rich boys are said to have been deprived of a mother's love at an early age, or they have been spoiled by an overindulgent father. Again, Alger draws a curious moral line between struggling for material success and simple greed. His good rich men go to church regularly and practice charity, albeit in rather small doses. The bad ones think about nothing except money, and how to get more of it.

As though this were not enough, Alger frequently deplores the idle life of the idle rich in their Fifth Avenue mansions, contrasting it with the misery all around them in New York. Here, one supposes, Alger was betrayed by the plain facts of life he saw about him every day. The rich were, for the most part, ostentatious, grasping, idle, unscrupulous and all the other things he said of them. In the absence of a large middle business and professional class, most other New Yorkers lived in circumstances ranging from grinding poverty to humble struggle. They were, in fact, no more virtuous than the rich, by and large, but Alger depicted them as living in an atmosphere of sweetness and light, content with their simple lives because their hearts were pure. Yet Alger implies that they would be happier with money. Whenever a hero is elevated to fortune, the epilogue discloses him as dispensing enough largesse to less fortunate relatives or friends so that they will be able to live in circumstances approximating his own.

These contradictions and others make it impossible to take Alger seriously, if anyone were tempted to do so. Andrew Carnegie was a far better prophet of the American Dream than Alger because he had traveled the distance from poverty to wealth, understood both worlds, and was able to write about them realistically. Moreover, his idealism was on a far higher plane than that of Alger, who talked vaguely about philanthropy in his books and gave his own money away with no sense of direction, or even of common providence. Carnegie believed in the American Dream—that a boy could rise, as he had, to wealth and position, but for him that was not the end of it. A rich man, he said, at that point had an obligation to society to use his wealth for the betterment of mankind.

It is ironic that Alger lived in an era when there were enough real products of the American Dream to provide examples for any ambitious boy, yet he could only create the fantasy world of rags to riches, which nevertheless made him successful because it was also the fantasy of so many American boys. He might have written about the careers of such eminences as Peter A. B. Widener and Gustavus Franklin Swift, who rose from meat markets to wealth; or of Thomas Fortune Ryan, who began as an orphaned and penniless boy on a Virginia farm and in twenty years had a seat on the New York Stock Exchange; or John D. Rockefeller, a boy from an Ohio village who became one of the nation's first billionaires. These examples were everywhere in nineteenth-century America, yet Alger wrote about the street boys of New York and their melodramatic, implausible rises to fortune, which in fact actually occurred to a negligible number of them.

Why did millions of Americans prefer the fantasy to the reality? The answer is, of course, the reason for the success of so much popular fiction in that century or this—the inability of the mass mind in America to face reality. Just as we invent a version of American history to satisfy our own image of ourselves, so we prefer the Ragged Dicks of literature to the real heroes of the American Dream. Until the muckrakers came along at the end of the century, everyone wanted to believe that the great entrepreneurs of business were like Alger heroes. When a later school of writers tried to depict historical figures as something more than stereotypes, they were called debunkers. We talk about reality in popular fiction today, but it is more often a pseudo-reality because the truth would be too harsh and unpalatable for mass taste. As a people we cling to our images, and, as Alger's public did, we still prefer our dream world to the real one.

As we have seen, Alger doubted the validity of the American Dream himself and materially aided the virtue and hard work of his heroes by melodramatic devices which helped them over the critical line between struggle and success. Americans themselves, even as they dreamed with Alger, must have doubted too. They saw virtuous and hardworking people all around them who died still virtuous, working hard until the day they expired—poor. Obviously not every butcher's boy in a meat market was going to wind up as Peter Widener and Gus Swift had done. There were uncounted thousands of farm boys who were not going to get any nearer to the Stock Exchange than the nearest grain elevator, no matter how hard they worked. Other ingredients were needed—sometimes luck, sometimes talent, and always and overwhelmingly a relentless drive and a willingness to sacrifice everything else in life for the great game of business. The winners had one thing in common: they were utterly devoted to business in a way unimaginable to other people, who considered work as an unavoidable means of making a living, not as an end in itself.

That much has not changed. The most successful entrepreneurs are still those to whom business is totally absorbing, to the exclusion of nearly everything else, although the twentieth-century reorganization of society has altered the lives of these people, too. We are still a nation that worships material success, and, in spite of all the hypocrisy to the contrary, the values of the materially successful remain our national values. But the recasting of society has now so altered the original American Dream that it has little resemblance to what it was in Alger's day. We have organized the dream, applied the dogmas of sociology and psychology to it, carefully channeled it into acceptable procedures which can be weighed and measured at every point. The unpredictable human element exists only at the top, where the struggle remains. But it is a struggle for power, for position, for satisfaction of the ego, not the old-fashioned struggle to bridge the awful gap between rags and riches. That is gone with the dream. The wish now is to be reasonably comfortable and secure, with enough money for an automobile, a television set and the down payment on a house.

It was a powerful dream, a compelling fantasy while it lasted. It made Alger a successful writer in his own time and one who was read avidly for generations afterward. It elevated failing magazines from deserved obscurity to mass readership, and mass acceptance of what they printed. It was a prime factor in the spectacular rise of the advertising industry, and in the success of many giant enterprises. It has been, indeed, a vital part of the fabric of American life.

In a history replete with irony, it is perhaps most ironic of all that a man like Horatio Alger, Jr., should have been the chief prophet of the American Dream. Yet there is a curious logic about it, because Alger's life was built on just such fantasy materials. Twice in his life this balding, unimpressive little man, with his conventional ways of living and thinking, embarked on romantic adventures so far removed from every principle he expounded that his readers would have been profoundly shocked had they known of it. This apostle of success considered his own career an abject failure, and so it was by the standards he himself celebrated. He could not comprehend the impact his books made on his fellow Americans. Frustrated as a serious novelist, he thought of himself only as a writer who had hit upon a successful formula in the market for boys' books.

It was a strange life, Alger's. The books he wrote tell us a great deal about him, and even more about the world he lived in. Their lasting popularity over so long a period of time in our history makes them worth a closer examination, and the life of their creator equally merits a reevaluation. Considering them together, perhaps, will cast some additional light into the dark corners of our national consciousness.

PART TWO

ALGER THE MAN

CHAPTER 1

A PSYCHOANALYST searching for clues to what was eventually the total disorganization of Horatio Alger's personality would have to look no further than to the classic psychologic mainspring of human mental ills, the man's father and mother. In Alger's case, these two represented between them nearly all the ingredients necessary to guarantee their son a maladjusted life.

The father, Horatio Alger, Sr., was a Unitarian minister cut from the New England cloth. Spiritually he was the descendant of those rebellious men who renounced the true faith brought over from England and went off into the wilderness, away from the orthodoxy of Boston, to establish their own splinter faiths. There they repeated the authoritarian sins of orthodoxy, exactly as the rulers of the Bay Colony had done as soon as they were free of the Church of England.

The senior Alger epitomized the basic evil of this cycle. As a Unitarian he was a symbol of freedom from the orthodoxy which still held New England firm early in the nineteenth century, although dissent was becoming popular enough to be fashionable. Yet not even the Mathers could have surpassed the orthodoxy which Alger forced down the sometimes unwilling throats of those who made up the Unitarian Society of Chelsea, Massachusetts. If these refugees from the Trinity had thought to escape dogma, they had not reckoned with Mr. Alger.

In the Alger character there was no room for compromise. Except for the little matter of the Trinity, he took the Bible as meaning exactly what it said, and he conceived of his own role as God's servant to save souls and no nonsense about it. There were those in his congregation who grumbled that the pastor seemed to think of himself more as a partner than a servant.

He was a formidable figure even at a tender twenty-six, when his son was born. Tall and thin, his nose cut on the lines of a catboat under full sail, hollow-cheeked, ears standing out large from his head as though to catch every last whisper of sin—that was Horatio Alger, Sr., as he marched about the precincts of Chelsea and of Revere, a few miles to the north, where he lived. His march had something of arrogance in it, befitting God's partner, and his manner had little of comfort for those who sought spiritual consolation. A sinner had only to look into those icy blue eyes, set wide apart in a pale, almost gaunt, face to know that when the thin, wide lips opened they would utter intimations of hell.

To Alger there was so much sin in the world that hell was in danger of overpopulation. Sometimes when he lifted his nose into the air and sniffed, he appeared to be smelling sin afar off. But never very far, because there was little in the world that Mr. Alger did not consider sinful. He did not even trust the purity of his friends in the ministry, and as for his parishioners, their every move outside the church was viewed with suspicion. Alger referred to himself piously as a sinful man, like everyone else, but it was plain that he did not really mean it.

It was equally obvious that Pastor Alger's major sin was pride. Few of those who knew him, however, comprehended how monumental that sin had grown to be. For Alger had a plan which he had thought about and prayed about. It was nothing less than to be the spiritual leader of America, and on his right hand he intended to have his own begotten son as his helper and heir.

The virgin he took to consummate this major purpose of his life was also a New Englander, Olive Fenno. Alger considered her as little more than a slave in the house, and fortunate indeed to be the biological mechanism he needed to acquire a son. She was utterly submissive to him, to a degree unusual even for those prefeminist days. Once when she attempted to reenter their burning house to save a personal treasure, her sewing basket, Alger imperiously forbade it. It was God's will that the house and everything in it be destroyed, he said. By one of God's little ironies, however, it was Olive who was responsible in the end for destroying his master plan for Alger Junior.

Under such unlucky parental stars, Horatio the younger was born on Friday the thirteenth, in January, 1832, at the most inconvenient time, since it was the one night of the week his father always set aside to prepare next Sunday's sermon. He did not permit his son's coming to divert him from his schedule. There was no need in any case to pace the floor, in the manner of ordinary fathers. He was not overly concerned about Olive, and there was none of the ordinary suspense about the newborn's sex. Olive would not dare to give him a girl.

"The boy has arrived as I expected," he wrote to an old friend in Chicago, after the event. "It was a *strenuous ordeal* and I am earnestly trying to accommodate myself to the new order of things. Needless to say my work has *suffered* enormously and some months will elapse before all is normal again. His name will be Horatio, after me, not as a concession to any vanity of mine but rather as a reminder to him that I shall expect him to continue the religious endeavors I have begun but in a *larger, broader* manner."

He took the baby's training under his personal care immediately, except for the drudgery of it, which naturally he left to Olive. Even when four other children followed—Olive Augusta, James, Ann and Francis—Alger Senior gave them no more than perfunctory attention. It was the firstborn whom he intended to make in his image.

There were setbacks from the beginning. Little Horatio stubbornly refused to talk at first; he appeared positively stupid. His sister Olive, a year younger, was talking before he opened his mouth intelligibly. The father was annoyed and frustrated, but he persisted, employing his own superior methods of child instruction. These consisted of singing hymns to the boy and telling him Bible stories. When the nurse who had attended his birth suggested that the boy might learn more rapidly from fairy tales, she was fired at once.

"I was hired to raise a child, not a cathedral," she snorted and left little Horatio to his fate.

By the time he was eight, the boy was more cathedral than child, a living monument to his father's pedantry and zealous purpose. He was knowledgeable in American history and geography, a formidable speller, an able mathematician, conversant with Plato, fluent in Latin, thoroughly familiar with the Bible. He was also exhibiting an early symptom of personality disorganization: he stuttered badly.

Besides all this, Horatio was unutterably lonely. He spent much of his early childhood building with large blocks, and no doubt a psychiatrist studying him at that stage would have derived further clues from the fact that he built the same structure again and again—towers which he erected block upon block until they toppled, whereupon he would quietly, unemotionally, start building them up again.

At home he was under his father's piercing eyes most of the time, but when Senior had to be away on the Lord's business, in Boston or New York, Olive did her best to give the boy that love and affection which her husband was incapable of giving. It was natural for Olive to do this, as a gentle woman who truly loved the firstborn son of whom she saw so little, but it only complicated young Alger's problem. These moments with his mother had the aura of guilt about them, yet he treasured the feeling of being in her arms and knowing the warmth of her love. They sensed each other's loneliness in the drab, stern world Alger Senior had created for them, and without having to explain the intensity of their feelings, they instinctively reached out to each other. As the boy lay in his mother's arms, they sometimes cried together in love and sympathy.

No wonder Horatio Junior did not, as the educationists say, identify with the group when he went to school. His little schoolmates gave him the savage, primitive treatment children accord to those who are not like themselves. He was excluded from games, teased, made to suffer indignities large and small, poked fun at, and of course given an odious nickname—"Holy Horatio." The other boys wanted to humiliate him, to see him cry. For his part, he wanted desperately to be like them, to join their fun, but he knew that his father wished it otherwise. Alger Senior considered that he had created a superior child, and he enjoyed seeing him stand grave and aloof from the others, always immaculately dressed.

If he had seen him in the classroom, he would not have been so complacent, for Alger Junior was already displaying the hopeless split in his character. He had his brilliant days and his dull days, and then there were days when his memory inexplicably deserted him and he could not begin to answer questions to which he would have responded easily another time. He was frightened by these sudden, terrifying lapses, when he had to stand dumb and empty, like an idiot, before the teacher's smiling exasperation. When he escaped at last he would fly home to Mother, hoping to find her alone so they could cry together before his father came home.

Any quick flash of normalcy was immediately suppressed if it was observed. Once, goaded to the limit by his tormenting classmates, Horatio did what he had never done before and turned on them. Astounded, they fled the scene except for one young bully on whom Horatio was wreaking all his pent-up rage and frustration when his father happened by, and instead of taking his son's part, removed the boy to his study where he explained, with prayers and exhortation, the meaning of the Biblical injunction, "Forgive them, for they know not what they do."

Horatio was already more than familiar with everything the Bible had to say. He could not help it, because he was compelled to sit quietly and attentively beside his father to watch Pastor Alger write his lengthy sermons, and when they were done, the minister read them back to his captive audience, requiring the boy to write down a synopsis of each one after he had heard it. Father and son ate breakfast and supper together and alone; the rest of the family could eat when they pleased. They went for long walks together in the country, and, whenever they paused to rest, Horatio Junior would be subjected to a brief examination in the Scriptures. He had to travel to Chelsea every Sunday with his father and sit in a front pew.

The almost demoniac possession of the son by the father went on year after year, driving the boy into a rigid loneliness and a desperation he seldom had a chance to express. He had a "company answer" his father had taught him to repeat when there were guests and the proud pastor asked him to declare what he was "going to be." Like an automaton, Horatio would repeat: "I shall be a teacher of the ways of God, a preacher of His commandments, a liberal thinker, a loyal citizen." But when his mother asked him, as he lay reading or when they were alone together, he would look at her with pitiful eyes and cry out, "I don't want to be anything, Mother, honest, I *don't*."

Students of psychosomatic behavior will not be surprised to learn that eventually Horatio contracted a severe case of diphtheria and nearly died of it. His mother nursed him day and night, and temporarily her influence completely displaced her husband's. But when it was over, she as easily relinquished the reins again. Olive undoubtedly saw with more or less clarity what was happening to her son, but she did not have the courage to defy her husband. She could give young Horatio sympathy but nothing else.

The father appears in the son's books in various forms, but probably most often as the sober, moral, respectable businessman who gives advice to young men, full of good examples and modern instances. These characters cannot resist pointing morals at the drop of an incident, and in this they are exactly like Alger Senior, who could not even see his son, in a rare moment of normal play, build a snowman without pointing out to him when the sun melted it how transitory are the works of man when confronted with God's permanent instruments.

Alger Senior was shaken by his son's nearly fatal illness, but his concern was entirely selfish. He wrote to his Chicago friend: "I cannot tell you what anguish I endured as I witnessed the little body wasting away with fever. God be thanked that he has survived and is once again on the road to sturdy health. I forbid myself to think what I would do without the lad. So far I have devoted my existence to his upbringing and the progress he has made in his studies has been most *gratifying* to an infinite degree. God willing, some day he will be a credit to *His* name."

If Horatio Junior had been a serious writer, he would have crucified his father as soon as he set pen to paper. One thinks of Stendhal, and of course a dozen others among the great writers, not to mention the literary patricide (and matricide) which is common currency in contemporary writing. But from the first Horatio demonstrated that his father had done his work all too well and forever deprived him of vitality. It is evident even in the childish piece that marked his first appearance in print, at thirteen, in the columns of the Revere *Gazette*.

The fatuous father considered the event a vindication of his training and an early expression of his fondest hopes. "In a community as small as ours," he confided to a friend in Boston, "nothing occurs to disturb the tranquillity of our lives and I am without the means therefore of informing you of any events of extraordinary significance. Were I to pass by a *certain small occurrence*, however, I would not be doing justice to my oldest boy whose diligence in study has already won recognition from our weekly press. He has developed a *flair for writing* which is most remarkable for his years, and this without an iota of instruction or advice from anyone. I must ask you to pardon my enthusiasm, if it seems such to you, for I am *very proud* of his accomplishment and look forward with eagerness to his further achievements."

The *Gazette*'s editor seemed no less happy about it. He wrote in an editorial precede that he deemed it "an honor to publish in the columns of this journal a tale written by a child of our community who has not yet celebrated his fourteenth birthday. Horatio Alger, Jr. is the author of an entertaining piece entitled, A Race Up The Hill, which, through the generosity of his esteemed father, we are privileged to present to our numerous readers."

The story itself is a fairy tale, of a kind the author was forbidden to read. It went as follows:

"A boy was waiting at the bottom of a hill for some one to come and play with him. Soon he heard whistling and was happy because he thought a friend of his was coming. The whistling came from the wind which was blowing about the fields and at first the boy was ready to weep because he had no one to play with. The wind kept whistling and the whistle seemed to say, 'Come, little boy, *I* will play with you.' The boy listened hard and was sure he heard the words. This new companion made him full of joy even if he could not see it.

"So he jumped about and ran merrily about the trees with the wind singing and chasing after him. The fact that the boy ran ahead of the wind pleased him very much. He was proud and challenged the wind to a race up hill.

" 'Well, well,' cried the wind, 'let us start.'

"The boy ran as fast as he could run. The wind was close behind him. 'I win,' said the boy as he stopped. 'I beat the wind.' The wind grew angry at hearing the boast and whistled by him and did not come back to play."

What a heartbreaking revelation that tale would have been for anyone with the perception to understand Horatio. The boy waiting at the bottom of the hill for someone to come and play with him, and ready to weep "because he had no one to play with," then the race with a playmate in which Horatio acted out one of his childhood wishes, and at last the poignant ending, "and did not come back to play"—these were the telltale signals which would have meant a call for help to another generation of teachers.

But there was no one to listen. There was only Alger Senior, writing fatuously to his Chicago friend: "The moral of the narrative is readily discernible. It is in reality a sermon which says, 'Thou shall not set thyself against the word of the Lord.' "

Whether it was the stimulus of finding himself in print and an individual at last, or whether it was only the normal rebellion of early adolescence, Alger Junior at thirteen began to resist his father for the first time. Rewarding his son for the *Gazette* story, the pastor went up to Boston and came home with a clergyman's suit exactly like his own which he had ordered made in his son's size. Horatio flatly refused to wear it and never did.

This act of defiance astonished both father and son. Senior found it incredible and incomprehensible; Junior found his unexpected success heady. Apprehended a little later in the act of playing with the family cat, Duff, when he was supposed to be spending his usual compulsory half-hour of morning meditation, Horatio fought again against his father's peremptory banishing of Duff from the household. Senior had to compromise and permit Duff to return to the house, although not to Horatio's room.

A third conflict between father and son is a psychoanalyst's delight. After the bout with diphtheria, Horatio's doctor had ordered him to get some exercise, which his father's stern discipline had always denied him. If he thought this reprieve meant that he would be allowed to play, or try to play, with the other boys, he was disappointed once more. Pastor Alger's idea of carrying out such therapy was to build a swing in the backyard.

At first Horatio was more than happy to settle for any contrivance that would get him into the open air in a nonclerical, nonlearning role, but when he tried the new swing he found to his dismay that he suffered from motion sickness and promptly vomited after every excursion with it. Reluctantly, he announced that he would have to give it up, but incredibly, Alger Senior would have none of it. He knew of no better way to keep the stomach clear, he said, and the boy must have his exercise.

This time Horatio tried a new tack. He went directly to his

mother, who would not have dreamed of confronting her husband on the issue, but with more guile than she had ever exhibited before, took Horatio's case in turn to the doctor, who declared that certainly the boy should not swing if it made him sick. Once more Senior was overruled.

By this time Horatio was fourteen and ready for prep school. His departure for Gates Academy, in Marlborough, was marked by a letter from Senior to Frederick Winslow Wilson, the assistant headmaster, which is a masterpiece of irony, considering everything that had gone before. "I hold the belief that the environment of an educational institution should stimulate that which the students are accustomed to at home as closely as practicable," the father wrote. "I hope and believe Horatio will find under your jurisdiction all the comforts he has had in the past. Again I urge you to communicate with me instantly if he fails to accommodate himself to the new regimen. I am *utterly concerned* with his well-being."

No doubt he was, in his pathological way, but if Horatio had seen the letter he would have shuddered at the idea that life at Gates Academy was to be just like the one he had left at home. He was, in fact, determined that it would be different, now that he was out from under his father's domination.

He was not surprised when the other boys found him strange and uncongenial; that had always been the case and he was used to it by this time. But he was resolved to change it if he could. He endured the freshman hazing without complaint, loaned a half-dollar to a classmate, and before the first term was over, he had become what he had never been before—a member of the group in good standing.

In the semiscientific jargon of a later day, Horatio overcompensated. It was the familiar story of the minister's son who turns out to be the leading hell-raiser in the school. Alger's biographer, Herbert Mayes, summarizes the new boy's transgressions. Horatio, it appears, "was admitted to all the councils, took part in all the games, conspired to break the windows in the home of Obadiah Albee, headmaster of the Academy, and when caught and threatened with expulsion for his share in the crime declined to name the other culprits; he never hesitated to let his friends copy their lessons from him or had scruples about reciprocal indulgences. He helped to build bonfires which threw the residents of Marlborough into a panic of fear. On a dare he swallowed a penny; on a double dare he swallowed two pennies. And when an Abolitionist stopped in the town long enough to deliver a lecture on the abomination of slavery, he assisted magnificently in inciting a riot though he and his youthful confederates were committed to anti-slavery doctrines."

News of these activities reached Senior from time to time, and he responded with letters of exhortation, which were followed by new outbreaks, no doubt in direct result. Nor did Pastor Alger know the worst of it. Horatio was emerging from under the heavy hand of his father's religion. He no longer read the Bible, wasted no time in prayer and meditation, and was one of the ringleaders in a school plot to skip Sunday chapel and go on a picnic instead. The plan was thwarted temporarily by an alert faculty, but the boys simply postponed the project to a better Sunday. In this interval, Mr. Wilson wrote another letter to Senior, relating Junior's latest delinquencies in as delicate a manner as he could summon.

The response from home was typical of both father and mother, whose letters arrived on the same day. Opening his father's, Horatio was hardly surprised to read: "That a boy who has been the recipient of such profound attention as you should forget all the principles of honor and decency *distresses* me fearfully. Can it be you have no thought for the approval of your God nor for my desires? I must request you again with all the fervor at my command to forget the selfish impulses which come to you and think of living a life that will redound to the glory of God."

When he opened his mother's letter, he could almost hear her soft voice saying, "I am sorry that Mr. Wilson has found grounds for complaint about your conduct. Perhaps there is some reason which I cannot understand, but I know that you will not resort to wickedness for its own sake. Try to be a better boy for I should be unhappy to think of you in trouble. I miss you more as the weeks go by. Think of me always as your affectionate mother."

Neither of these letters restrained Horatio from joining the chapel-skipping Sunday picnic expedition, when it was finally accomplished. But it ended on a note which momentarily sobered him. The wayward boys were caught in a violent thunderstorm, in open country, and while they huddled together, terrified, the lightning blasted a tree to the ground nearby, sending one susceptible truant into hysterics. At that moment early training asserted itself and Junior performed an act which would have pleased Senior inordinately. He got to his knees and addressed his cowering comrades in the commanding way his father might have done. "Come, let us pray," he said. It was not a plea; it was an order, and they prayed, except for a scoffer whose noncompliance earned him a punch in the nose from Horatio.

Whether it was this evidence that the Almighty was watching him in the absence of his father, or whether it was the result of growing up, Horatio survived his two years at Gates Academy, which was considered sufficient preparation for him to enter Harvard. At sixteen he was translated to the Yard and another new world opened for him, far more glittering than the last, and one that unfortunately pointed the way to his ultimate destruction.

CHAPTER 2

Nothing about Horatio Alger becomes too difficult to believe after a time, but his entry into Harvard is almost like a chapter from one of his own incredible tales. He had no more than walked into the Yard when he was set upon by a boisterous crowd of sophomores who welcomed him to the university by dragging him around and abusing him until he fainted. He supposed it was only part of the regular hazing.

That had been his fate through his public school years, and during his first days at the Academy, but he must have been surprised to discover that Harvard was no different. To the sophomores, however, one supposes he was still the strange-looking new boy he had always been—a little taller, his face somewhat more melancholy, with the air of having come from another world. His appearance at Harvard was the more unusual because in his hasty packing he had been unable to cram everything into his luggage, and what was left over he had stuffed into his pockets and strapped to his person until he looked like an itinerant junkman. No wonder the sophomores had greeted this apparition with whoops of joy.

Nevertheless, when he had recovered, Horatio contemplated Harvard with undiminished anticipation, and pride that he was actually enrolled there. He began a diary at once and wrote on its first page: "I, Horatio Alger, signed the roll and am now a scholar at Harvard! I promise to do my best in every subject and uphold the learning of this great place! Everything that happens I will keep a record of in complete detail so that I will be able to see progress made and be guided accordingly."

The diary descends from this high plane almost at once and becomes a detailed and dull record of Horatio's movements, set down with that passion for minute notations which was part of his mediocrity. He carefully noted when he took a bath and when he changed his underwear, and on his rambles around Cambridge he could scarcely have been more pedantic: "Walked for half an hour in the sunlight and watched the sparrows. Walked for twenty minutes and studied the trees—could pick out the oak trees and elms but found I have much information to learn. Very few people out for walking, counted only seven in three hours. Tired then and went back but purchasing a pair of shoes first.

Made bath ready and fresh underclothes and put on shoes, not very comfortable but will be very soon. Read in Isaiah and some in Exodus. My head burned and lay down until Mrs. C. returned."

He had returned to reading the Bible, after the first wild days of rebellion at the Academy. His father's rigid teachings had begun to reassert themselves. He was also beginning to struggle with sex, another result of his early training, and in his inability to come to grips with it, there were further indications that Alger Senior had done his work all too well. The "Mrs. C." of his diary was his landlady, a middle-aged widow named Frances Curran, whom Alger frequently referred to as "a good woman." She mothered him by cooking him goodies like chocolate cake, darning his socks, and doing little favors for him, for which he was pathetically grateful.

Reading between the lines, it is possible to believe that Mrs. Curran's loneliness interfered with her role as Horatio's mother, in which her young lodger had cast her, as she grew more and more accustomed to having a man in the house again. The climax came one day, which Horatio recorded with pious horror in his diary: "She stood in the doorway as I passed to my room and had on very little and I might have seen her bare but I did not look. I shall move to where there is greater respect for decency."

He did so at once, but he leaves us with the tantalizing speculation that his new landlady, a Miss Mullins, was as lonely as poor Mrs. Curran. Leaving his second place after only three days, he writes mysteriously, "Am not satisfied. I must be more careful where I go."

Obviously he had to find a house with a man in it, if he meant to preserve his honor. The man he found was Floyd Thurstone, "an agreeable gentleman with white hair," with whom he began a relationship curiously like those in the Alger books where an elderly man befriends and helps a poor, struggling young boy. The situation was reversed in this instance, for it was Mr. Thurstone who was poor and struggling. He had taken a roomer because he was scarcely able to keep up the heavy mortgage payments on the creaking two-family house in which he lived, particularly after he had made a foolish investment in a Philadelphia bookstore which turned out badly and brought him to the edge of disaster.

Learning of this circumstance, Horatio behaved like an Alger hero. He entered an essay contest at the college and worked hard day and night to win the prize of forty dollars, so that he could help his benefactor. His paper, "Athens at the Time of Socrates," did win the prize and Horatio did give the money to Mr. Thurstone. If Alger had been twenty years older and writing the script, he would have presented it just as the flinty banker was about to foreclose the mortgage. Forty dollars would not have made much of an impression on Mr. Thurstone's mortgage, but he was in such serious circumstances that he took the money anyway, with the deepest gratitude.

Horatio had good reason to be grateful on his own account. In escaping from possibly predatory landladies, he had found a man who could give him the sympathetic friendship he had never enjoyed from his father. His diary is full of the many ways in which Mr. Thurstone had become a part of his life:

"Last night we talked about the slaves and he stated he once owned many slaves in the State of Georgia but some of them were burned in a fire and he gave the others their freedom so that he could come North and earn a living for himself. . . ."

"He hears my lessons and helps me in mathematics. Also he reads poetry that is a pleasure to hear."

"He is a devout Catholic. At six o'clock we drove in his cart and I was very happy. He is pleased to look at the stars and is old and kind. He inquired after my plans for the future but he does not think I should be a minister. Once upon a time he must have been a teacher for that is what he thinks I ought to become and if he could live over again he said he would be a teacher to the slaves. Later we ate cookies and talked of philosophy."

Mr. Thurstone encouraged his young lodger to study languages. "It is a joy to be familiar with foreign tongues," he said, and Horatio took it as gospel. In practice, however, he discovered that French was the only foreign tongue he really enjoyed learning, although he also did well in the classical languages, Greek and Latin, and in Italian. He did not do well in German. Nevertheless, as a Harvard scholar, Horatio fulfilled some of the early promise he had shown and stood tenth in his class of sixty-two at the end of his studies.

Unlike the wild days at the Academy, Horatio's life at Harvard was sober and withdrawn, much as it had been in childhood. Except for Mr. Thurstone, he had few friends. One was the son of the next-door neighbor, a rich shipbuilder named Chapman, whose son Alexander was getting his education privately from a tutor. "Lexy" was the first rich boy Alger had ever known, and he bore little resemblance to the stereotype Horatio later created. He was soon the closest friend Horatio had ever enjoyed, so close that the boys spent a good deal of time planning how they might spend their lives together. "We have considered the advantages afforded by the practice of law, and we agreed to proceed with study at once," he reported at one point, and again, "Lexy thinks we ought to be shipbuilders and start a branch of his father's business in London. Tomorrow we may talk with Mr. Chapman."

The boys considered and discarded one plan after another. Once they thought of establishing "an academy for the advancement of knowledge in the sciences." Again, even more ambitiously, they thought of "establishing a powerful organization which will undertake a wide study of the negro problem and what can be done to reconcile the views of slave holders and non-slave holders." It was not even beyond them to "embrace a career in politics."

But the heavy hand of his father still lay upon Horatio. He was pricked on by his conscience from time to time to consider the ministry. "Nothing is more necessary to mankind than an understanding of the vital influence of religion," he assured himself solemnly, "and I would be unwise to forego the privilege of serving the needs of my fellow men in the capacity of spiritual adviser."

It was an ambition his friend could not share. Lexy, it appeared, was a scoffer. Religion, he told Horatio, "is a barrier to mental growth. He assured me that a minister is too much concerned with the trivial concerns of his followers to be able to keep in touch with larger affairs." Lexy was ready to abandon Horatio to religion and move on to those larger affairs, if that was going to be Alger's real mission in life. "He has decided to go South and buy a cotton plantation," Horatio recorded, but whether with anger or regret, he does not say.

The inseparable friends separated, Chapman to die at Antietam, fighting the defenders of those lush plantations for which he had longed in austere Cambridge. Before they parted, however, Lexy had given Horatio what was to be at once the greatest joy and the deepest sorrow of his life. He introduced him to his cousin, Patience Stires.

They were almost of an age, Horatio seventeen and Patience only a little younger. The day-by-day entries in his diary from the moment he met her, on October 4, 1849, reveal his swift descent into the bottomless pit of love.

"She is an agreeable girl," Horatio recorded their first meeting. "She wore a yellow bonnet. Her eyes are hazel and sad."

A week later: "Patience has dimples and her teeth are white as snow. Lexy is fond of her. I am fond of her too. Tomorrow we shall walk together."

A little later: "Patience is a good Latin scholar. She is slender and lovely and this afternoon she informed me her desire is to learn to sing. I think she sings beautifully now."

Patience had changed his world by Christmastime. Not only was he hopelessly in love with her, but he could not tolerate anything or anyone that infringed on the time he might be with her. No longer could he find any pleasure in Mr. Thurstone's company, and even Lexy was transformed into one who was "always propounding great schemes which no sensible person would listen to, much less make an effort to consummate." Yet only four months earlier, before religion had begun to interfere, he had not only listened to Lexy's schemes but was full of plans to realize them.

It might have been better, though more immediately painful, if Patience had rejected him, but she declared herself as much in love as he was. Naturally, they agreed to get married.

Both families were agreeable with one exception. Consistent to the end, Horatio Senior said no, flatly and unequivocally. "I have made up my mind to marry Patience Stires," Horatio wrote to his father from Cambridge, but it was his father who had made up *his* mind, even before he read these words. "I am behind in my studies, father," Horatio went on, innocently compounding his crime, "and have even lost interest in French, my favorite study. By this time I know my own feelings and have no doubt Patience is the only girl I will ever love. The world seems centered in her. I could never forget her—not as long as I live. Some part of me would be missing."

It was all true, but to Horatio's father it sounded like the fervent moanings of every lovestruck young man in history, and he refused to take it seriously. As far as he was concerned, his son was a fool and Patience was "a chit scarce old enough to walk abroad alone, much less think of matrimony."

Angry and impatient with such nonsense, he hurried over to Cambridge and gave his son a stern moral lecture on his duty to God and conscience. Everything he had done for him, he said, had only one purpose, to prepare his son for the ministry, and now Horatio was talking about throwing away past and future. The least he could do would be to wait until he had his degree and was safely embarked on his proper career as a Unitarian minister.

Sadly, dutifully, Horatio agreed that he was bound to wait that long, and he told his love: "My father is convinced we ought to wait, my darling Patience. That is not what I want to do even if the suggestion is sound. What is the value of love if lovers allow business to come between? I am ready to withstand the displeasure of my father if you are willing to be satisfied with the meager living I can earn because I suppose I will be a clergyman.

"Be sure to meet me on Sunday. I will wait for you in the regular way at Corsings at four o'clock and then we can go over our plans and make decisions for the future. Do not fail to be there because I shall be waiting, and leave you now, thinking of you in the meantime with the greatest love."

Patience may have been only seventeen, but she faced the heartbreak of her life with the insight and composure of a veteran in the amatory wars. She met Horatio and listened to his protestations and said good-bye to him, and when she got home she read without surprise a letter from his father, advising her in his usual sententious manner that women who really loved their men did not stand in the way of their careers. Patience knew something about love. She knew that this was the end, and she did not prolong it with indignities to herself. She did not write to Horatio again.

He was profoundly hurt and puzzled. His instinct was to think her inconstant and renounce her, but he was honest enough with himself to know that was impossible. "The young lady I hoped to marry seems to have changed her mind," he wrote home. "At least I do not hear from her. I have been taught the meanness of being a hypocrite and the lesson comes in good stead now. I am obliged to speak honestly and say that I still feel the same toward her. If she comes back I will surely ask her to be my wife. In the meantime I am devoting myself to study as much as possible. I am sure she will return and this makes it easier for me to do my work."

With Patience gone from his life, Horatio began to slip back into his old, withdrawn way of living. He read much and talked to fewer people than ever. His complacent father heard of this progress with satisfaction; he believed smugly that Horatio's straying feet had been turned back to the proper path. But in fact, his son's inward contemplation and constant reading were having exactly the opposite effect. Horatio was moving away rapidly from religion toward a new world which began to dawn before his dazzled eyes.

"Am reading Moby Dick," he confided to his diary, "and find it exciting. What a thrilling life the literary must be! Imagination and observation—these I take to be the important requisites. Would it be desirable for me to take up writing as a life work? The satisfaction resulting from a beautiful story must be inspiring —a story that rouses readers to a new sense of the fine things of life. Have I the ability to write? Why not—if I am conscientious and observe closely all that goes on about me?"

Now he was truly torn, as graduation approached, between writing and the ministry. Horatio Senior, having disposed of Patience, found himself confronted unexpectedly with a less tangible and more formidable enemy. He tried threatening, but his son had long since passed beyond that kind of influence. Then the pastor pulled out of his ministerial bag all the tricks of cajolery which had served him so well in and out of the pulpit. They did not impress Horatio, who had heard them before.

They agreed, at last, on a compromise. Horatio would go into the ministry, but by agreement he would be permitted to take up writing as a sideline. The harassed father had no more than sighed his relief, however, than Horatio was off on another impulsive tangent which rekindled his ambition. A Greek Literary Society was formed at Harvard among the undergraduates and the lonely watcher, no doubt to his surprise, was asked to join. It took only the first meeting to excite him again. As he told his diary that night, one of the aims of the society was "to promote interest in the best reading *and* writing among young people for the benefit of all literature." He was "excited and eager" over the prospect, and in fact pledged himself "to continue my efforts even after graduation and to work toward the establishment of scholarships or prizes for the best literature produced by our members. Everybody anticipates a spirited association. How can it help but be so! All my spare time I intend to devote to it."

The Society collapsed within three weeks, under the weight of final examinations, but by that time it was too late for the senior Alger to save his son. He was committed to the literary life. When he was awarded the bachelor's degree in 1852 and the choice lay clearly before him, he crushed his father by refusing to go on to divinity school at the pastor's expense. He preferred to try the world on his own terms and be a writer. "Holy Horatio," it appeared, was holy no longer.

It was not an easy road, he soon realized. He got a job teaching languages at night in a Boston private school, which gave him enough money for food and lodging, and most of all, the daytime leisure to pursue the Muse. His pursuit was purposeful. In company with two other hopeful authors, Joel Evans and Joseph Parke, who roomed above him, he set off every morning after breakfast to absorb the life of Cambridge and vicinity. By agreement they went in different directions, returning later, like reporters on a newspaper, to write down whatever they had seen and heard.

None of the three worked harder at this game than Alger, who was a veritable Dickens in his approach. He began to fill his notebooks with capsule descriptions of people known and unknown to him, from the flower peddler on the corner to, prophetically, the hunchbacked figure of a newsboy on Tremont Street. "I shall soon start to organize an army of people for my books," Horatio wrote purposefully, and he did.

A stroke of luck pushed him deeper into the literary life than he had hoped to attain so soon. Norman Mayo, the editor of a new religious-literary weekly, the *New England Review*, hired him as an assistant editor. It was a strange relationship, and a mistaken one, as Mayo soon found out. Years later he wrote: "I felt sorry for him. I kept him with me because I felt sure he would find no other place to go. To look with disapproval on one of his suggestions was to invite the saddest expression in his eyes. He did not talk much, but when he did it was with enthusiasm. Most of his projects were impractical. It was impossible to make him understand that publishing has a business side—that finances are as important as writers. Alger was, I am afraid, most incompetent notwithstanding his unbounded faith in his own capacity. His chief fault, I think, was that he could not get started. Even when he possessed a sound idea he was at a loss what to do with it."

With this shrewd observation, Mayo came close to the core of Alger's troubled life. Horatio never got started at anything he truly wanted to do. The success he did achieve was not what he wanted. Over him lingered constantly the dread figure of his father, confusing him, inhibiting him, bringing to nothing the impulsive enthusiasms that moved him from time to time. Sometimes these impulses were at least in a constructive direction, even if he did not have the ability to carry them out. More often they were foolish, even irrational.

When the *Review* had to close after a brief, unhappy career, it was undoubtedly more of a blow to him than it was to Mayo. Incompetent he might have been in the editor's eyes, but the magazine had been his life. He wandered about disconsolately, out of a job, out of spirits, often hungry. "Today I had three slices of bread and a pot of tea," he reported grimly in his diary. He would not ask his father for money—not yet. Like a Skid Row outcast, he took to frequenting church again an Sunday because it was such a warm and comforting place in contrast to the bleak, cold austerity of his room, where there was as little food as fuel.

One day, contemplating this contrast, he must have concluded that his ambitions were mistaken. Hard as it might be to admit it, there was the possibility that his father was right after all. "No doubt I was unduly optimistic about literature—no doubt I was mistaken," he wrote bravely, if sadly, and came meekly back to his father with the promise that he would now go to Harvard Divinity School and behave himself.

Horatio Senior was elated and more than willing to forgive. Thus, three years after his graduation, Horatio found himself back in school again. To all appearances he was a changed man, earnest, sincere, dedicated, hardworking, and so he remained for the first two years at Harvard Divinity, praised by his teachers and his gratified father.

Then, inexplicably, he began to change again. His father was exasperated beyond measure, and puzzled as well, when the reports began to come in that Horatio's marks were lower by the term. From being head of the class he began to sink toward probation, in spite of warnings and reproofs. Once more, too, he began to spend his time alone—restless, moody, vague and inaccessible. The school encouraged him to go home and take a rest, but he would have none of it. There were only two months before graduation, and the worried father prayed that his strange son would not disappoint him again.

Senior would have been dismayed if he could have known what was going on in Horatio's mind, revealed only in his diary. He was thinking about writing again, about the joys and satisfactions of the literary life. "I will stay out the time in order to graduate," he concluded. "I figure the past three years have been wasted but I will receive my degree as something to carry through the years to remind me of my folly." His father was spared this revelation.

But once more one of the bizarre coincidences that appeared almost as often in Horatio's life as they did in his books disrupted his plans. Two old classmates from Gates Academy suddenly appeared in Cambridge one day and called upon him. Gilbert Ramsbotham, by this time twenty-seven years old, had grown up to be a large, happy young man with an inclination to the bottle. His companion, Martin Embry, was Gilbert's opposite, as he had been in school, a quiet, introspective boy who wanted to be a writer. These two unlikely friends were on their way to London and Paris for a junket; they had stopped to invite Horatio to join them.

The temptation was overwhelming. Through most of his years at Harvard, Horatio had dreamed of going to Europe, particularly to Paris, and his literary ambitions had since fed the dream. But there was the dreary fact of his poverty. Reluctantly, he had to say no to his friends, and tell them why.

Next day, like an episode from an Alger book, Floyd Thurstone died. In his will, the old man remembered with gratitude the prize money Horatio had generously given him, and left his young lodger two thousand dollars, a watch and a ring. In a day when a dinner in a fine restaurant cost less than a dollar, it was a fortune. Now there was nothing to stop Horatio from joining his friends—nothing, not even his graduation. He did not wait for the exercises. When his father and mother, knowing nothing of what had happened, arrived for the graduation ceremonies, they found Horatio's room empty. He was gone, without a word of explanation or apology, and the fatuous father and the poor, subdued mother were left to contemplate the ruin of their ambitions and sympathies.

CHAPTER 3

"I expected something more than the common sort of place it is," Alger said of London, mercilessly revealing his poverty of imagination. "Why, so far as I can see, nothing ever happens here."

What Embry thought of it he does not say. Ramsbotham spent most of their week in the city getting drunk and enjoying himself as he did everywhere, while the other two roamed the streets. They had heard much of Dickens without reading him, and unconsciously emulating Boswell, they sought him out, not stopping to ask themselves, as Boswell did Johnson, "Whether a man's being forward in making himself known to eminent people, and seeing as much of life, and getting as much information as he could in every way was not yet lessening himself by his forwardness." For them the question remained unanswered, as well as unasked. Dickens was never at home, although they called several times.

After a week of tramping about in constant London rain, the three were ready to sail for Paris, but as they were about to board the Channel steamer, Alger suddenly began to plead with his friends to go back to London and stay another week. They were amazed and indignant, and wanted to know his reason for such a mad request. When he gave it, they thought him madder still. Horatio told them seriously that he meant to be a writer, and since he might someday write stories with an English background, it was his duty to go back and take notes.

To Ramsbotham, the idea of Horatio as a writer was excruciating. He roared with laughter and gave his friend an impulsive nudge in the ribs—"as fierce as an ox's kick," Alger reported, and added half-contemptuously, "the fellow is such an unthinking brute." They went on to Paris.

Expecting so much, Horatio was again disappointed. The City of Light was wet and cold and foggy, exactly like London. "It doesn't come anywhere near to what I looked for. It is just like another city," Alger wrote home to his brother James. "This talk of gaiety is false—everything is quiet and moral, and though I did not expect to find a bedlam I anticipated something entirely different—more vivacity and less routine."

Horatio never made a worse judgment. If he could have known what Paris was really to mean to him, he might have fled precipitately after the first day. As it was, he may have had some queer premonition. When Ramsbotham, after a few days of inaction, insisted on going out on an evening expedition to find the gaiety Alger had already branded as false, he had to be satisfied with Embry's company. Horatio gathered that the goal of Ramsbotham's expedition was to be sex as well as liquor, and with his characteristic prudery, in which fear was mixed with his father's admonitions, he begged off.

Next day began one of the strangest periods of Alger's life. His friends had found the "real Paris" they had been looking for, and next morning and the next and constantly thereafter they told him of the girls, the drinking and the splendid times they were having. It was every young man's dream of what Paris ought to be—every young man except Horatio. He was alternately appalled by what he considered his friends' immorality and the forbidden passions their stories stirred in him.

Now there began a struggle between sacred and profane love, between the ironclad morality his father had instilled in him and the natural desires of a man who had still to know sex of any kind. There was more than a little of the pathological in this struggle. Horatio was determined to preserve his virtue intact, then and always. He would have surrendered it to Patience, his ideal love, but since her loss he intended to remain virginal. He thought and spoke of all this like a woman disappointed in her first love and thereafter resolved to be an old maid.

In his frantic effort to avoid temptation, he took to leaving the apartment in the morning, while his friends were still asleep, and staying away until he hoped they would have departed for another night in the fleshpots. He roamed about the city, scarcely seeing it, preoccupied with his tumbled thoughts. He walked beside the Seine, inspected the Louvre, and explored the bookstalls without buying anything.

His wandering progress led him to a few new acquaintances. One was Emmet Colvin, whom he met by chance, and who told him about Spain, for which he experienced one of his sudden enthusiasms, as quickly extinguished by his confused state of mind. Another was Arnold Stuart, whom he met through his landlord, and who told him stories of exotic places and people, to which Alger listened with vicarious pleasure. It was typical of Horatio's fear of life that his friendship with Stuart ended when he found him one day in an epileptic fit. Frightened and sick, he avoided Stuart afterward, and spent what time he was willing to give to anyone else with a German named Morris Gutterman, who planned to go into business in America and asked him a thousand questions until Horatio was bored to distraction.

Eventually, of course, he remembered that he was going to be a writer someday, and he began to make notes of what he saw and heard. Again, these notes disclose the poverty of his mind. "A big place and I didn't stay there long," he wrote of Notre Dame. Most of the other glories of Paris had no interest for him, and the notes he made on them were so sterile that he despaired of their value and tore them up.

One day somebody told him about the Morgue, describing it as a place where newspapermen and other writers were sure to find stories. He hurried to these gloomy precincts, somehow got himself admitted, and among the dead found living sex.

She was Elise Monselet, a figure no more romantic than he was, small and inclined to fat, regarding him with a pair of calculating blue eyes in which there was more sad knowledge of the world than guile. Elise had come to the Morgue on a mission straight out of a *chanson*, like the ones she herself sang in a café. Her lover had deserted her, suddenly and without explanation. That had been weeks ago. Unwilling to believe herself deserted, she had come to see if his unidentified body, no doubt self-destroyed for love, was lying on a slab. It was not, but a live American loomed before her as a possible substitute.

Elise was a practical girl. She knew that her café act would never make her rich and famous; it was her mimicry, not her singing voice, that kept her working. Meanwhile, away from the café, it was pleasant to live with a man who could help with the bills as well as entertain her after work. She was not a prostitute, only a girl who took one lover at a time until circumstance or propinquity drove them apart. Seeing Horatio in the Morgue, she decided, for reasons which may only be imagined, that he would be the next occupant of her apartment.

The conquest was ridiculously simple, hardly worth the effort of a worldly woman like Elise. She collided with him accidentally, accepted his apology, and before he knew it, they were outside the Morgue and walking away together, chatting as though they had known each other for years.

As they walked, Elise saw a friend and hailed her, anxious to introduce her American conquest. The three stood talking, and by another of the coincidences which haunted Alger's life, his friend Ramsbotham appeared, on an idle stroll, and was duly introduced to the girls. Ramsbotham assessed them both quickly, and before Horatio quite realized what was happening, his friend had disappeared with Elise's friend—straight to her apartment, as it turned out, where he lived from that day. Alger saw him only once more during his stay in Paris.

As for Elise, she discovered that the conquest of Horatio was not quite as complete as she had thought. No doubt this simple, direct girl, with healthy appetites, hardly knew what to make of a man who showed no inclination at all to go to bed with her. She saw that he knew nothing of Paris, of women, or in fact, of life. Elise had never been cast as a mother, but Horatio stirred her hitherto well concealed maternal feelings.

Naturally, she did not intend to go on being a mother for any longer than it might take to educate Horatio. He came to her café, listened to her sing, and basked in the glow of celebrity when she came to sit with him between appearances. A feeling of manly pride, something he had never experienced in his life, stirred in him as she sat at his table, regarding him fondly and coldly rejecting the invitations of those who wanted her to dance or drink with them. Horatio was not good at either drinking or dancing; he only wanted to sit and watch Elise. At night, when she had finished, he took her to her door, wished her a fond but polite good night, and departed, leaving her frustrated and baffled.

One night, however, after they had gone to a ball at which Elise had done all the dancing, she insisted that he come up the stairs to her apartment. It was a sad-comic scene, the biology reversed, Elise pleading with him to come in, Horatio protesting that really, no, it was late and he had better be getting home. At length she lost her temper, and whether Horatio was afraid she might wake up the house and disgrace him, or whether the idea she was conveying so plainly pushed him, fainting, past the point of further resistance, we will never know. At any rate, he followed her inside, and there he was lost forever. His diary recorded the first astonishment and delight, as well as the second thoughts that followed immediately.

"Feb. 4th. I was a fool to have waited so long. It is not vile as I thought. Without question I will be better off physically, anyhow I have sometimes thought so. She is more passionate than me. . . .

"Feb. 6th. I ought to know more. Elise makes fun of me. She says she knows I wanted to . . . I am learning things from her.

"Feb. 7th. Should I go on and is it right? What makes it wrong? She doesn't think it is wrong and nobody else does, only I.

"Feb. 10th. I won't do it again. If nothing else, from now on I will be clean. I *shall*. They may laugh but I will leave if anything they say to me. I want to be alone and I don't want to see Elise. She must leave me alone. I want to get away somewhere anyhow. My head aches."

Unless one knew Alger, it would be difficult to believe a man had written these lines.

For days he stayed away from her, miserable, struggling with himself, and apparently trying to find some kind of rationalization for doing what he had been told from infancy, with hammer strokes of rhetoric, was forbidden. One night he found it, and as soon as he had scrawled down this exciting philosophical revelation in his diary, he hurried to the café. Behind him, on the pages of his little black book, he left the excuse he was making to himself and his father:

"I want to live to be great. Suppose it is vain—all great men are vain. What have they got that I need to be like them? Whatever it is I will see. If I insist with myself why shouldn't I be, as well as the rest of them? It is just something that grows inside and I can feel it just as surely as I am writing. It seems to depend on doing what you want because all of them are that way. I will do *what I want* hereafter, least I can do is try. They say true genius has no bounds as to conventions. Genius has prerogatives. Then I will have prerogatives too."

The liberating effect of his rationalization was no less than miraculous. Having anointed himself a genius, and therefore no longer bound by convention, Horatio dived into the fleshpots headfirst and disappeared from ecclesiastical view. He drank, he learned to dance, he sang in a loud voice unrecognizable as his own. He was, indeed, the life of the café. At night he made himself and Elise happier than either one had believed was possible at the beginning.

As they came to know each other better, they made pleased discoveries. She learned that Horatio's consuming ambition was to be a writer, whereupon she disclosed to him that her real interest was not the café and her career there, or even sex, as he had supposed, but literature. This little doll-faced blonde was, Horatio learned with astonishment, more widely read than he was, and much more knowledgeable about authors. She quickly sensed his lack of brilliance, and their conversational relationship became like their sexual one—Elise the aggressor and teacher, Horatio the passive learner.

Passive he might be, but he was fascinated. Elise talked with passionate enthusiasm about the great French writers of the day —Victor Hugo, Dumas père, Balzac, Henri Murger—and she was equally well informed about Dickens, Thackeray and their contemporaries. Sometimes she took him to cafés where the literati of Paris gathered to drink and gossip and argue. Horatio sat quietly in the background at these affairs, because he had nothing to say to such people, but Elise traded anecdotes and arguments with them as an equal, while he listened with wonder and excitement. He loved to hear stories about Eugène Sue, de Musset, Gautier and the others whose lives and loves were discussed so freely, in a way he had never known. This, at last, was the literary life he had dreamed about back in Cambridge. It was all he needed to confirm his ambitions.

His friend Embry, who now had to live alone, wrote to his sister about Horatio: "Times are when he comes and goes without seeming to know that he is doing either, as if he were preoccupied with weighty affairs that mere mortal man cannot expect to grasp. Why, Mary, it is weird to see the far-away gaze that haunts his eyes even when the rest of us are engaged in violent talk—he just sits and stares and says nothing for so long that his doze becomes noticeable and some of us are willing to believe he is posing. He is no poet and has no breadth of imagination that I have been able to discern, yet he does once in a while advance a startling suggestion; viz., last night he inquired of the advisability of three authors, presented with a stipulated set of circumstances, moulding them into a story and having their separate versions printed together, in such manner affording the readers a glimpse of how their minds react. I have also seen him begin to expound other ideas but he seldom finds himself able to work them out completely in his mind. In other words, his thinking seems to break down before it gets very far ahead. He isn't much to look at, nor entertaining to be with, and still I can't help thinking he is not an ordinary person. He may be above, or he may be below, but I have no doubt he is not average."

Horatio baffled Embry, as he did so many others. He looked and acted like such an uncomplicated, rather dull man that it was always a surprise to find a complex human being of whom almost anything might be expected. To anyone who had known him before, it would have been shocking enough to find him living with a Parisian café singer, but no one could have anticipated the next bizarre turn of his life.

He fell precipitately into the hands of an English Circe, a powerful woman who took him completely in hand.

Where Elise had used simple guile, Charlotte Evans was bold and forthright, as the masculine role she played demanded. Again biology was reversed. Charlotte saw Horatio in the café where Elise worked, and marked him for her own; he appeared to attract women with this particular psychological structure. In his diary he recorded that Charlotte had approached him "brusquely and noisily, engaging in conversation, later asking me to dance, which I politely rejected."

Charlotte was not an easy woman to reject. Besides her determination, she had certain other assets, including gray eyes, black hair, provocative lips and a figure that made poor Elise's deficiencies all the more noticeable. She was an aggressive, sensual woman, who for complicated reasons meant to have Horatio. Elise made the mistake of underestimating her, and so did Alger. It must have been a surprise to both of them when he disappeared with her.

She took him to live with her, and in this new relationship he was utterly dominated by a woman who absorbed him and controlled him in a manner chillingly reminiscent of insect behavior. Cruelly, she compelled him to go back with her to the café and sit through Elise's act. Elise carried it off like the sadly experienced woman that she was, Charlotte had her triumph, and poor Horatio suffered a traumatic experience that deepened his love-hate feelings toward his new mistress. Or, it would be more accurate to say, *he* was *her* mistress.

Their life together was stormy. Sometimes she was so voluptuous, so lovely, that he was lost in passion, and an hour later he might be lashed by her violent temper, which she made no effort to control. It was the kind of life Charlotte enjoyed; in Horatio she had the perfect foil for her own twisted psyche. But for him, living had become a constant torment. Once he tried to flee from her, but she brought him back and gave him the kind of moral sermon his father might have delivered, and as he had with his father, he yielded.

Horatio considered himself trapped. He wrote disconsolately

in his diary: "Tonight she had another crying fit but what for or what is the cause I don't pretend to know. I don't think she knows herself—just stupidly hysterical and screaming enough to hurt my ears. Always, always, *always* yelling. I am under no obligations to her but how can I get away?—she would find me again and pester me to death. Maybe I would like to choke her!"

He knew that he would never do anything of the kind. Instead, he fell into his characteristic lassitude, unable to do anything or think clearly. He was beginning to think that his miserable state might be the just retribution for his Parisian immorality, and that, too, contributed to his anguish.

Like a bolt of lightning came a message from that safe moral world he had left so far behind. It was a letter from his mother, saying: "I have had no word from you for six months. I do not know whether you are well or even if you are living, which I pray to Heaven you are both. What have I done to have you not think of me at all? Though you may not think of me, I think of you each day. You are always in my heart. There must be some good reason why you have forgotten.

"All here arc well and wondering where you are, though your Father is angry you should be so silent. Write to me, my boy, for I bless you and keep wishing you were back. Keep your faith in God, for He is good and will care for you if you remember Him."

That was all he needed to propel him out of his lethargy. He prepared to leave at once, but kept his plans secret from Charlotte; he did not dare tell her he intended to go home. He made his farewells, as he described them in his diary: "Said good-bye to Embry. He is surprised that I am leaving. I am not so surprised as glad. Went to see Elise. She was sad and kind. Kissed me farewell. I do not love her at all but I like her simple ways. Now my task is to get away without seeing Charlotte."

But he had made a mistake in trusting Embry. He had no more than breathed the first precious winds of freedom aboard ship, congratulating himself on his successful escape, when Charlotte stood before him, accusing and triumphant. They were on the way to America together.

CHAPTER 4

Alger was a pitiful figure as he contemplated New York again from the deck of the boat that was bringing him home in late November, 1861, after nearly a year in Europe. It is difficult to understand what the masterful Charlotte, standing beside him, a handsome figure, saw in this thin, sick man. He was down to 110 pounds; he looked seedy, ill and beaten down.

Desperation, however, had given him more wit than usual. As they left the boat, he told Charlotte, in the classic manner, that he was going across the street to buy a newspaper, and as soon as he was out of sight, he fled. Undoubtedly she had thought him incapable of such a thing. There was no way to trace him, because Horatio had thoughtfully ordered his luggage sent on to Massachusetts. A woman of Charlotte's resources could probably have tracked him down if she had cared to but in a promising new city, full of potential victims, she may have thought herself well rid of him. In any case, she never saw him again.

As for Alger, trembling in the early winter cold without adequate clothing, there was only one thought in his mind, and that was to flee to home and Mother. He sent word ahead and got on the first train he could find. To his relief, he found his mother waiting for him alone at the station with the news that he would be spared the dreaded confrontation with his father, who was traveling on the Lord's business, a trip which would take him several weeks. As for Olive, she was so overwhelmed with joy to have her son home that she would not have thought of reproaching him with anything.

Horatio basked in sweet forgetfulness. He strolled about town, ate and slept, got his health back, wrote poetry, told his mother carefully edited tales of life abroad, and waited for his father's return with intermittent apprehension. He had no illusions about his father's welcome. There would be lengthy tours through the fields of self-righteousness and repentance, prayers and meditation, followed by the certainty that *now* he would be expected to enter the ministry. As though to confirm his thoughts, his father, having been informed of Horatio's return, wrote to Olive:

"On the 23rd I shall reach Boston and promptly go home, in order that we may spend Christmas together. It will be good to see you after this extended absence. As for my wayward son—need I say, dearest Olive, how anxious I am to see him again! I trust he has seen sufficient of the world to stay at home hereafter and settle himself to useful endeavor. I have in mind a church which will soon seek the services of another minister."

Resolutely, Horatio told his mother that he was as determined as ever to be a writer, and quietly he left home before his father arrived, to be frustrated once again.

Having made the decision and gone to Boston to carry it out, Alger had no way of fulfilling it. He had no job and little money; much of the time he was hungry. Under the circumstances he could hardly turn to his father, and his crippling timidity kept him from applying for jobs which he might have been able to do.

He was saved, quite naturally, by a coincidence, in the true Alger style. One day while he was wandering about Boston, disconsolate and almost starving, he encountered another old classmate from Gates Academy. This was Alfred Wright, who heard his sorry narrative and generously invited him to come home with him and stay as long as he liked.

Once more Alger found himself in a different world. Wright, a rich liberal, spent most of his time promoting the Abolitionist cause, to which he was passionately devoted. An accomplished speaker, he made antislavery harangues night after night to audiences in and around Boston. While Horatio, a conservative by nature, shrank from such a wholehearted commitment, he was made at least somewhat aware of the strong tides running in his native land, about which he had known almost nothing until that time. But he listened to the speeches, passive as always, without being drawn into the issues that inspired them, and without really understanding them. Horatio was merely bewildered by the events of the early months of the conflict. The approach of war meant chiefly that he was about to be ejected from his warm nest, since Wright prepared at once to close his house and join the army.

Adrift again, Horatio found a tutoring position in Cambridge, teaching French and Greek to Wilbur Cross, a fifteen-year-old boy who was profoundly uninterested and thought only of the war. Oddly, it took a false rumor to rouse the same thoughts in Alger. One day his pupil arrived in a state of agitation with the news that a Confederate army had driven President Lincoln out of Washington. The two hurried down to the post office, where the latest bulletins were posted, and there they found it was only a rumor, but suddenly a spark kindled in Horatio and he found himself involved in the war, much as he had been in other enthusiasms.

Carried away, he organized a drill corps and began marching as many as a hundred boys around in a field, listening with pleasure when they addressed him as "captain," and wielding a violin bow in lieu of a more violent weapon, while they performed their drills with broomsticks and a few rifles. At the beginning, he knew as little of military routines as they, but he had an army manual and taught them from the book.

Horatio enjoyed every minute of it, commanding "Alger's Army of Up-and Comings," as some spectators began to call it.

It never occurred to him to enlist and take part in reality; in the fantasy world which he occupied most of the time, he considered what he was doing a splendid service to God and country, and since he was having so much fun doing it, he had no intention of giving it up.

But reality intruded. His pupil's father discovered that his son was learning no French, and, although Horatio earnestly explained that the boy was doing well in the Army of Up-and-Comings and could expect to be made a sergeant, he was fired. Wilbur immediately ran away and enlisted in the Massachusetts Volunteers. Alger wandered over the Charles and into Boston again.

He found the city in a turmoil. News of the early Union defeats had arrived, the call for volunteers was out, and there was a rush to the recruiting stations. Carried away again, Alger rushed too, but once more coincidence intervened. While he was hurrying to enlist, he fell and broke his arm. He appeared next day, nobly, but as he expected, he was refused for active duty. Unexpectedly, however, he was advised that he could, until his arm healed, act as a civilian recruiting officer.

It was one of the longest bone-healing cases in medical history. Month after month he attended amiably to his clerical duties with his arm in a sling. Sometimes he permitted abashed young men about to sign up to believe that he had been wounded. But a letter from his ex-pupil fired him up again. It appeared that Wilbur, too, was enjoying himself. He wrote: "I am having a great time. Johnny Popetetsky is here and we send salutes. We are hoping for a battle quick and I am trying to be a corporal and I hope I am, which I should be. Some have lice and get their hair cut off. Everybody cheered us like a king in Philadelphia. You should be a general I guess. The niggers are funny here. I wish there was target practice but most we do is march. Send me a letter as every one gets them."

Perhaps it was the line about being a general which stirred him, but in any event, Horatio's arm was healed and he was ready for the front. The Boston recruiter ordered him to join Company F, of the Massachusetts Volunteers, at Pittsfield, but when he arrived there, he found that the company had marched off to the war. He found them in Philadelphia and went on in their company by train toward Washington, still not enlisted, still not in uniform.

At this point the role of coincidence in Alger's life approaches the incredible. He might have gone on to Washington, been thrust into uniform, and shot shortly thereafter, but as the train plunged on through the night toward the Capitol, it plowed off the rails and disintegrated in a shower of steam. Horatio picked his way through the dead and dying, unhurt. As he stumbled about in the dark and confusion, another train, following close behind, hurled itself into the wreckage. As other men were added to the list of killed and maimed, Horatio was thrown clear—and broke his arm again.

Back he came to Cambridge, and found shelter at the home of his former pupil, where Wilbur's mother had been compelled to take in roomers, with both father and son away in the army. His life there is described in a letter to her husband by Mrs. Cross, and it has a familiar sound.

"My guest is still with me," his landlady wrote. "I see little of him, however, for most of the day he keeps to himself, usually staying upstairs, as quiet as a mouse, going out for a few hours in the night. He acts strangely—that is, so reserved and oppressed. One thing, I suppose, he is worrying about paying us for rent. He is about two months back now but I haven't the heart to remind him. He looks honest and I think if he had the money he would pay. Unless you think it advisable I won't mention it to him. Last night, while he was out, I went into the room to get a book and the desk was open and a pile of papers on it. It was impossible to make out anything he was writing because he has to use his left hand and I imagine he must find it hard to read his own writing. But there was something about every slave his own master and something about the church as a power for arbitration. Maybe he is an author and I should feel proud to have him here!"

Horatio was, indeed, beginning to be an author. Painfully, with his left hand, he was jotting down ideas for books. Mrs. Cross did not see it, but already there was a brief synopsis on his desk of a book which, fifteen years later, was to be *Young Captain Jack; or, The Son of a Soldier.* The synopsis read:

"Boy living with Mrs. Alice Ruthven. Thinks she is his mother but she is not. His mother perished in a storm years before and his father is also supposed to be dead. His father is living, however, and is an officer in the Union army. The son, Jack, learns Mrs. R. is no relative of his after all. Later a man appears in the village in search of papers on a nearby island where a ship foundered years before. He is seeking papers belonging to Jack's father which will establish his—the villain's—claim to a fortune which should rightfully go to Jack. Foiled by a negro servant; and Jack, who has formed all his young friends into a company and drills them, meets an attack of Confederate infantry and is being beaten back when reinforcements arrive headed by a man who proves to be his father and who in the end marries Mrs. Ruthven who has taken excellent care of Jack."

Alger was, in fact, already an author. In 1856 he had published a volume titled *Bertha's Christmas Vision; An Autumn Sheaf,* dedicated to his mother, and containing short sketches interspersed with poetry. He may have been, a year later, the author of a slim narrative poem published in Boston, titled *Nothing to Do,* inspired by William Butler's famous *Nothing to Wear.* This poem is of doubtful authenticity as an Alger item, although its style, bad as it is, and its general feeling speak of Horatio.

In any case, he was preparing during these days in Cambridge to write his first full-length book, *Frank's Campaign; or, What Boys Can Do on the Farm for the Camps,* which appeared in 1864 as his contribution to the home front. Its characters and a good many of its incidents were drawn directly from his drill corps days.

Meanwhile, he had to earn a living. Mrs. Cross was not importunate but he was aware of his debt. Fortunately he found the ideal position, doing research for a lawyer, Roscoe M. Carpenter, who had a Boston office and also worked in his Cambridge house. It was easy, pleasant work and Horatio soon made enough money from it not only to pay his back rent, but to save a little. He was restless, filled with vague longings and discontents, and again uncertain about what he should do with his life. Certainly there was nothing to detain him in Cambridge, and, as soon as he had enough money, he quit his job and came down to New York late in June, 1863.

The city was as turbulent as his state of mind. Tides of discontent flowed through it, stemming from the political and economic dislocations of the war. New York had never been enthusiastic about the Union cause. It was saturated with still unassimilated Irish and Germans who had come over in the great immigration waves of the thirties and forties. Jammed into squalid slums on the East Side from the Battery to the shanties of Goat Hill, where the Grand Central area lies today, these people were exploited by the politicians, condemned to menial jobs for the most part, and suffering from the high cost of wartime living. They had no strong feelings about the slavery issue. On the contrary, there was a powerful undercurrent of resentment running among them at the time of Alger's arrival because they feared that the advancing Union armies would further depress the labor market.

There was an ugly mood in the city. Gangs roamed the East Side, and the entire length of the Bowery was not a safe place for a law-abiding citizen to be, even in daylight. Every variety of sin was doing a flourishing business. The war and its issues seemed no more than a nuisance and a cause of bad times to a good part of the population.

Horatio noted the state of the city in his diary: "New Yorkers are not giving the support to the War as Boston is. People here talk mostly about high prices for commodities and they wish the War would end one way or another." Aware of the tension and the prospects of trouble which were causing open anxiety among many citizens, Alger characteristically went directly to the top, to Chief of Police Thomas C. Acton and volunteered his help in case the peace was disturbed. Chief Acton may well have wondered what help this earnest, ineffectual little man intended to give him, but he thanked Horatio and told him no help would be needed. The chief had deluded himself into thinking that he had the situation well in hand.

But the city was waiting, and what it was waiting for was the application of the President's Conscription Act, which had been passed in March. As the hot, muggy summer closed down on the steaming streets, talk of the impending draft curled up from the saloons and front stoops like smoke from a smoldering fire. Hate was in the air—hatred of Lincoln, hatred of Negroes, hatred of the poverty that fed their discontents.

Into this powder keg on a still July morning fell the match of the first draft call. A silent, sullen crowd heard the first names drawn: O'Connor, McCarthy, Desmond, Hogan, Muldoon, and names other than Irish, but the list was bound to be heavily weighted with the Irish majority. Nothing happened that day, however, nor on the next, a Sunday, during which large, muttering crowds of men gathered everywhere on the East Side in front of the saloons or blocking the streets. The clammy, penetrating humidity which had gripped the city for days was fraying nerves.

Then, on Monday morning, came the explosion. A mob that began gathering at daybreak until it numbered nearly ten thousand began to move from its meeting place in the construction work at the lower end of Central Park down Fifth and Sixth avenues, turning east at Forty-fifth and Forty-sixth streets until it was massed before draft headquarters, the provost marshal's office, at Third Avenue and Forty-sixth Street.

At eleven o'clock the front door opened and a detachment of policemen took up their stations. The drum was placed in plain sight, and the draft officials appeared to call the names. Four were drawn in an ominous quiet. Then one was read that brought a stir, like the first gust of wind in a storm. It was the name of a man widely known as a leader in the Black Joke Volunteers, a notorious fire company, most of whose members had long criminal records. A pistol shot rang in the sodden air. At the signal the mob rushed upon the marshal's office building, signaling their advance with a fusillade of stones that broke most of the windows. While the police held back the first onslaught, the provost marshal escaped out the back door with his files. Then the rioters broke into the building, overwhelmed the police, sacked it and set it afire. With that act, the war moved from the fields of Gettysburg to New York.

Alger recorded his view of the Great Draft Riot in a report that later appeared in a book called *Our Police Protectors*, by A. E. Costello, and in a letter to his mother. In the first he wrote:

"For three days and three nights the rioters maintained a reign of terror. They sacked houses in great numbers, demolished the offices of the Provost General, burned the colored orphan asylum, attacked the police, and chased the negroes—women and children even—wherever they appeared on the streets, and when caught hung them on the nearest lamp-post. They tore down and trampled under foot the National flag, and robbed stores in open day. The Secretary of War ordered home the regiments doing duty in Pennsylvania, but ere they arrived the climax of atrocities had been reached, and through the combined action of the police and the citizens, together with the slender military force at the disposal of the authorities, the riot had been substantially quelled. The police displayed admirable address and undaunted bravery against overwhelming numbers; they were under the command of Thomas C. Acton, President of the Police Board, who issued orders with the coolness and skill of a trained military veteran."

To his mother he wrote: "I have never imagined anything so

terrible as the scenes which are being enacted here. Thousands of men and women have gone out of their minds. They storm the streets, many of them armed, breaking into stores, attacking peaceful citizens without cause. They refuse to abide by the draft regulation and everything is in a fearful turmoil. There is no such thing as loyalty to country—the President is condemned and the South lauded. No one knows where it will end.

"Yesterday afternoon I saw a hundred men attack a defenceless negro who ventured out. He was beaten unmercifully and nearly killed with kicks and blows. I felt like leaping into them—but what could one person do? For there was no one other than myself who seemed to feel like interfering. I do not know whether he was dead at the time or not, but they carried him to a post and hung him, cheering throughout as though they were attending a celebration. I grew sick at the sight and could have fainted. So disgusting—so revolting! Still now I am dizzy from the effect and have not eaten since. Loyal citizens will answer this outrage by joining the army without delay and tomorrow I shall be among them."

It had all been too much for Horatio, and how well his mother knew it, reading between the lines. So strong was her feeling that she persuaded her husband to go down to New York. At least he could see his son before Horatio went into the army—if he did. But he would not be going. His father found him deliriously ill, with a sickness which a doctor diagnosed as pneumonia.

Pneumonia it may have been, but there seems little doubt that a large part of his malaise, and the other mishaps which had afflicted him since the war began, had their psychic origin in the conflict that must have tortured him, his conscience propelling him toward the war and his natural timidity making him unconsciously shrink from it in horror. Seeing his father again must have seemed to him like opening a gate to the past, offering a straight, secure road to a resolution of his conflict by returning to the world he had foresworn, the world of his father. By the time he was well enough to travel, he was on his father's arm, shakily making his way to a train that would take them home to Massachusetts. His father was well satisfied. At last—at last—he was certain the boy would become a minister.

CHAPTER 5

On the eighth of December, 1864, Horatio entered the ministry, ordained as pastor of the Unitarian Church in Brewster, Massachusetts. He had come to this decision while he convalesced at home, telling himself that the horrible scenes he had witnessed in New York were convincing proof that the need of the world was the word of God. He intended not only to save souls, but to console them.

His first sermons were models of Northern patriotism, full of praise for Lincoln and fervent exhortations on behalf of the Union. The little group of worshipers who gathered to hear him thought him "gentle, solicitous of the welfare of others, and humble as it behooves one of the Lord's servants to be."

He had intended to give up literature completely, but he could not keep himself from making notes for stories on the margins of his sermons. Moreover, forces again were at work in his life to change it and direct him back to the only way of life that ever truly interested him. By a chance meeting whose circumstances are unrecorded, he met William Taylor Adams, a man whose own life had been what would later be known as "a Horatio Alger story," and who would be Alger's nearest rival as a prolific writer of stories for boys.

Adams was a Massachusetts boy from Bellingham, whose father later became the owner of the Lamb Tavern in Boston, and then moved to a farm in West Roxbury. There Adams endured the hard life which was commonplace in those days wherever men worked the soil. He had little time to go to school, except in winter when farm work was light, and then it was so cold in his room that he had to turn the pages of his textbooks with mittened hands. Fortunately he did not also have poverty to battle, as did Alger's heroes and the real-life business entrepreneurs of the century. His father was able to give him private tutoring and to send him traveling about the country, after which he became a teacher.

When Horatio met him, he had been teaching in the Boston public schools for twenty years and had resigned to write, and to edit magazines for young people. His first editing venture was *Student and Schoolmate*, which had been founded ten years before by uniting two struggling magazines—*Student*, of course, and *Schoolmate*. Adams took over the editorship from N. A. Calkins and began looking for new writers. Presumably he was attracted to Horatio's work as a result of reading *Frank's Campaign*.

Adams invited Horatio to contribute, and in 1865 a few simple tales on the general order of *Bertha's Christmas Vision* appeared under the by-line of the Reverend Horatio Alger, Jr. A few years later, both men were writing books and magazine fiction steadily, Adams under the pseudonym that made him famous, "Oliver Optic." The difference between the two is well illustrated by Adams's versatility. He not only wrote 126 books and thousands of short stories, considerably more than Alger's output, but he edited three magazines at various times, produced love stories under another pseudonym, "Irving Brown," travel sketches as "Clingham Hunter, M.D.," and miscellaneous pieces as "Old Stager." Unlike Alger, he never used his own name.

"Oliver Optic's" books had millions of boy readers who were devoted to him, and many of the things he wrote were curiously like Horatio's—one, for instance, was the "Onward and Upward" series—but he somehow never achieved Alger's enormous popularity, never became the enduring household word.

In Cambridge, as both started their careers, it was Horatio who thought of Adams as the successful one. He was grateful for the opportunity to sell his simple stories, and seeing them in print stirred his ambition anew. He began to outline longer tales, book length; one of them was the first intimation of *Ragged Dick*. The more he thought of writing, the more his enthusiasm waned for helping suffering humanity from the pulpit, and he began to regard the ministry as a dead end. He could not bring himself to think of ending his career in such blameless and obscure piety. In March, 1866, he resigned his pastorate and moved to New York. For his father, it was the final, crushing blow.

For Horatio, however, it was the beginning of what he now considered to be his proper life, for which he had always been meant. He was certain he would never deviate again from the pursuit of literature. The Boston publisher, A. K. Loring, who had brought out *Frank's Campaign*, had urged him to write other books for the same market, and he had obliged while he was still in Brewster with *Paul Prescott's Charge*, published in 1865. Now, free of any other commitment, he roamed the New York streets in search of material from life to feed his inadequate imagination, and produced in rapid succession during 1866 the curious *Helen Ford*, and *Timothy Crump's Ward*, his first attempt at an adult novel, which Loring published in paper wrappers in the popular "Loring's Railway Companions" series—a paperback original, as it would be known today.

Early in 1867, discouraged by the comparative failure of *Timothy Crump*, he returned to the boys' market with *Charlie Codman's Cruise*, and that year began to write as a serial for *Student and Schoolmate* the story of *Ragged Dick*, his best book, which appeared in 1868 and is recognized today in the Grolier collection as one of the hundred most significant books published before 1900.

It was *Ragged Dick* that brought him to the second love of his life, the Newsboys' Lodging House, where he found the material for the books that were to make his reputation. The details, however, are not clear. The story is that Everett Jansen Wendell, an ex-Harvard athlete who had been hired by the superintendent, Charles O'Connor, to bring order into the postwar confusion of the House, had read *Ragged Dick* as a serial in *Student and Schoolmate,* and invited Alger to use the material provided by the House because he considered Horatio's moral tales exactly the right kind of reading matter for the tenants.

If this story were true, it would be difficult to explain Alger's introduction to *Ragged Dick,* in which he expresses his indebtedness "to the excellent Superintendent of the Newsboys' Lodging House in Fulton St., for some facts of which he has been able to make use." This would indicate that Alger was already familiar with the House before he wrote *Ragged Dick,* although the explanation may lie in the fact that the published book was a rewritten and expanded version of the magazine serial. It is quite possible the serial was written from observation outside the House, and the book had the benefit of his new acquaintance with the institution.

In any case, Horatio was aware at once of the material he had to draw upon as soon as he came to New York to live. The city was overrun with hundreds of homeless, footloose boys who had been mustered out of the Union Army, where they had been drummer boys. They ranged in age from twelve up to sixteen or seventeen, and were making a precarious living as bootblacks, delivery boys, newsboys—all the occupations which Alger was to celebrate in his books about them. In his preface to *Ragged Dick,* Horatio noted that he planned to write a series "intended to illustrate the life and experiences of the friendless and vagrant children who are now numbered by thousands in New York and other cities."

City officials and the police were aware of the problem the children presented, but the corrupt political life of the city was not likely to produce any solutions. Their savior was Charles Loring Brace, who had founded the House in 1853, and now invited the wandering drummer boys to make it their home in New York.

Brace was a philanthropist whose career had paralleled

Horatio's in one respect. The son of a distinguished Connecticut family, he had followed his family's urgings and studied for the ministry at Yale Divinity School, but he had discovered that his true interests were in New York, where he hoped to do something about the appalling delinquency of its younger citizens. He, too, was distracted by Europe, but far from being trapped in the Paris fleshpots, he became an international incident by going to jail in Hungary as a Kossuth sympathizer, released after thirteen courts-martial only through the intervention of the United States minister. After writing of these and other experiences in two books and bringing home a British bride, he turned to the task in New York upon which he had set himself. He founded the Children's Aid Society in 1853, or at least was influential in helping to found it. The Newsboys' Lodging House was one of the Society's activities, which numbered the establishment of other lodging houses, as well as industrial schools, sanitariums, summer camps and night schools.

Brace's philanthropy rested solidly on the principle of self-help; he was against any kind of charity likely to pauperize its recipients, consequently the House was not a home for idlers. It cost the boys six pennies for supper and five pennies for a bed at night. Superintendent Charles O'Connor was their father confessor, the diagnostician of their ailments, and their impartial adviser. With the help of Wendell, he established the new rules by which the House had to be run after the influx of drummer boys produced near chaos. They were expected to work, and most of them were either bootblacks or newsboys. They had to attend classes in elementary subjects at the House, which O'Connor taught. They were required to take a bath every week. Their reading matter was carefully supervised, and that was where Horatio, who was Wendell's idea of a model author, entered the scene.

Alger became virtually an inmate of the House himself. He had quarters at various times in other parts of the city, but his heart was on Fulton Street in the shabby rooms over the *Sun*'s offices, and there he came every day. After Wendell departed for other activities, Horatio and O'Connor became intimate friends; the superintendent shared his office, made his records available, and spent long hours talking with his new lodger. Alger treated himself as though he were a waif too, as indeed he was, in a sense. He began to stay on for supper, paying his pennies with the others, and if there was a bed available, he paid the fee and slept in it. O'Connor kept him constantly supplied with anecdotes and stories gathered from the boys, and Horatio himself was soon their friend and confidant, working a never-failing vein of plot material.

With every passing week, Alger sank deeper into the life of the institution. He did much of his work there, beginning now to turn out books in rapid succession, but he also fashioned for himself a way of living fully as strange as any of the earlier periods. His friendship with O'Connor was a closer relationship than any he had ever enjoyed. While it is dangerous to read into it more pathologic overtones than may have existed, there were strong elements of the homosexual in this friendship, at least on Alger's part, although there is no reason to believe it was ever overt. On the face of it, Alger appeared to be living a kind of existence which was homosexual in nature, if not in fact. He had renounced women and the conventional patterns of sex. As far as anyone knows, he had no women friends. All his time was spent either with O'Connor or the young boys who surrounded them.

The two men were familiar figures, in the House and on the streets. At night they spent long hours discussing the institution's program, and how to make it better. O'Connor put his feet on the desk and blew cigar smoke in the air, while Alger sat meditatively chewing candy, which he loved. On summer nights, they walked on Broadway and along the Battery, enjoying the cool air from the harbor and talking of their lives before they met.

As for the boys, they were much more perceptive about Horatio than he imagined. He thought they regarded him as their protector, a role in which interested adults had cast him and O'Connor, and one which flattered and pleased him. In fact, the boys knew him for an easy mark, and they took advantage of him in numerous ways. When he loaned them money in his usual generous manner, they often failed to repay him. Sometimes he even set them up in their paper-selling or boot-blacking enterprises, and never asked for repayment. At noon he would gather up several of the boys he knew were having a hard time and likely to be hungry, and take them to lunch with him. If a boy was missing, he helped the police to locate the wanderer. He could often be found riding about the city in a carriage, visiting the boys wherever they might be working.

For the ease with which he could be hoodwinked or imposed upon, they regarded him with a tolerant contempt, but nevertheless they turned to him for all manner of consolations. He sat by their bedsides when they were ill, and if a boy died, it was Horatio who gave the sermon and conducted the rites, in his best professional manner. If a boy did wrong, Alger was the last to believe him guilty, and on occasion he would get a lawyer to fight the case, if he thought an injustice was being done.

As time went on, he began to appear before gatherings of the boys at the House to give informal lectures, in which he sounded exactly like the moralizing old gentlemen in his books. For these occasions, however, Alger was transformed. Ordinarily a drab, careless dresser, he put on his best and most colorful clothes, and made himself generally immaculate. He seemed to rise from his physical insignificance, bring resonance and conviction into his ordinary rather quavering voice, and exhorted his young listeners to heights of attainment which, for the moment, he too apparently believed he had reached.

"Ten years from now most of you boys will be grown men," he told one such gathering. "You will be working in stores, some of you, and some will be in banks and others in manufacturing establishments. Some of you may be doctors and lawyers. My little friend Howard here told me the other day he wanted to be a soldier. That is a laudable ambition too. George Washington was a soldier and so was our late president Mr. Lincoln. There is no telling how far you boys can go. But you have to work hard and study. If you spend your time going to amusements you won't get anywhere and I know you want to get somewhere. You boys want to be respectable citizens, a credit to yourselves and to this great city. You want to have wives and children of your own. You want comfort in old age.

"I want to tell you boys to keep thinking ahead to the day when you get married. Some of you have been fortunate enough to come from homes where happiness was plentiful even if worldly goods were not. Think what it means to have a happy home of your own! Now can you have a home like that without the right kind of wife? Of course not! Well, to get the right kind you have to deserve her. Yes, you must make yourselves worthy and deserving. You don't want to go on living all alone by yourselves. You want families, many boys and girls running around you and you will be their father, bringing them up in a wonderful way."

It may have been difficult for some of the more astute boys in his audience to reconcile this stern-voiced upholder of home and family, dressed in a bright necktie and neat suit, with the unkempt figure who lived among them without wife or child of his own. No doubt it was even harder to equate him with another kind of Alger who was only whispered about among the boys, an Alger who sometimes put on a grotesque wig, wrapped himself in a cape right out of the Grand Guignol, and paraded down Broadway at night, bemusing the crowds who turned to stare at him. He had been inspired to this odd behavior by another Broadway character known as The Limekiln Man, an eccentric with a long beard and intense blue eyes, dressed in shabby clothes which were covered with white from the limekiln he slept in near Gansevoort Street. His frequent appearances on the street where everyone strolled made him a familiar figure, often mentioned in the newspapers. Possibly Horatio hoped to attract the same kind of attention and enjoy a vicarious fame in disguise. Unquestionably there were far deeper psychological motivations.

Parading in wig and cape was not his only eccentricity. He had an inordinate fondness for playing the bass drum in the Newsboys' band, and, although he was far from being a good performer the boys would never have interfered with his obvious intense pleasure. Whenever the band marched in a parade, the odd, adult figure of Alger and his drum towered among the urchins, an implausible spectacle.

O'Connor was uncomfortable about his friend's peculiarities, and when Alger first appeared in wig and cape, he must have doubted the other man's sanity. Loyally, he made excuses. Alger wore the disguise so that he might better get material for his stories, O'Connor said; it was a writer's prerogative. He could not explain the bass drum playing, however, and there were rude outsiders who thought Horatio was a fool, as well as eccentric. Owen Bailey, a New York *Herald* reporter, was among those who thought so. Like one of the bullies from Horatio's youth grown up, he sneered contemptuously at the band's devoted bass drummer one night, and Alger instinctively raised a threatening arm, a rare gesture for him. Bailey promptly knocked him down, and O'Connor banished the *Herald*'s man from the House forever.

Yet, for all his peculiarities, this was the same man who was becoming recognized in the country as a leading writer of boys' stories. *Fame and Fortune*, written at the House, had followed *Ragged Dick*, and Alger was beginning to get some of the literary acclaim he had dreamed of, although he thought little of it. These books were not what he wanted to do, he told Adams and his Boston publisher; he wanted to write adult books, great books which would stir and inspire his readers. They listened politely, and urged him on to new stories of struggling boys.

He yielded to their pressure and to the demand which was making it plain to him how much boys liked his work. They wrote to him from every quarter of America, from city and farm, telling him how much pleasure he had given them, and begging for more. Adults wrote too, particularly ministers and other "group leaders," as they would be called in a later day, who were working with young people. They were grateful for a writer whose books could be read as exciting tales, and yet preached morality on nearly every page.

Horatio did not care much about the opinion of the ministers, although he was always gratified by any kind of praise for what he wrote. But he did care about the letters from boys, and he was immensely pleased by the enthusiasm of the boys at the House, who naturally were enchanted with these books which reflected their lives in such familiar detail. The truth was that Alger liked boys more than any other segment of humanity, more than anything else in the world, and now he came to love one boy with a wholeheartedness he had never felt for anyone except Patience.

Alger first saw Wing in Chatham Square on a cold winter evening in 1873. A small gang of assorted children had invaded the neighborhood from an adjacent white slum neighborhood and were diverting themselves by attacking with snowballs any Chinese passerby they saw who might not be able to fight back. All had fled except for one small ten-year-old boy, who was being tortured by the mob. They had washed his face with snow, and when Alger came upon them, they were holding him to the ground and attempting to bury him with the stuff.

In that poor, inert figure lying half-submerged, Horatio quite possibly saw himself in his early school days, and even on that horrifying first day at Harvard. Only such a powerful motivating force would have made him behave as he did, so unlike his customary shrinking manner. He strode among the young ruffians, snatched them away, cuffed a few, sent them flying, and rescued their victim.

The little Chinese boy, terrified and half-frozen, could not speak any English. Alger thought he recognized "Wing" in his murmurings, and concluded that must be his name. Apparently he had no home, or if he had, he could not tell where it was.

Horatio carried him in his arms to the House, where O'Connor helped dry him out and feed him. He slept there that night, and every night for more than three years.

At first his rescuer was impelled toward the boy only by memory and sympathy. Next day he tried to find out if he belonged to anyone, but it appeared that no one even knew he was gone. He seemed quite alone in the world, and Alger found himself being drawn more and more to him. He had a shy smile, like Horatio's own, and he clung to his savior as much as he dared. Alger was conquered. Almost from the first, he treated Wing as though he were the son he would never have, and the boy repaid him with an unquestioning devotion not often seen in real sons.

Horatio took the boy completely in hand. He began by teaching him English, so that he would be the equal of the other boys. O'Connor protested, but Horatio would not permit Wing to go out and work, like the others; he paid all expenses himself. His refusal was based partly on a fear that Wing would be set upon again. Still, the boy could not stay inside all the time, so Alger paid a neighborhood patrolman, Timothy Grogan, to watch out for him whenever he went out. Grogan never let Wing out of his sight.

For nearly four years Horatio was idyllically happy. Never before nor after would he be in better health and spirits. Wing was growing into a bright young boy; he did not doubt that Alger was his father. Horatio thought there was nothing else now that he could ask from the world.

The end came with a blow so cruel it could hardly be borne, especially by a man like Alger. One August afternoon in 1877, he sent Wing on an errand, but the boy did not come back. By the time it was dark, Alger was frantic. He traced Wing's path as far as he could, and discovered that the message entrusted to him had never been delivered. He hurried to the police station to enlist Grogan's help, but it was the policeman's day off. His precinct captain assured Alger that Grogan would be assigned to the search as soon as he reported.

After a sleepless night, Horatio Alger resumed the search, with Grogan's help. The entire corps of newsboys was split into search parties, spurred on by Alger's promise of a twenty-five-dollar reward for anyone who brought news of Wing.

By nightfall of the second day of searching, Alger had lost his frantic zeal. He was collapsed into apathy, sensing that when the news came, it would be bad. Grogan brought it late that evening, when everyone was asleep except Horatio and his friend O'Connor, and it was worse than anything Alger could have imagined. Wing had run out into the deadly Broadway traffic in front of the German Thalia Theatre, near Spring Street, and a runaway horse had trampled him to death.

Overnight Alger was a changed man. What hair he had remaining turned white, and a flood tide of bitterness washed out most of what religion remained in him and all of whatever hopes he had for a happy life.

CHAPTER 6

Casting about for anything to occupy his mind after Wing's death, Alger began to explore the worst aspects of humanity in New York, as though to confirm his low opinion of the world. With Grogan as his guide, he toured the opium dens and gambling hells of Chinatown, brushing aside the prostitutes as he progressed from one smoky inferno to another.

In his new state of bitterness, he no longer took a moral view of these scenes, but saw them through the eyes of the serious novelist he hoped to be—the dream within him that not even the loss of Wing could vanquish. Chinatown might be the vehicle. "A vivid, startling picture of the Orient in New York," he noted down his burgeoning idea. "Chinatown, its dirt, its disease, chaos, brawls, crimes. Passion, lust, viciousness. A terrifying prospect. Sin and Sin and Sin. Yet some beautiful souls are there no doubt. And one of these has a dream. I will call the book *Opium, the Story of a Dream.* I must commence work at once."

The authority on Chinatown was reputed to be Henry Clapp, the jovial editor of a transitory publication called the *Saturday Press,* and Alger went immediately to call on him. Clapp, remarking that he hoped Horatio hadn't come on business, handed him a card he was just about to hang in the door. It read: "The *Saturday Press* is obliged to discontinue publication for lack of funds; by a curious coincidence, the very reason for which it was started."

Horatio began to talk about the book he wanted to write, but Clapp, a *bon vivant* who did not appear seriously concerned about the loss of his business, invited him to dinner instead. They went to Pfaff's, a German rathskeller on Broadway, near Bleecker, a place much loved by the city's writers and artists, who had made a Bohemian club of it. Clapp was one of its leading spirits. He introduced Horatio that night to Walt Whitman and a number of lesser lights who were drinking their way through heavy schooners of beer, interspersed with Charley Pfaff's noteworthy cheese sandwiches.

As the boisterous talk went around the table, some of it obscene, much of it literary, all of it informed with the cosmopolitan kind of knowledge only writers and artists could exhibit, Alger sat drinking it in, wholly absorbed. He had forgotten all about Chinatown. This was the literary life he had nearly forgotten, the kind to which he had responded so ardently in Paris when Elise had taken him to the same kind of place. Now, as then, he had to sit and listen because, after all this time, he had nothing to contribute to such conversation.

His silence created a sensation at the table, where interruption was an art, and the gathering was further stunned to discover that Alger neither smoked nor drank. They could hardly credit that he was alive, and Clapp spoke for all of them when he rose, and with an arm on his guest's shoulders, announced: "Behold, among the sinners doth a saint appear!"

The evening roused a desperate hunger in Horatio to be closer to such celebrities, to know as much about them as he could in the hope that someday he might be like them. He took to frequenting the Astor House, where every notable person visiting the city might be expected to stop, and where New York's own celebrities ate and drank. Alger paid a friendly desk clerk, Edwin Sterne, to keep him informed about who was in the hotel, and to point out to him the noted men and women who thronged the lobby. But he had lost what little daring possessed him to seek out Dickens in London. He only watched these famous people, and never dared to address them. He considered that he had nothing to say to them, and sadly, he was right.

If he could not mingle at the upper level, however, Alger was determined to mix as much as he could at what he thought was his own. That meant, to him, joining as many organizations as possible, an activity to which he was soon as addicted as other men were to cigars or alcohol. It was a time when those natural joiners, the American people, were proliferating clubs and societies of every description in staggering numbers, and Alger joined as many as he had the remotest excuse for joining. He belonged to the Actors' Benevolent Association, the Society for the Suppression of Vice, the Editors' and Publishers' Guild, the New York Police Captains' Association, the Association for the Development of Port Facilities, the American Education Alliance, the Bowery Boys' Club, the Quill Club, the Chat Club, the Ding Dang Dong Club, and he would have joined Ye Twilight Club if he had not committed the gaucherie at his first meeting of trying to talk about politics. The club was against every serious purpose in life except eating.

He would not have been happy in the Twilight Club, or in any other whose purpose was conviviality. Horatio was simply not a convivial person, and had never been gay except for that brief period in Paris. As his writing fame grew, he was becoming a symbol of morality in people's minds, and they began to treat him as one treats the minister making a pastoral call, carefully censoring their language and trying to keep the conversation on edifying subjects.

Almost against his will, he was a celebrity himself, but of a different kind from what he had anticipated. His books were regarded as a kind of one-man campaign for morality among the young, and their national popularity was making him as well known as Anthony Comstock or other professional reformers. Around his flag gathered all those in the nation who were against sin and for virtue. Every Y.M.C.A. library in the country boasted a lengthening shelf of his works. Next to the Bible, his books were most popular as Sunday school prizes. Any minister from the outlands visiting New York felt compelled by Christian duty to call on him.

It was widely assumed that he knew more about sin in New York than anyone else, although in fact he knew only of Chinatown and a few other places. The vast network of vice and corruption running from the Battery to Forty-second Street on the East Side was a mystery to him, except by hearsay. Nevertheless, Mayor A. Oakey Hall appointed him to the Anti-Vice Commission in 1871, and a later mayor, Smith Ely, called him in 1877 to join a conference on how to eliminate crime, one of the occasional gestures made in this direction by the Tammany syndicate that controlled it. No record exists that he ever contributed anything to the numerous commissions and conferences except to recommend that the police force be made larger. He made no attempt to take seriously the large issues raised by these appointments. It was enough to have the honor, which elevated his always sagging ego, and to take advantage of his civic eminence to ride the fire engines.

He had the constant satisfaction of knowing that he was famous, as book after book spread his name everywhere. True, he thought little enough of it; his mind was always on the masterpiece that remained unwritten, and the boys' books were only the means to that end. But he would have been inhuman if he had not enjoyed the fact that he was an American symbol. The "Horatio Alger Boy" was as much a stereotype in his lifetime as it was for decades after his death, and his influence in the nation was far greater than he knew. When a public official was caught with his hand in the civic cookie jar, there was always someone to observe in print that what was needed in public service were more men like Horatio Alger. People tended to confuse him with his heroes, so that he was regarded as a noble gentleman who was the unofficial head of a nationwide crusade for higher morality. If only they could have seen him in the Newsboys' Lodging House, or parading on Broadway in his wig and cape. . . .

Horatio did not fully realize at first how noted he had become, since he lived a relatively cloistered life on his familiar rounds in New York. He began to have an inkling of it when all kinds of people visiting the city came to call on him, often to ask his advice on how best to see the city, a subject on which he was widely regarded as an authority. That was natural, because Alger's books were full of street names and place names. A good part of *Ragged Dick* had been little more than a guided tour of the city. One reporter, Philip Bauman of the Brooklyn *Eagle*, called him a one-man Society for the Prevention of Getting Lost.

Always flattered by these visitors who came to ask his advice, Alger frequently showed the inquirer about town himself, even paying for the horse and cab on occasion. Whenever they passed a boy from the House on one of these excursions, he was sure to call a greeting to Horatio, and then the visitor went home and added to the Alger legend by relating how all the street boys in New York knew him, which was substantially true.

For a time Horatio deftly guided visitors to a curio shop he had bought in a characteristically odd way. He had stopped there one day to admire a flowerpot in the window, and, having made himself known to the shop's Hungarian proprietor, Albert Zotto, was doubly welcomed because Zotto's two sons were avid Alger readers. Horatio returned next day to meet the sons, but found on this second visit a greater attraction. It was a desk, a baroque affair with carved gargoyles, but Alger fell in love with it. Zotto refused to sell it, but he consented to let Horatio come to the shop and write on it. This he did for two years, until Zotto declared he was going to move back to Hungary and put the store up for sale.

It did not attract buyers. Anyone with the least business judgment could see that it was no more than a break-even investment, if that. But Alger bought it, for twelve hundred dollars.

After trying to run it himself for a month, Alger placed it in charge of two sailors who had been recommended to him as men anxious to settle down and start a business. When the sailors discovered what kind of businessman the owner was, the end of their management was easily predictable. They quietly went back to sea again, taking a good part of the store's stock with them.

By this time Alger had a new publisher, Porter & Coates, who had assigned an editor to look after him, one Donald Malone, because Horatio was now a valuable literary property. Following the departure of the sailors, Malone reported: "Finally he has given up that stupid store of his. We ought to have a contract which forbids him to do anything but write and then he ought to be locked in a cell to do it. He gets more ridiculous notions about doing things than seems possible. I think he prefers anything to keeping his contract because I find him anywhere but home and doing everything but writing. I am not sure we wouldn't do better to have a nurse here, instead of me, to take care of him. Unless he changes his mind I am to dine with him this evening and I will advise as early as possible about a new schedule. P.S. Alger wants to know if we would be interested in a novel from him. He says he has one in mind."

Alger did have someone to take care of him besides Malone. Since Wing's death, he had been living much of the time in various lodgings of his own, and he had a housekeeper, Katherine Marshall, whom he called Miss Kate, an old maid who fussed over him when he was sick with the respiratory illnesses that plagued him, cooked for him, and in general carried out the functions of a mother. Naturally, she appeared in his books, rather thinly disguised, as a mother.

He needed, however, someone to restrain him from making public appearances. His fame as a writer led to numerous lecture invitations, which he accepted in spite of his shyness because he thought it was all good publicity for his unwritten masterpiece, when it finally appeared. It never occurred to him that he might be one of the worst public speakers in the world, but it occurred often to his audiences, who did not know what to make of this seedy, diffident man who waved his arms and talked what was usually absurd nonsense. He would lecture about anything, no matter what the subject, with a splendid disregard for his own knowledge of it.

One of his victims was the Northeastern Conference of Ministers, whom he addressed at their 1877 convention in New York. The subject of the conference was new methods of religious education for the young, and Alger drew on his extensive knowledge of the boys at the House to assert what must have been shocking to the assembled clergymen—that religious training, while important, was no more so than a child's freedom to develop, and the loving understanding of his parents. Lack of it did not make boys leave home, he asserted positively, basing this claim on the knowledge he had gained from the newsboys.

Horatio was talking as much about the lessons he had learned from his own past as he was about the boys. Teach children that God is kind, not cruel, he advised the ministers; talk and eat and play with them before you try conversion. Here he was speaking to his father, subconsciously, but the assembled ministers were as rigidly doctrinaire as Alger Senior, and they listened with his impatient contempt for ideas beyond his understanding.

Innocent that he was, Horatio wrote to his father, with whom he had maintained a cool but continuing relationship: "Last week I addressed the body of ministers gathered here, and regret you were unable to attend. I was forced to the conclusion that the trend of my observations, though interesting to them, did not meet with their approval. That, however, was something I could not foretell in advance or I would have chosen something else. I hesitate to go into detail because you will hear from Mr. Parker all that transpired."

From rock-ribbed Massachusetts, Horatio got a cold reply: "From Mr. Parker I am led to believe that your address was invested with a radicalism hardly befitting the occasion. I agree with him that the need of the hour is for stricter discipline to counteract the ever-spreading tide of waywardness which we find exhibited in children in all walks of life."

A year later father and son met at what was a solemn occasion for the senior Alger. It was the semicentennial anniversary of the First Unitarian Church of South Natick, where he had been pastor for fourteen years. At his father's urging, Horatio had contributed an original hymn for the occasion, the first time he had tried poetry for several years.

It was a resounding success. The pastor from Needham, the Reverend S. W. Bush, reported later that decorum was forgotten "while the men and women gave vent to their approval in the form of violent applause. The author himself was present and accepted the hearty testimonial in a becoming manner." Mr. Bush pointed out to the author after the service that two lines in the first stanza, "Thy people, shielded by Thy care,/ Have walked in peace these fifty years," was puzzling, inasmuch as the Civil War had occupied four bloody years of the half-century, not to mention the War of 1812 and the unpleasantness in Mexico. "Poetic license," Horatio told him loftily.

Horatio did not often go up to Massachusetts. His father still tried to direct his affairs by writing acid comments about his stories, but he no longer had any fear or much other feeling for the old man. Two years after the Natick ceremony, however, he came without hesitation in response to a letter in which his father drove the final nail in an old coffin.

"My dear son," he wrote, "I have just come from a visit to a Miss Stires for whom, if recollection serves, you evinced an attachment when you were a boy. She has been living in Concord and has come here in the hope of seeing you again. The woman is seriously ill and I would be derelict in my duty if I failed to comply with her request and inform you of her desire."

While the train carried him through the Connecticut and Massachusetts countryside, Horatio must have thought bleakly of that letter, mingled with his sad and loving memories of Patience. "You evinced an attachment," indeed. He had told his father plainly that he would never love another girl, and it had been true. She was the only woman who could ever have made him happy; how different his life might have been if they had married. And to think that she, herself, had never married, perhaps waiting all these years to hear from him.

He reached Concord in a hysteria of grief and anticipation, but once more he was too late. Patience was dead. After the funeral, he returned desolate to New York, hardly able to work again, in spite of the clamoring of his publishers.

In little more than a year, death again brought him back to Massachusetts, where he had known so much grief. This time it was his father, and even in death the man had the capacity to make his son feel guilty and unhappy. Only a few months before his death, they had quarreled for the last time. Horatio's biography of Garfield, *From Canal Boy to President,* had appeared and his father had written sourly: "You did not sufficiently emphasize the religious training he had. You could do a more estimable service to the country by giving all possible prominence to religious traits which have been instrumental in shaping the lives of its leaders."

Horatio was stung by this letter to make the kind of reply he usually avoided: "Dear Father, You perhaps know a great deal more about Garfield than I do. I am sure the possibilities of the subject have not been exhausted. I shall look forward to reading your own life of him."

Alger Senior was already ill and did not reply. Horatio took the silence to mean that his father was hurt or angry, or both, and overcome with remorse, he wrote a friendly, conciliatory letter to heal the wound. His father got the letter on his birthday, November 6, 1881. That night, not long after midnight, he was dead and Horatio never knew whether he died reassured by the letter, or still angry.

Often it seemed to Alger that no matter where he turned, or what he did, matters turned out badly, except for the boys' books which he constantly produced, sometimes in two or three weeks, for a constantly increasing and clamorous market. There was, for example, his excursion into the children's theater movement, two years after his father's death.

At a Fourth of July celebration in City Hall, he met a woman named Virginia Barry who had been trying unsuccessfully to establish a children's theater in Chicago. Alger heard her story with more than ordinary interest; he was fired up again to one of his impulsive enthusiasms. He told her she must establish such a theater in New York; they would do it together. Miss Barry was not optimistic; the project would require a great deal of money, she said. But not long after, Alger met a rich German named Gustav Reinbeck and succeeded in interesting him as a sponsor.

Alger had a large plan for the theater. He and Miss Barry would write the first play to be produced in it, a drama based on Lincoln's life, with a cast of newsboys from the House. Reinbeck agreed to finance this venture, and after six months of research, Horatio and Miss Barry were ready to do the actual writing. About that time, however, Alger found himself so far behind his own schedule of boys' books that the importunate publishers were buzzing about his ears. He explained the situation to them, and they suggested that he use the material he had collected for a book about Lincoln. In two weeks he had done it: *Abraham Lincoln, the Backwoods Boy*. When Miss Barry heard about it, she was justifiably incensed. She pointed out that Alger had used material which she had helped gather to write a book for himself, instead of the play they had agreed to do together. She washed her hands of the children's theater and of Alger.

Discouraged but not ready to give up, Horatio tried to write the play alone. He discovered that he was without any playwriting talent whatever, and concluded that the best way to handle the material would be a musical play for children. He would outline it and someone else could write it. But no one was interested in such a proposition.

Undaunted, Horatio went to Reinbeck with a new proposal, much vaster than anything he had yet conceived. The little play about Lincoln had now grown to be a pageant which would encompass nothing less than the entire history of the United States until that moment. Subtly, Horatio had solved the writing problem by constructing his pageant as a wordless panorama, in which the principal effects were to be attained by means of scenery. Unbelievably, Reinbeck agreed to finance this venture too.

With the usual energy he mustered for his short enthusiasms, Horatio went to work. He marshaled a squad of newsboys and began making them into pageant figures. Meanwhile, he hired a sign painter named Binsky to do the scenery, upon which so much depended. Binsky, it appeared, was utterly innocent of any knowledge of theater design, a fact obvious even to Alger, who noted that his rendition of Henry Hudson discovering the Hudson was "awfully atrocious" and his conception of the Indians on Manhattan Island made them look "like Hebrews."

What with one delay and another, the preliminaries to producing the play had taken two years, and at this point Reinbeck's patience was exhausted. He withdrew his support. There was nothing else for Alger to do but abandon the project. To himself (and his diary) he rationalized the experience, as always, putting it down as something which would certainly help him to do the real work he intended to begin any day, the writing of a great novel.

One cannot help viewing Alger as a pathetic figure in his futile thrusts and parries at life. To his millions of readers he was a superb moral figure, a master storyteller, a success. To those around him he was a baffling, often disturbing individual. To himself he was a man with a mission still unfulfilled. Meanwhile, he alternated between trivial amusements and moments alone when his mind tottered a step nearer complete disorganization.

He went to Barnum's Museum. He rode about town on the horsecars. Always he was an inveterate follower of fire engines. One night he came home and wrote in his diary: "Gigantic conflagration on Pearl Street. Warehouse in flames that reached the clouds. A beautiful, clear evening so that everything visible. A dangerous task to go through the flames and smoke but the brave men did and I was of a mind to applaud. Two men injured, one with a broken skull and taken to the hospital, and one lady slightly hurt by part of wall that fell to the road. Rode back on engine."

Later that night, unable to sleep because of the fire's excitement—a state that would have been familiar to any psychoanalyst—he paused from a restless pacing of his room and sat down to his diary again. Drawing a line under the previous entry, he wrote: "Later, much later. I am not alone now. Wing is with me, and Patience. I see them clearly again here beside me. Is Patience talking? *Is Patience talking!* God, do I hear her voice! Do I hear Wing? Or are my senses leaving me?"

He was moving slowly, irresistibly, toward an inevitable climax in his life, but there was still a long road to travel.

CHAPTER 7

In the sorry catalog of Horatio Alger's failures, one success shines among the rubble. It was his assault on the padrone system, the despicable exploitation of children by Italians who bought young boys in their native country, had them exported to New York, taught them to play on harps or violins, and then sent them into the streets to beg. The padrone took all the money they earned, and beat them if they did not earn enough. Alger's exposé of this vicious racket was *Phil, the Fiddler,* his favorite book and one that played a major part in helping to crystallize the public indignation that eventually ended the system.

Alger did not initiate this crusade; he seldom initiated anything. It was a result of the personal outrage of George Nelson Maverick, who operated a department store in Newark. Somehow he learned of the padrones and their victims, and began writing indignant letters to the newspapers about them. The letters were ignored, which infuriated Maverick. He looked about for support and hit upon Alger, the authority on street life in New York, as everyone supposed. If Alger knew about the racket, he had never been aroused by it or written anything about it until Maverick communicated his sense of outrage and sent Horatio into one of his states of enthusiasm. He set out immediately to gather evidence, to be presented to the proper authorities.

That Alger had little conception of what he was looking for when he began is evident in his first report to Maverick. "Now this is getting to be a serious matter," he says, with an air of pained discovery. "The evidence of malicious treatment which I have seen so far, if it is a fair sample, is unholy and must be stopped. The leaders must be punished. Why, I saw a boy fourteen years old, weighing fifty pounds, starved and weak, also mentally deficient. I met him at ten o'clock at night, afraid to go home. He only had collected sixty cents. Dear friend Maverick, let me find further evidence of this padrone business and I swear to you that if more of it is like what I know now, I will not rest until the curse is wiped away and until every right minded man and woman screams in protest at this foul thing whose stench makes me sick. Let me uncover other facts of like import and I will not rest until New York is purged and every mishandled child set free."

Fired once more, Alger plunged into his investigation with the persistence and skill of a good reporter. He enlisted an Italian boy named Giacomo and followed him about, making careful notes of everything he did, and drawing from him a detailed story of the life he was compelled to live with his padrone.

With the evidence compiled, Alger went to Charles Loring Brace for help, but Brace was off on a crusade of his own at the moment, against the exploitation of children in factories. He suggested Charles E. Whitehead, counsel for the Children's Aid Society. Alger took his appeal to Whitehead, who proved to be as unresponsive as the newspapers had been to Maverick, which drew from Horatio an angry letter, rare for him.

"It is not my business to question your good motives nor have I any desire to do so," he began, and proceeded to do just that. "But it does occur to me," he went on, "that regardless of the pressure of other matters calling for attention, you would find time to take up the business I have discussed with you with your associates. You are no more willing to see a child die unnecessarily than I am, yet your lack of diligence in attending to my request fills me with annoyance, if I may say so.

"If the Children's Aid Society is what its name implies, then I cannot be wrong in assuming it has strong obligations to convert all its facilities for eradicating the dastardly evil which I have called to your attention. Your negligible response to my pleadings leaves me with the assumption that duty is not being performed somewhere.

"I wish to put three questions in writing for which I respectfully solicit an early reply.

"First, will the Children's Aid Society take steps to eradicate the padrone system from New York?

"Second, to what extent will it exert its efforts?

"Third, when will its support begin?

Title page from Horatio Alger's "Luck and Pluck Series." Young boy leaving farm. Woodcut.

"Luke rescues Mrs. Merton."

LUKE WALTON

BY

HORATIO ALGER, Jr.

AUTHOR OF
"BOUND TO RISE," "BRAVE AND BOLD," "PAUL THE PEDDLER,"
"JULIUS THE STREET BOY," "THE YOUNG SALESMAN,"
"THE YOUNG OUTLAW," "PHIL THE FIDDLER,"
"THE CASH BOY," "SLOW AND SURE," ETC.

N Y B Co

NEW YORK
THE NEW YORK BOOK COMPANY
1911

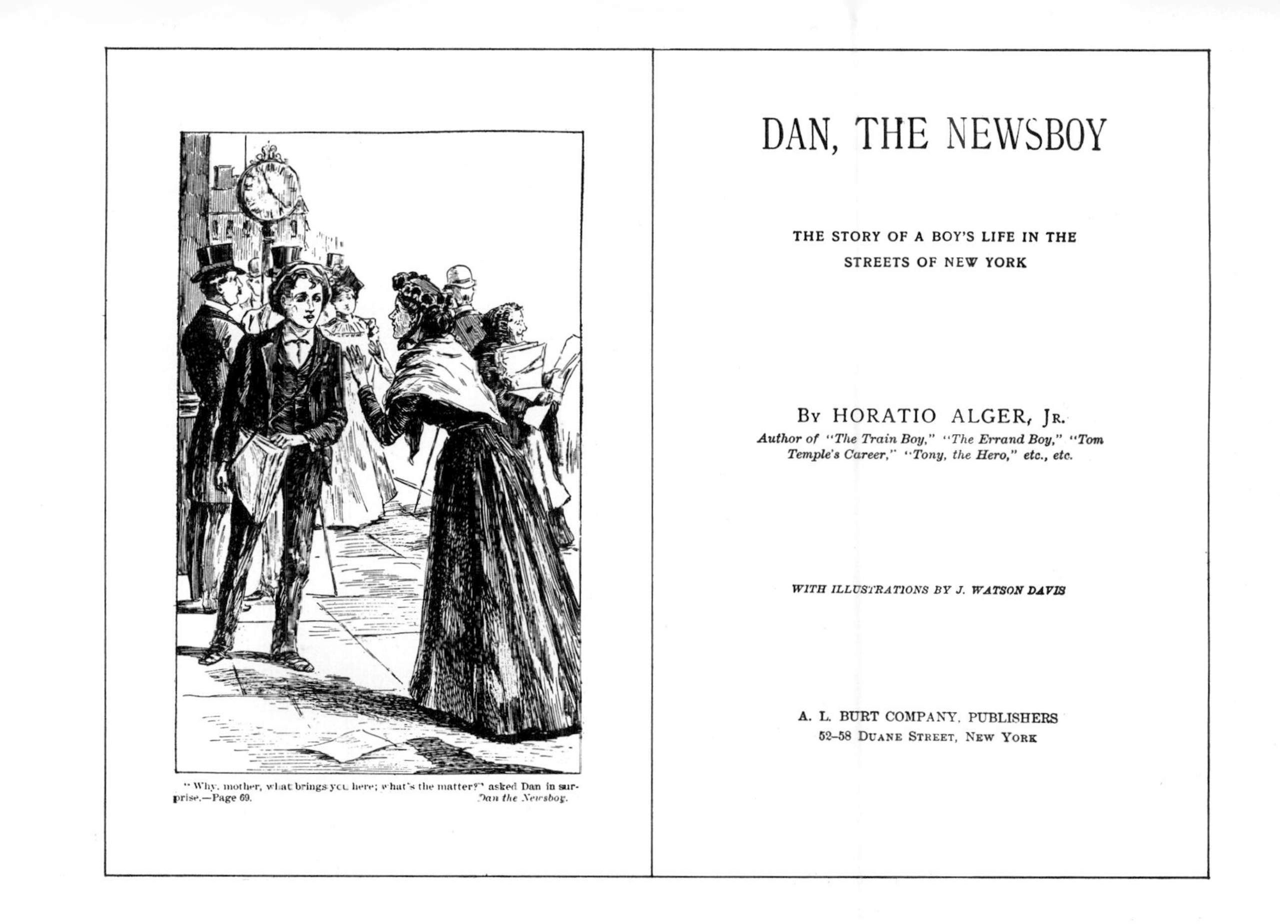

"Why, mother, what brings you here; what's the matter?" asked Dan in surprise.—Page 69. *Dan the Newsboy.*

DAN, THE NEWSBOY

THE STORY OF A BOY'S LIFE IN THE STREETS OF NEW YORK

BY HORATIO ALGER, JR.

Author of "The Train Boy," "The Errand Boy," "Tom Temple's Career," "Tony, the Hero," etc., etc.

WITH ILLUSTRATIONS BY J. WATSON DAVIS

A. L. BURT COMPANY, PUBLISHERS

52–58 DUANE STREET, NEW YORK

"Smash yer baggage, Mum?"—from the "Ragged Dick Series"

Newsboys' Lodging House, New York City

STRIVE AND SUCCEED;

OR,

THE PROGRESS OF WALTER CONRAD.

BY

HORATIO ALGER, JR.

AUTHOR OF "RAGGED DICK," "FAME AND FORTUNE," "MARK, THE MATCH BOY," "ROUGH AND READY," "CAMPAIGN SERIES," ETC.

LORING, Publisher,

COR. WASHINGTON AND BROMFIELD STREETS,

BOSTON.

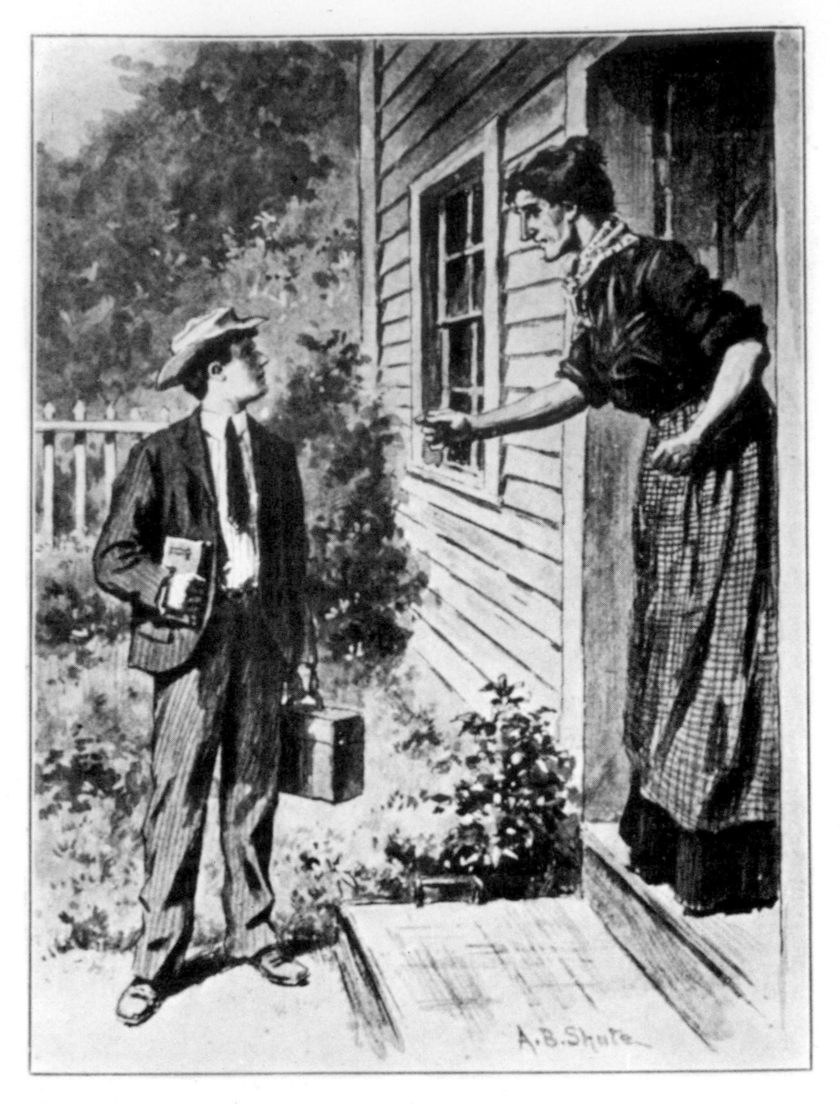

"Books! You get right out of this doorway!"—from *The Young Book Agent; or, Frank Hardy's Road to Success*

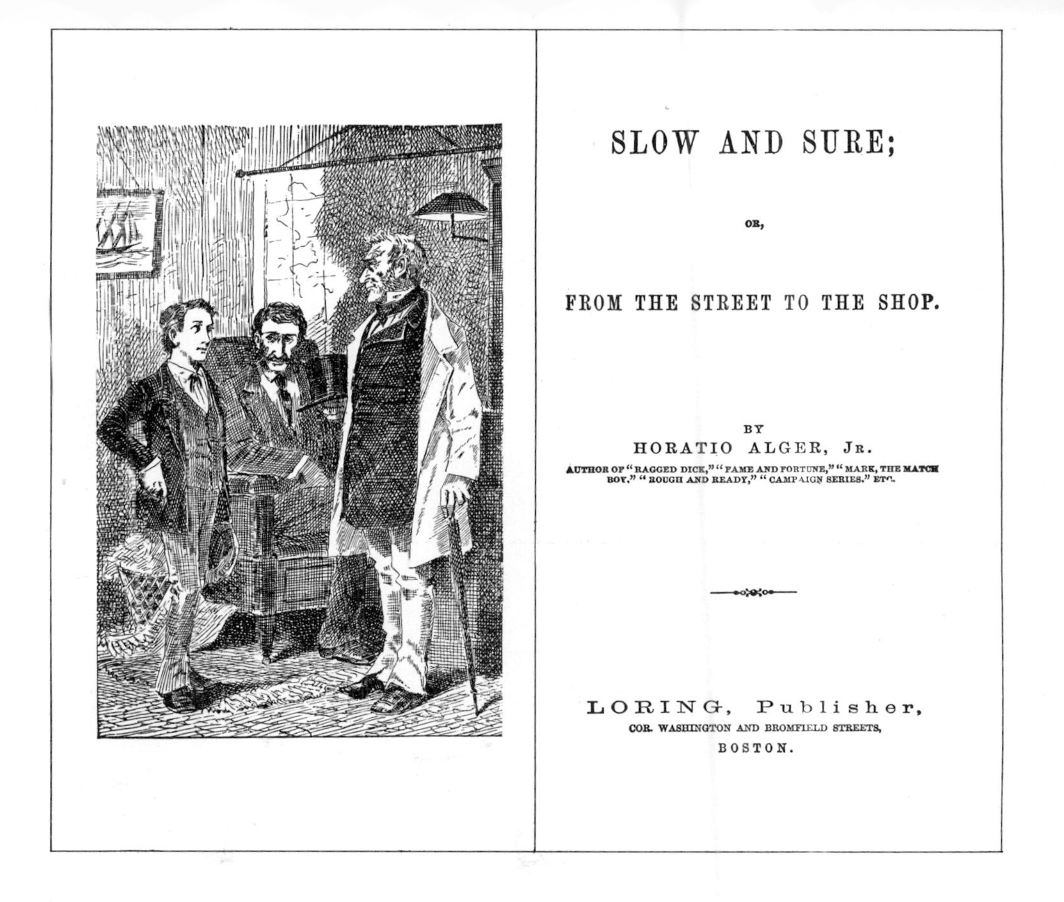

SLOW AND SURE;

OR,

FROM THE STREET TO THE SHOP.

BY

HORATIO ALGER, Jr.

AUTHOR OF "RAGGED DICK," "FAME AND FORTUNE," "MARK, THE MATCH BOY," "ROUGH AND READY," "CAMPAIGN SERIES," ETC.

LORING, Publisher,

COR. WASHINGTON AND BROMFIELD STREETS,

BOSTON.

"I will sell my shares for sixty thousand dollars," said Walter.

STRIVE AND SUCCEED

OR

THE PROGRESS OF WALTER CONRAD

BY

HORATIO ALGER, Jr.

AUTHOR OF

"STRONG AND STEADY," "TRY AND TRUST," "BOUND TO RISE,"
"RISEN FROM THE RANKS," "BRAVE AND BOLD,"
"WAIT AND HOPE," "SLOW AND SURE," ETC.

NEW YORK
NEW YORK BOOK COMPANY
1909

"In concluding this correspondence I wish to add one final note of warning: Brutal men are beating little boys to death and the responsibility for this ungodly condition rests with men like you and me."

Mr. Whitehead declined the responsibility; the Society was doing everything it could about the plight of children in the city, he said. Alger hesitated, not knowing where to turn next, but Maverick urged him on. "Conceding the advisability of having the full cooperation of a society well organized and with trained investigators," he wrote to Horatio, "yet a cause is not lost and should not be forsaken for lack of it. Personally I believe that if the public be made aware of what is transpiring, it will overnight wipe out the padrones. You have enough facts on hand now to talk them out of existence. A few well attended meetings should turn the trick. Why don't you go after them? You will have humanity in your debt if you do."

Horatio felt himself inadequate for the role in which Maverick had cast him. He was no tiger, to "go after them," not even with the enticing prospect of placing humanity in his debt. But he was too far into the crusade now to back out. He returned to collecting evidence.

One set of facts was missing: a firsthand look at the headquarters of a padrone, and an interview with one of these exploiters. Alger picked one at random, a man named Salvatore Gioletti, and went to see him. Gioletti threw him out as soon as he learned why Horatio had come. Optimistic about his investigative ability, Alger went back again, and this time Gioletti intimated that he would be lucky to be alive if he did not mind his own business. Grimly, Alger returned a third time, prudently bringing a policeman with him. Gioletti let them in and for a moment Horatio was almost sorry he had succeeded.

"Revolted by the sight of it," he wrote, "the dirty, filthy sight of it, the foul stomach-turning smell of it, with two or three boys sprawled sick on the floor, half lying in their own vomit." The spectacle rekindled his flagging enthusiasm for the crusade.

He burned with holy zeal to stamp out this cruelty, as he always did when he saw a boy physically persecuted. That had been his introduction to Wing. Always, one supposes, he saw himself as a child, reliving with shame and anger the humiliations he had known. The visit to Gioletti's removed any hesitation he had about carrying out Maverick's urgings to hold mass meetings.

Herbert Mayes, Alger's biographer, has given us a memorandum about the first of these meetings, which he extracted from the memory of Max Seligson, a New York tailor. Seligson recalled:

"I was out of work at the time, as I remember, walking on Second Avenue near the Battery. I saw a notice in a store window about a protest meeting. I don't remember what the sign said but I had nothing to do that night, so I went. Twenty-five or thirty people were there when it started, on a corner on Catherine Street, and there were many more—two or three hundred—before it ended, who stood around when they saw the other crowd. I remember Alger because I heard he was a writer and I paid strict attention. Somebody talked before he did. I don't remember what he said exactly but it was about padrones and the way they mistreated boys. There was a fight when a man yelled he was lying. A cop came and that was the end. Then some of the people signed a petition which was handed around, asking for a law for keeping padrones out of the United States."

The second meeting was held in Lamartine Hall, which Maverick had hired. It was an enthusiastic meeting, Alger reported, attended by about five hundred people who signed a petition to the governor; several of them offered money for the fight. There followed a succession of similar meetings in every part of the city, until Alger and Maverick had succeeded in whipping up a public issue.

They were incensed by the attitude of the police, particularly Alger, who had always been a friend of the force as a result of his relationship with Grogan. The argument of the police officials was that they had no law available to clean up the padrone system, but the real answer was widespread bribery and corruption in the department and in the courts. Padrones were arrested on occasion, when specific charges were brought involving actual assault on one of the boys, but few of them were ever convicted.

Alger wrote an eloquent indictment of the police failure. "Honor seems foreign to our police officers," he charged. "This is no mysterious plot that must be dug for to be found. One does not have to search for it far and wide. It is unnecessary to employ scouts and detectives. Why, see here, it is open and above board, on the surface, right in front of everybody's eyes. The next time you hear a violin playing, look out of your window and gaze hard at the boy who is playing it. See the paleness of his face. See the rags he calls clothes. Get close and you will find more bones than flesh. And happiness! Try and see a glimmer of it anywhere in him. Talk with him as I have done and learn what he has to look forward to in this life which under ordinary circumstances is not too beautiful."

He was even more eloquent in a set speech he wrote, with Maverick's assistance, which never failed to bring down the house at the mass meetings, even when it was delivered in Alger's unconvincing public manner. Other and better speakers elicited ovations with it. They called it "the Christ speech," and it was in the vein of the rouser with which William T. Stead, the British reformer, was to excite the Middle West when he depicted what would happen "If Christ Came to Chicago."

"Our officials are supposed to be Christians," ran the peroration, "but are they Christians who blind their eyes to villainy on the one hand and extreme suffering on the other? What must God in heaven think of those who live in luxury and contentment while helpless children, torn from their homes in a distant land, are suffered to waste away and enter premature graves for want of the commonest necessities of life? Suppose Christ Himself were to take charge of our civic affairs. O, my friends, just think of that. Christ the head of our government! Would He be content to dress in a uniform and walk with His head high and let these cowardly padrones pass unnoticed? Would He not stop and lend a hand to the boys who wept for succor?"

In time the real operators of the padrone system, probably the Mafia itself, were annoyed by the public uproar which Alger and Maverick had instigated, although they had little reason to think they would actually be harmed by it. They began a counterattack, employing the usual methods—the warning letter, the threat of death, paid rowdies to break up the mass meetings—but these attempts, which Horatio saw to it were well publicized, only stirred up the public more. Then they resorted to more direct means. Alger was set upon repeatedly in the streets, and once he had to be rescued—ironically, by the police. Like the coincidences in Horatio's books, they were just in time. Horatio had been beaten about the head, and his attackers were preparing to finish their work with knives.

It was a measure of Alger's intensity about this crusade that he did not consider running away, as his fearful nature would ordinarily demand. He was heart and soul in it, as he had never been before. His life was in imminent danger, and he knew it, yet he persisted, even when the padrones' thugs invaded his room on Seventeenth Street, and nearly ended his career.

"I heard a knock on the door and rose instantly to open it," he described the incident, in a letter to his friend O'Connor, who was on vacation in Vermont. "I was startled to see the hall in darkness—which had never been without gas before. 'Who is there?' I called out, but got no response. Thinking this strange, I stepped out into the hall and was set upon by, it seemed, a hundred pair of hands. I shouted for help when a blow across my face stunned me, and then another and another—a hail of blows, each administered with such force that I fell into unconsciousness. I can tell you they pained me severely.

"Regaining my senses I deemed it prudent to say nothing, merely resolving to await developments. I was carried back into my room and for the first time was enabled to get a glimpse of the assailants. One of them I recognized—an Italian with whom

I had remonstrated but two or three days before. He was, I surmised, the leader of the ruffians. Altogether there were four of them—ugly, desperate looking ruffians, whose every other word, whether in Italian or English, was an oath. Shutting the door they arranged themselves around me while I sat on a chair and asked if I was ready to listen to reason. I considered it prudent to reply in the affirmative, hoping thus to gain time and possibly be favored with the arrival of Maverick who I was expecting at any moment.

"Salvini, as I later learned the name of the leader to be, then informed me that if I would agree to desist from further activity no further harm would befall me. On the other hand, if I continued—he made no definite threat but from the way he paused and the ominous glint in his eye I knew that neither he nor his confederates would stop short of murder. While I contemplated a reply I heard—and they heard at the same time—steps upon the stairs. During the instant's silence that followed I called out with every vestige of strength there was in me. The men were panic-stricken. Pushing me aside as I leaped to my feet, they jumped to the door and disappeared down the stairs, each in greater fear than the other."

Incredibly, Horatio persisted. He carried a pistol to protect himself, and gloried in the publicity he was getting. Horatio was a man transformed in those tense days, belligerent in a way quite foreign to him, deeply and sincerely committed to eradicating cruelty and injustice. He made ambitious plans. When he was successful in New York, as he was certain he would be, he intended to stamp out the padrone system in the other American cities where it flourished.

He cast about for help, and thought of turning to his father (it was a few years before the old man's death). Perhaps Alger Senior could enlist the powerful help of the church in his behalf. "If you can manage it," Horatio wrote hopefully, "it will have a salutary effect on our efforts. A petition signed by all the Unitarian ministers you can get together, and by all members in their respective parishes, will be a big step toward getting other denominations to follow suit. Once the religious element voices its disapprobation nothing can stand in the way. The press will be forced to take up the cudgels and slay this awful terror wherever it exists in the country."

But again Horatio was disillusioned by his father, and by organized religion. Alger Senior found a dozen reasons for not rallying to the cause. It was a police problem and had nothing to do with religion, he said; ministers should not be involved in these civic affairs. Nor did he have any hope that the Unitarians could rally other faiths, with whom they were in bad repute in any event. They would only be laughed at for being concerned about immigrants who should not have been permitted to come to America at all.

After this rebuff, Alger turned to the source of national publicity for his cause, which he should have thought of at once—one of his own books. Nothing was likely to muster public opinion more quickly. Once he had thought of it, Horatio went to work and turned out *Phil, the Fiddler* with his usual speed, no more than three weeks in this case. The result was gratifying, like the reception of *Uncle Tom's Cabin* in miniature. Letters poured in from everywhere, nearly a thousand of them; sermons were preached; editorials were written; Alger was hailed as a crusader for morality.

As a book, *Phil, the Fiddler* had little merit. It was not even written with the angry conviction Horatio had given to the "Christ" speech, and which illuminated his letters and diary entries about the problem. Somehow, when it came to writing a story, he could produce nothing but the flat, pedestrian prose which characterized all his work. Yet he wrote the book with all the intensity he could summon. Here are some samples:

> Most of the little Italian musicians to be found on our streets are brought from Calabria, the southern portion of Italy, where they are purchased from their parents, for a fixed sum, or rate of annual

payment. . . . Even where the contract is for a limited term of years, the boys in five cases out of ten are not returned at the appointed time. A part, unable to bear the hardships and privations of the life upon which they enter, are swept off by death, while of those that survive, a part are weaned from their homes, or are not permitted to go back.

The little Italian musician must remain in the street till near midnight, and then, after a long and fatiguing day, he is liable to be beaten and sent to bed without his supper, unless he brings home a satisfactory sum of money.

These boys are wont to regard the padrone as above the law. His power seems to them absolute, and they never dream of any interference. And, indeed, there is some reason for their cherishing this opinion. However brutal his treatment, I know of no case where the law has stepped in to rescue the young victim.

And this white slavery—for it merits no better name—is permitted by the law of two great nations. Italy is in fault in suffering this traffic in her children of tender years, and America is guilty as well in not interfering, as she might, at all events, to abridge the long hours of labor required of these boys, and forcing their cruel guardians to give them some instruction.

Of one hundred Italian children who are sold by their parents into this white slavery, but twenty ever return home; thirty grow up and adopt various occupations abroad, and fifty succumb to maladies produced by privation and exposure.

Phil's story was read with horror and increased the public agitation for reform of the padrone system, but even so it is doubtful if Alger's crusade would have succeeded had it not been for the coincidental revelation of the Mary Ellen case, which shocked New York. Mary Ellen was a little girl whose plight was discovered by a volunteer social worker in the tenement district, who learned of it through a neighbor of the child. The neighbor, a dying woman, told of hearing the girl beaten day and night by her stepmother, and the visiting lady resolved to rescue her. She got no encouragement from the police, nor even from her minister, but she was able to persuade Henry

Bergh, president of the Society for the Prevention of Cruelty to Animals, that he should intervene. Armed with a warrant, Bergh invaded the tenement and found a scarecrow of a girl, scarred and bruised and beaten beyond belief, barely alive.

This story was a sensation in the newspapers, many of whose readers were instantly reminded of Phil, the fiddler, and the other cases Alger had told about at the mass meetings. Enough political pressure was generated by the resulting indignation to compel the New York legislature to pass in 1874 the first statute ever enacted anywhere for the prevention of cruelty to children. When the Society for the Prevention of Cruelty to Children was subsequently created, it was able to use the legal power given to it by the state to end the padrone system, along with numerous other abuses.

For once it was a clear-cut victory for Alger. As he wrote so often, right had prevailed over wrong.

CHAPTER 8

By an irony peculiarly appropriate to Alger's life, his greatest fame did not come until after his death, but in the decade following his father's passing, his popularity reached a peak that was sustained while he lived and made him by far the most popular writer of children's literature in the country.

One of the chief reasons for his surge of popularity in the 1880's was his meeting with the incredible Frank Munsey, whose own life might have been a plot for one of Horatio's books. Munsey came from Augusta, Maine, which had become, more or less by accident, a publishing center, particularly for mass circulation mail-order periodicals. Young Frank was in charge of the telegraph office in Augusta, but his mind was on the town's chief business and he spent all his spare time studying how the magazines operated.

Eventually, as he sat idling over his telegraph key, a splendid idea came to him. He would go down to New York and start a weekly for boys and girls, which would beat out its numerous competitors (Alger's success had inspired a small industry in this field) by using bright lithographed covers and numerous woodcuts inside to lure young readers who might be deterred by too much type.

The fact that he was penniless did not deter Munsey, just as it always failed to daunt an Alger hero. One of the talents which enabled him to title his autobiography *Forty Years—Forty Millions* was his ability to sell an idea, and he sold his initial idea to a broker in Augusta whom he knew so well that he persuaded this hitherto astute money manipulator to promise $2,500 of hard cash for a venture which at that point was no more than a vague plan in a telegraph boy's head. Then he wrote to a young man he had known in Augusta who was now in business in New York and extracted another promise from his friend for another thousand. Munsey himself had saved up $500 and that was his contribution—that, and his talent and enthusiasm.

It must be said for him that he spent his own money first. After he had paid out nearly all his $500 to acquire manuscripts, he stepped off the train in New York, in the autumn of 1882, with only forty dollars of it remaining. Almost immediately he learned something about friends and promises. Both the broker in Augusta and the man in New York failed to keep their bargains, which helped to make Munsey the cynical and ruthless businessman he eventually became.

Not unlike Horatio's bootblacks and newsboys, Frank Munsey found himself alone in New York, without money or friends, his only asset a pile of manuscripts. He made the rounds of the publishers, steadily discarding the portions of his plan that were expensive in the hope of attracting some support. Now he talked of a five-cent weekly with only a few pictures and a generally moral and inspirational tone.

As usual, he talked well. E. G. Rideout, the publisher of *Rideout's Monthly* and two magazines for women, listened to him and consented to add Munsey's idea to his string. The first issue appeared on December 2, 1882, as the *Golden Argosy*, subtitled "Freighted with Treasure for Boys and Girls." The chief treasure in its eight pages was the first chapter of an Alger serial, titled *Do and Dare; or, A Brave Boy's Fight for a Fortune.*

After about twenty issues, and just as *Do and Dare* was reaching its conclusion, Rideout's small empire collapsed and he declared himself bankrupt. Here Munsey demonstrated the acumen which was to make him a fortune. He bought his magazine from the receiver for what Rideout owed him as its editor. There followed a brief period of struggle, during which Munsey wrote part of the magazine, did all the editorial work, and handled its meager business affairs as well, meanwhile borrowing $300 from an Augusta friend to keep going. He did not miss an issue, and in little more than a year he was on firm ground, able to hire an editor for $10 a week.

As a writer, Munsey was by this time a shameless imitator of Alger. He called the second serial he wrote for the magazine, *Afloat in a Great City*, and backed it with a $10,000 advertising campaign. Apparently it was a formula that could not miss. Munsey's circulation jumped until he was making a clear profit of $100 a week, well on his way to the ultimate forty million. Of course he had been compelled to borrow more money to finance his campaign, and he was still $15,000 in debt, but with the daring which always characterized his business ventures, he disdained caution and increased the size and subscription price of his magazine, meanwhile distributing 11,500,000 sample copies.

When he came to write the story of his Munsey Publishing House, Munsey described his spectacular rise that began where Alger's stories usually stopped. "Five years of poverty, five years of awful struggle, and now the earth was mine!" he wrote. "Rich at last, richer than I had ever dreamed of being—a thousand dollars a week net, and every week adding to it by leaps and bounds—fifty thousand dollars a year, and all mine—next week sixty thousand, then seventy, and a hundred—a million, maybe—GREAT HEAVENS, AND IT WAS ALL REAL!"

It was not as simple as he made it sound. After Munsey's second campaign, his magazine had a circulation of 115,000 and it was bringing him in $15,000 a week in profits, yet he was compelled to juggle his finances in a way that would have sent him to jail if he had been unsuccessful. The turning point came when he realized that he could make more money by putting out magazines for adults, with a line of cheap books on the side. Children grew up too rapidly, which was bad for an entrepreneur trying to establish a stable circulation, and in any case they did not buy things and so advertisers were reluctant to use the pages of publications like the *Golden Argosy*. The more subtle arts of advertising persuasion had not yet been developed.

Munsey's own stories were already appearing as books, consequently he had the beginnings of a new business. He could also use the work of other contributors, including Alger. But he needed a magazine, too, and in 1889 he launched *Munsey's Weekly*, changed simply to *Munsey's Magazine* after a little less than three years. It was highly successful. He was then able to change *Golden Argosy*, which had nearly expired, into an adult monthly, and its circulation shot from 9,000 to 40,000. It became, as Frank Luther Mott has noted, the first successful all-fiction "pulp." By 1907 it had a half-million circulation and was making $300,000 a year.

As for *Munsey's Weekly*, it became a vehicle for both the publisher and Horatio. Sometimes their stories were indistinguishable as far as plot and tone were concerned, although Munsey was the better writer. Yet the imitator was never as successful as the originator. Alger bumbled along in his own dreadful style, building larger and larger audiences, which

Munsey increased considerably when he started his own book publishing business, establishing a fifteen-cent series by Alger and the other imitators, most of them originally published in the pages of *Argosy*.

The *Weekly*, however, did not prosper. It lost more than $100,000 in slightly less than three years, and Munsey converted it into a monthly. Alger was its only well known contributor while it lived, and his work was its primary attraction for readers.

These magazine and paperback sales not only contributed substantially to Horatio's already formidable popularity, but inspired still others to imitate him. William Taylor Adams and Munsey were already leaders in this thriving business. Now a third one was added, Edward Stratemeyer, who emulated the Alger heroes he had read about assiduously while he was clerking in his stepbrother's tobacco store in Elizabeth, New Jersey. His emulation took the form of trying to write books like Horatio's and Adams's.

Stratemeyer once asked Alger, whom he came to know, for the secret of his success, but there is no record that Alger gave him an answer. It is doubtful if he had any idea. He enjoyed his popularity, but he still disdained what he was doing as no more than a means of making money while he prepared to write his Great Novel. Stratemeyer had no illusions about *his* future. Once he had learned the formula, he began to reap a harvest only slightly less than Alger's, although millions read his books who did not know his name. Any middle-aged reader in mid-twentieth-century America will have heard of the "Rover Boys' Series," Tom Swift, and the *Motor Boys*, and the *Bobbsey Twins* continued by other writers under the pseudonym of Laura Lee Hope. They may even remember the "Old Glory Series" (*Under Dewey at Manila*), or the "Flag of Freedom Series," or the "Boy Hunters Series." But few will recall that Edward Stratemeyer wrote them, under his own name or as Captain Ralph Bonehill or Arthur M. Winfield, two of his pseudonyms.

At one point the line between Horatio and his chief imitator becomes so dim it is still the subject of controversy. While Alger was alive, both wrote for Munsey and both published in magazines and paperbacks, but Stratemeyer was always conscious, presumably, that Alger was more popular. There is no other reasonable explanation for what he is said to have done after Alger died, which was to write no less than eleven Alger-like books and pass them off as part of Horatio's posthumous published product, published under the Alger name. Both Stratemeyer and his publishers asserted that Alger had given his rival the plots, but Frank Gruber, Alger's most meticulous bibliographer, does not believe it. These eleven titles, Gruber notes, are still carried as authentic Alger items in most bibliographies, and they are, incidentally, among the most difficult for collectors to locate.

So great was the market for boys' books in the last ten or fifteen years of Alger's life that there was more than enough money and fame to go around among Horatio and all his imitators. Alger enjoyed the money, although he failed to hang on to much of it. As for the fame, he found himself in constant touch with his public through the post office, as well as their personal calls on him in New York.

There was the usual spate of inquiries from inquiring readers, of a kind still common. "Do you think 'The Tale of a Ruined Career,' of which I am enclosing a copy, shows talent?" writes one. "I have never written stories before but I feel there is something in me—some power—" another muses hopefully, as so many thousands have done. The queries from would-be authors were innumerable: "Would you be kind enough to advise me whether the end of a story is more important than the beginning?" This, to Horatio, whose style and technique contained nearly every possible flaw! He basked in the admiration of those who thought he was wonderful—they were far in the majority—and he suffered under the lash of the inevitable, and in his case inexplicable, critic who wrote, "Your stuff is abominable and has a derogatory influence on the young mind." The writer came to call and present his case in person, but Alger refused to see him. In later years the caller's son did his best to get Horatio's books removed from every library within his sphere of influence. The argument was that Alger's stories prevented young people from developing a taste for the masterpieces of literature.

The young people themselves were his best and most numerous correspondents. Horatio loved them all. He tried to answer the problems with which they presented him and respond to their complaints, like that of the Milwaukee boy who complained of the arithmetic in Alger's tales. It was too explicit, he said. Other letters told of real-life situations which paralleled those in his books. One boy wrote: "My father is like Squire Tarbox. He is mean and stingy and gives me no money to spend." Such letters usually ended: "Shall I run away?" It was difficult for Horatio to say no; his heroes usually did.

The parents wrote too, asking for advice from this man who clearly knew all about boys. "Charles is an only son," wrote one. "He is aged sixteen, proficient in geography, and has made up his mind to be a sailor. Should I let him be a sailor? Is there any future to being a sailor? Will you let me know how much money sailors earn? Are all sailors bad? Would there be too great a temptation to evil for a boy of sixteen to withstand? Thank you in advance, Mr. Alger, for your kind attention."

Often his replies were in verse. When people asked for a poem, he gave them one, usually no more than a couplet in his customary exquisitely bad style, but a poem nonetheless, which he did his best to adapt to the writer's situation. Thus a girl whose doll had been broken was no doubt soothed to get this sententious advice:

> "Think of your Dolly as she was at her best
> And she will be happier in Heavenly rest."

The ecclesiastical note was still present in much of what he wrote, prose and poetry. Early training was impossible to obliterate. He coined this aphorism, consequently, for a young man who wrote that he was the sole support of his father:

> "His soul draws nearest unto God above,
> Who to his brother ministers in love."

Sometimes the couplets were simply extensions in rhymed doggerel of the advice which saturated his books, as this to a boy on his birthday:

> "To man's estate you'll succeed;
> As a man, strive to lead."

On occasion bathos crept into these couplets—a conventional and sentimentalized longing for the wife and children he did not have, as in this to a widow left with numerous children to support. He meant it as consolation:

> "The future will be filled with light,
> Children dear will make it bright."

As happens to many authors, Horatio had at least one correspondent to whom he wrote regularly and never saw, a Vermonter named Wallace Borden, who had once been a newsboy and was now rich and retired—the living proof of Alger's thesis. For eleven years these two men carried on an intimate correspondence, but never attempted to see each other. They talked about their daily lives and problems, like old friends. Borden spoke often of his wife, to whom he was devoted, and Horatio came to feel that he knew her almost as well, although she did not join the correspondence. When the news came that she had died, Alger wrote to his friend a letter which, as his biographer observes, was sentimental but "surpasses anything he ever put in print." The letter read:

Dear Borden, All dreams end, all flowers lose their color, all stars twinkle but a while. The shades of night are drawn on the glories of the serenest day.

I am sorry. I have lost a friend. I, who never knew her, never spoke a word to her—feel her absence. Her loveliness and passive charm I appreciated through you. Through your eyes I was aware of her nearness. I heard her voice and saw her smile.

Try not to grieve. I think she would be happier to know you will not grieve. Keep in mind the happy years you spent with her and be not angry with God for calling her. Rather thank Him for the day He gave her to you. Cherish the memory of that day as even I cherish the memory of a long ago day.

In the face of your loss do not despond. Try to smile a little, though sadly. Bear bravely and cheerfully what more life has in store. Some day you will meet again.

Alger himself was not doing well at bearing bravely and cheerfully what life had done to him in taking away Wing. After the boy's death he slipped again into the apathy which had claimed him so often before. He needed a change, and his Boston publisher, A. K. Loring, was ready with the motivation for it. Loring pointed out that his sales were dropping in the East but rising West of the Mississippi, and he suggested that it might be a profitable switch of markets to write stories of the West for Eastern boys.

The suggestion was like a light thrown into the gathering darkness of his life. He had fallen into a restless pattern of living, moving frequently (as many as seven times in a year), tutoring occasionally to break the monotony of writing, and wandering about the city in a preoccupied gloom that made him an easy mark for hoodlums. Occasionally he had a brief flash of enthusiasm for something, like attacking saloons, but it was soon over. He was constantly subject to the respiratory attacks that troubled him all his life, a reflection of his disturbed psyche.

Even without Loring's idea to motivate him, it was clear to Horatio that he ought to get away for a time. He made his will, leaving everything to the House, accepted gratefully a diamond scarf pin from the friends who came to say good-bye, and turned toward an America he had never seen.

On the train crawling sedately westward across the pastures and mountains of Pennsylvania, he fell into conversation with a man sitting next to him, and as had happened often with him, this chance conversation led to another diversion in his life of a kind which could only be described as pathological. His new friend was Samuel Albee, who heard about Wing with more than ordinary sympathy because his only son had died the year before at twelve. Albee was drawn to Horatio, as so many people were without quite knowing why, and invited him to stop off and visit him for a few days at his home in Cincinnati. Alger, who had no particular plans of his own, accepted the invitation with his customary gratitude for any kindness shown to him.

He met Samuel's wife, Paulina, and was drawn into a domestic situation which would have made a normal man uncomfortable. The Albees, who had been married fourteen years, behaved toward each other like honeymooners, having been drawn together even more closely by their son's death. Mayes describes it as a "household quiet with the beauty of love and sorrow joined." In the evening the Albees had a ritual which never varied. Before they went to bed, Paulina played the piano, which she did well, and when she finished Samuel embraced her and took her hands in his own. Alger would listen to the music, as enchanted as the husband, and in the closing moments of the ritual, as Mayes puts it, "when Samuel stretched out his arms and reached for his wife, he was wont, for Patience and Wing, longingly to stretch out his own."

Apparently it did not occur to Albee that there was anything inappropriate about his guest's behavior, or his ready willingness to settle into the routine of the house as though he were ideally happy with this *ménage à trois*. Alger did not resent it when Albee suggested amiably that he would be married and have such a happy home life himself one day, although he had been fiercely resentful of the same kind of talk from his father, remarking, "I suppose it would be a shame for me to knock you down—you just don't know any better." He had been as blunt with his sister, telling her that, "on the question of marriage, please save your suggestions. I don't want them, I won't listen to them, I have no use for them."

Albee and his wife, innocent of these deep feelings in their guest, tried to make a match for him. They introduced him to a twenty-two-year-old charmer named Doris Stuart, and as always, Alger was the passive recipient of an assault by an aggressive woman. With some echoes of Charlotte Evans, he was besieged for a week by Miss Stuart, who then left the field as defeated as the others. Horatio told Albee she was too fat, which of course was not the real reason for his coldness.

Significantly, the only one of Albee's friends in whom Alger showed interest was Arthur Bishop, a pleasant young man who appeared to have nothing to do in the world but to lounge about and be amiable. Horatio was puzzled by him, but he had the feeling that Bishop, too, suffered secret sorrows. If he did, they remained unknown.

What happened to remove Alger at last from his refuge with the Albees is unknown. Presumably it was nothing more than the realization that he had, after all, started for California and ought to get on with it. In due time he arrived in San Francisco, having encountered no more cul-de-sacs along the way, and was immediately lionized by the Friday Afternoon Club, an organization of women, mostly dilettantes, who were interested in writing and writers. They asked him to come and recite a ballad he had written long before, called "John Maynard," which had become one of the favorite "declamations" of schools and societies everywhere in the country, and was included in every popular collection of verse. The first stanza ran:

> "'Twas on Lake Erie's broad expanse,
> One bright midsummer day,

The gallant steamer *Ocean Queen*
Swept proudly on her way.
Bright faces clustered on the deck,
Or, leaning o'er the side,
Watched carelessly the feathery foam
That flecked the rippling tide."

At that moment, as Alger described the poem later for the December, 1895, readers of *The Writer*, a sailor discovers that the steamer is on fire. "He carries the terrible news to the captain. A sailor named John Maynard is at the wheel. As the flames make rapid progress it is seen that the only hope of safety is to steer the ship to land. Under the captain's order John Maynard undertakes the dangerous task. They are within half a mile of shore.

"But half a mile! Yet stay, the flames
No longer slowly creep,
But gather 'round the helmsman bold
With fierce impetuous sweep."

"Implored by the captain to remain at the wheel for five minutes more, John Maynard does so," Alger wrote. "In brief, he succeeds in his task, but as the steamer touches shore he sinks in death beside it. He falls a victim to the flames, but the passengers are saved. It will be seen that the story is a striking one."

This last modest estimate scarcely calculated the effect "John Maynard" had on the ladies of the Friday Afternoon Club. Not only were they overwhelmed by the spectacle of the great poet from New York reading his work in person (obviously, they were not followers of Ragged Dick and his friends), but the president of the club, whose name was Marion Lambert, insisted that Horatio stay with her and her sister Grace at their home while he was in the city.

Thus began another curious episode in Horatio's curious life.

The Lambert girls were maidens over forty who lived with their father, at the moment on a long trip to Texas. They were lonely without him, and Alger became the substitute. They smothered him with the same attention they had given their father. Neither had anything else to do. Grace had once been a nurse and Marion had amused herself writing fairy tales, but now they devoted all their time to making Horatio happy. In time they became aware that Alger had little to give back to them, either in the way of sexual attention or simply in entertaining their friends, who were invited to meet the noted author from New York and went away again thinking him a very dull man for all his fame.

By a circumstance fortunate for Alger, their father came home, a garrulous old gentleman who began boring Horatio at once with endless tales of his experiences as a miner. Alger was not so bored, however, that he did not perceive Mr. Lambert's value as a mine in his own right—an endless source of information about the West, which was the business purpose of his trip. He began to make notes, and from them drew nearly all of what he needed later to write his books with a Western setting.

Alger's Lambert period came to an end with the arrival of Bret Harte in San Francisco. Harte, too, was invited to address the Friday Afternoon Club, and the fickle Lambert girls at once turned their affections to him.

This rejection, trivial though it seems on the surface, was apparently the final turn of the screw in Alger's personality disorganization. Little evidence remains to show what happened, but it appears that Horatio was obsessed by a sense of failure and could not orient himself around any place or person. He left San Francisco and stayed for a time in a small town in the foothills of the Rockies, living by himself in a hut, like a hermit. He learned to ride, and otherwise occupied himself with long walks into the hills, while he examined dismally the sorry facts of his life, trying to determine honestly, to his own satisfaction, whether he had been a failure in everything that counted. To him, his obvious success did not matter. This man who was read and admired by millions could think of only one thing remaining in life that mattered to him. He wanted to write—not stories for children, but a great, burning novel.

Perhaps to begin on that long delayed effort, or perhaps because he wearied finally of solitude and the West, Horatio returned to the East, there to carry the disintegration which had begun in San Francisco to a fantastic and nearly disastrous conclusion.

CHAPTER 9

Horatio did not linger in New York. He was ill, seedier in appearance than ever, not fully able to cope with the realities of daily living, and still unwilling to end his self-imposed estrangement from everything he had known. He hurried off up the Hudson to the village of Peekskill, on its heights overlooking the wild prospect of the river, and immured himself in the house of an old and respected family. There he might have lived undisturbed, with what result no one can say, if he had not been drawn into a situation so unbelievable it can be explained only by his mental condition.

This final episode in a life filled with disasters began with a murder. The victim was Jeremiah Hardy, a Peekskill man who had been shot and robbed. For some reason suspicion turned on his widow, who was arrested and charged with the crime. In denying it, and while she was in a state of hysteria, Edith Hardy told the police she had seen a prowler in the neighborhood before the crime. Acting on this information, and undoubtedly looking for a suspect on whom they would be more likely to pin a conviction, the police arrested Horatio.

He fitted their qualifications. He was a stranger in town, of whom no one knew anything; he looked poor and untidy and sick; and when questioned, he was not coherent. They took him to Mrs. Hardy, who identified him positively, and Alger was thrown into a cell. Before the day was over, the real murderer came forward and confessed the crime. Before Horatio was released, however, the police tried to find out more about him. He was not reticent. He told them he had been in California recently, had been ill there and for a time had suffered amnesia; he was not yet well.

The police believed all this but they flatly refused to credit it when he told them he was Horatio Alger. They knew of Alger's books and his formidable reputation, and thought of him as one of the literary lights of New York. They could not reconcile that image with the forlorn, broken figure who sat dully before them. However, they took into account the fact that he was living with a respectable family, and since he was not a vagrant, they decided to let him go with no more than a cursory investigation, putting him down as a harmless eccentric, which may have been as apt a summary as any.

Meanwhile, Edith Hardy recovered a bit from the shock of her husband's death and *her* false arrest, enough to write a full account of her troubles to her sister, Una Garth, who lived in Europe with her husband Russel and a brother, Eugene. The whole family sailed for home at once when they got the news.

While they were en route, Mrs. Hardy also experienced severe sensations of guilt about Horatio. The injustice of her arrest had been transferred, with even greater injustice, to a wholly innocent victim, and it had been her fault. She wrote a note to Horatio, saying, "I am afraid that I was unwittingly the cause of the unpleasant experience which befell you recently. I do not know what amends I can make but I do wish to express my regret and ask your indulgence."

Alger did not think to raise his eyebrows over that "unwittingly." There had been nothing unwitting about it. But he was always quick to forgive, and instantly responsive to kindness, and whatever had been the circumstances, he was certain Edith Hardy meant to be kind. He wrote her a polite answer, minimizing his own experience and sympathizing with the hard lot which must now be hers. If there was anything he might do to alleviate it, he concluded formally, he hoped she would call on him.

He was surprised to learn there was, indeed, something he could do. Mrs. Hardy wrote back to inquire whether he knew of someone in New York who could enter into negotiations with the insurance company on her behalf. Characteristically, Horatio felt he could not answer this request without a discussion, and forthwith presented himself at Mrs. Hardy's door.

They were both agreeably surprised. Horatio had groomed himself for the occasion, much as he did for his appearances before the newsboys, and looked quite presentable. Mrs. Hardy, no longer hysterical and distraught as she had been at their unfortunate first meeting, appeared to be a charming, kind lady, They had an amicable discussion. Horatio suggested his friend Charles O'Connor as a New York intermediary, and promised to ask his help, after which he shook hands with his hostess and departed.

A few days later, while he was on one of his lonely walks, he encountered Mrs. Hardy again, and she invited him home for tea. After that, in his usual fashion, Alger infiltrated what remained of the Hardy household and became almost a daily visitor. He and Edith were friends. He found her so sympathetic that for the first time in long months he began to come out of his apathy and exhibit some signs of his old self. As for Edith Hardy, she too was lonely and welcomed a man to gossip with, particularly one who appeared to have no slightest intention of making a sympathetic pass at a bereft widow. She talked to him eagerly of her sister Una, and her happy anticipation of the Garth family's arrival. Una, she said enthusiastically, was like no woman he had ever seen, a female of such intelligence and beauty that she was not to be believed unless viewed. After hours of such ecstatic description, Horatio could scarcely wait to set eyes upon the paragon.

On the second night after Una's reunion with her sister, he had his opportunity. It was a fateful moment. He looked upon Una and was lost, as he had not been since Patience—more significantly, as he had never been in his life. For the first time he was instantly consumed by a leaping fire inside, as though all the powerful, conflicting forces which had been raging in him for so long had coalesced into a brilliant incandescence. She was wearing white silk, a dress which emphasized the tantalizing fullness of her fortyish figure. Her smile and her eyes drew poor Horatio as though they had been the glittering fixation points of a master hypnotist. He saw humor there, and warmth and sympathy—everything in the world he thought he needed.

As the evening went on, he could scarcely pay polite attention to Una's talkative brother Eugene, and even less to her husband Russel, who watched Alger with an immediate distrust and suspicion which, as it proved, were well founded. He could not miss the glances his wife and Horatio were exchanging, glances which expressed quite frankly their interest in each other. Whenever he tried to join in the conversation, directing a somewhat acid remark in Alger's direction, no one paid the slightest attention to him. This in itself was not unusual. Russel Garth was a man whose life was absorbed by business, in the manner of the true nineteenth-century entrepreneur, and he was not at ease in social situations. About love he knew nothing at all. An American representing a Chicago company abroad, he had learned nothing from years of living in Paris and elsewhere on the Continent except how to be successful in his business. He had neglected Una in the usual style of the busy businessman, and worse, did not know he had done it.

The transformation that evening made in Alger was one that might better have been applied to Russel Garth. The husband, only momentarily disturbed, slept peacefully. Horatio slept not at all. He was not only carried away, but a force was working so powerfully within him that for the first time in his relations with women he was impelled to be the aggressor. A resolve was growing in him to possess Una, one way or another. He did not think for a moment of difficulty or danger. In fact, he scarcely thought of her as married.

Next morning he appeared at the Garth house with a bouquet of flowers he had picked himself in his landlady's garden, but found the whole family out. He was waiting for them on the porch, holding his flowers, when they returned. Mrs. Hardy invited him to stay for lunch, and he stayed—on and on, through the afternoon and evening, while Russel viewed the scene with increasing irritation and the others watched with amusement. For Horatio and Una were plainly courting each other, under the noses of everyone. When Russel grumbled privately to his wife that he thought Horatio was a damned fool, Una responded by going out for a walk alone with her new friend.

So began one of the strangest triangles in the history of love. It would be difficult to imagine two suitors so inept in the amatory arts. Una's worldly knowledge more than made up for what they lacked, but the behavior of the men remains inexplicable. Horatio courted Una as though her husband were not there, and Russel never offered to punch him in the nose, nor did he argue the matter out with his wife. It was as though she were not his wife at all, and he and Alger were meeting on equal terms as suitors. Mayes believes Garth might have behaved differently in Europe, where he felt himself on familiar ground; in Peekskill, he was merely baffled and angry.

Discretion was forgotten after a few days. Una and Horatio rode together, walked together, talked together while virtually ignoring everyone else, openly flirted, exchanged little gifts —in brief, behaved like lovers. Mrs. Hardy no doubt was aghast to observe what she had set in motion, but by this time it was too late, and Horatio had forgotten Edith too. He had, indeed, forgotten everything and everyone except Una.

To her he unfolded the splendid literary plans which had once entranced Elise, and she listened to them, thrilled, because she too was much interested in literature and regarded herself as a well read woman. It never occurred to her that a man as noted as Alger was for his children's books might not be able to produce the Great American Novel he talked about so ardently. She could not have been more sympathetic, and poor Horatio believed that at last he had found the understanding and inspiration of which he had always dreamed. As for the childless Una, she found in Horatio at once a hero and a son.

Russel decided that the only way he could end this embarrassing and disgraceful situation was by taking Una away. He announced that he must return to New York, and the whole family left hastily. But Horatio was only momentarily diverted. Within two days, he had also departed for New York, and found rooms near where the harried Russel had come to rest. By this time, however, Una had come somewhat to her senses. Alger would have plunged on as he had before, but Una insisted that they see each other secretly. She was convinced that Russel, aroused at last, would have no more of this affair if he knew it was continuing.

They began meeting each other every day. Horatio showed her about the city, and took her proudly to the Newsboys' Lodging House so that she could meet his best friend, O'Connor, who reported later that he liked her, but with reservations. He did not elaborate. Horatio would not have cared about O'Connor's reservations in any case. He had never been happier in his life.

Soon, inevitably, they were meeting in his room, where they talked endlessly. Surprisingly, nothing else occurred for a time. They embraced each other occasionally and held hands; one supposes a good deal of what was known in those days as "fondling" took place, but they did not sleep together. Una was not altogether at ease, for one thing. She had begun to worry about her husband, and once ventured the idea that it might be better if they did not see each other again. Seeing the stricken look in Alger's eyes, Una repented at once. The affair went on as before.

After a month of these tortured, happy meetings, Russel Garth unwittingly made everything easy for them. His firm called him to Chicago, and he went with no particular misgivings, thinking Horatio back in Peekskill and forgotten by Una. He had no more than gone when O'Connor, with equal innocence, helped the affair further by persuading Alger to buy a farm, meaning it to have just the opposite effect. He wanted to get Horatio out of the city, and, as he supposed, away from Una.

For the happy lovers, it was an ideal solution. Horatio bought the farm and asked Una to come and live on it with him while her husband was away, which might be for some time, and she accepted gladly, joyously. She could hardly wait to give herself to him now.

But having given herself, she knew him better, and as so many others had experienced before her, to know Alger better was to value him less, to be puzzled by his oddly mingled strengths and weaknesses, in which the weaknesses were so much stronger. Sometimes his childish solemnities amused her. Quickly, too, she sensed that he was far from being the writer he hoped and planned to be. It was not difficult, knowing him well, to perceive that he had neither the talent nor the imagination to do what he planned. Innocently, she proposed that he take on a collaborator. Then she saw quick resentment flaring in his eyes, and knew that he had not the least doubt of himself. But even with the more intimate and sobering knowledge she had of him, Una Garth continued to give him all the love she possessed, and Horatio returned it in greater measure. It was he who loved the more.

Their rural idyll came to an end with the arrival of a letter from brother Eugene, who reported Russel's imminent arrival from Chicago, en route to Europe and remarked, in passing, that he too was about to leave. The lovers scarcely had time to get back to New York. Una anticipated her husband by only a few hours, but she was happy to see him still unsuspecting, busy with plans for their return to Paris in a few days.

Alger, naturally, was preparing to sail with them, if not on the same ship then one immediately following, but when he examined his bank account he found that his long dalliance with Una, during which he had written virtually nothing, combined with the unproductive time in California, had reduced his assets to a dangerous point. He could not possibly afford to go abroad unless he completed some new books. There was no alternative. He and Una had a tearful parting in his room, and she went away with his promise to follow as soon as he could. Horatio did not know it, but Una's love was already on the wane.

The transition to his old work schedule and a life without Una was unspeakably dreary for Alger. He was lonely and found it almost impossible to write. Moreover, as a result of the blazing idealism which Una had stirred in him again, he could not be satisfied with anything but the best even in his books for boys. He started a new one, then threw away the few chapters he wrote as unworthy. O'Connor tried to help him by suggesting a trip to the farm for rest and quiet writing, but he made a serious mistake by remarking bluntly as they discussed Horatio's problem that Una had done him no good. That precipitated their first, and last, quarrel, which ended with the contrite note O'Connor found next morning: "Forgive me. I am not well."

It seemed he could write nothing, only letters to Una, which he turned out at the rate of at least one a day, and not all of which he mailed. Their tone grew more passionate, more frantic when there was no reply from Paris. "Can you have forgotten, Una darling?" he pleaded. "Has all that passed meant nothing?"

When she answered at last, her reply was cool and sensible: "For heaven's sake, my dear, be more discreet. Suppose that Russel should come across your letters! What would I do? I have not forgotten and I will not forget—but pray store up your feelings until you can see me. It will be better not to correspond at all and I must ask you to consider this quite final. Only when you are ready to come, then send me word, but let even that be casual."

He knew she was right, and momentarily had some insight into his folly. The sobering effect of her letter succeeded in getting him back to his former routine, but nevertheless his second attempt at a new book also ended in failure. It was not until he had started the third one, *Frank and Fearless*, that the words began to flow again in his familiar, easy, artless way. He finished it in two weeks. His publisher paid him an advance royalty immediately, and Horatio put it all in the bank except for the absolute minimum amount he required to exist—and except for fifty cents, which he spent on a set of building blocks, the kind he had played with in his childhood. When he was not writing, this fifty-one-year-old child built the endless towers he had spent so much time constructing as a boy.

Following O'Connor's suggestion, he retired to his farm for more work, living quietly but driving himself to make more money. By a customary coincidence, material was waiting on his doorstep. He found a young man, eighteen, living near him in a tent, to which he had been exiled by his father, who had thrown him out of the house when he had proved to be a spendthrift at college. The boy told him his story, and Horatio thriftily converted it into *Walter Sherwood's Probation*. He did not even bother to change his neighbor's real name.

This book was so immediately successful that it made Horatio prosperous almost overnight. Pausing only long enough to collect his royalties, he began to pack. He wrote Una a one-sentence letter that was a model of discretion: "I am coming." And he was off.

Una's feelings about their reunion may be judged by a letter she wrote to her brother Eugene in Italy soon after Alger's arrival. "Why must he regale me with his crises?" she inquired petulantly. "Was there ever a man with such a mania for complaints! On Tuesday he arrived in the city and has besieged me ever since. I can't be rid of him though by now he should know I have no interest in his projects. He has taken rooms across the way and attempts to watch my every move. Twenty years ago this might have amused me, but you will agree—unchivalrous brother that you are—that I am beyond the age of kittishness."

She had also gone beyond Alger; she was, in fact, bored with him. Yet she could not help responding to his pathetic devotion. In the letter to her brother she wrote of their reunion: "His tears fell over my hands and as fast as they fell just so fast did he kiss them away. Can you imagine a more ridiculous procedure? If the passion were momentary I would not mind it, but he repeats and repeats his intention of staying near me. What, dear Gene, am I to do?"

Fortunately for Una, her husband was on a business trip to Germany. She could debate her problem for a time without the pressure of a jealous husband, and after Alger's first wild expressions of ardor, she found it easy and convenient to slip into something of the routine they had known before. He lived nearby and called every day promptly at eleven, lingering with her over luncheon, and then expressing his devotion by doing her little services which made him seem sometimes almost like a servant in the house. Their affair was resumed on a somewhat lower key, complicated further by Alger's health, apparently a chronic bronchitis or some other respiratory ailment. Una was constantly worried that he might become really ill—not for his sake, but because of the serious complication that might ensue.

The complication that did occur was her husband's return, and the warning letter which preceded it. Somehow Russel had found out about Alger's return—possibly from Eugene, who wanted the affair ended for his own reasons—and he wrote: "I am not at all pleased to hear that your friend Horatio is in Paris, and I hope I have the good luck to find him gone when I arrive. Minister he may be but man he is not. I swear the more I think about him the more I am convinced he is one of the impossible ragamuffins he writes so much blather about. If he intends to remain in Paris you must let him know I am not inclined to see him. With your usual good sense you will understand that I don't want him around under any circumstances."

Anxiously Una conveyed this information to Horatio, apprehensive of what he might say or do. To her surprise, and perhaps to her slight pique, he observed that it would be both inconvenient and indiscreet for him to remain so close at hand and risk being discovered. He would move, he said, and did that week.

It was two months before Una saw him again. She did not know whether he was alive or dead, and although her passion for Horatio had long since dwindled, she was still involved with him in a way she could not have described to herself, in which pity, memory and curiosity were mingled. As he had done to others, Horatio had left her with an exasperated unwillingness to let him go. Living with him was like reading a book so bad that the temptation to put it away was conquered by a persistent curiosity to learn how it ended—that is, the same feeling one has on reading an Alger book today.

At length a melancholy and disturbing note reached Una. "I have been a sick man," Horatio advised her, "and but for you should be willing enough to take my chances with my God. There is, however, something that will not let me go; it keeps tugging at my heart and spinning in my mind. I feel sure it has come at last—the idea, the story, for which I have been waiting. To what besides your encouragement can I attribute this success? For success I am sure it will be.

"I should like, dearest Una, to walk alone with you and tell you the story as it is forming in my mind. It will be called 'Tomorrow' and concerns a man who goes to the guillotine in place of his friend. The scene will be the French Revolution and I have already begun to collect facts for the background. The whole prospect of the book excites me. I am anxious to see it under way. Cannot I persuade you to meet me, to talk—to talk? Let us go somewhere for a day. Just a day? For old times' sake, *please*."

It was an appeal Una could hardly resist. She had not known

that the return of her husband had convinced Alger their love was hopeless, but if he believed it, as his long absence and the tone of his note implied, it made her feel somewhat more secure. And after all, they *had* been lovers, and now he was ill and needed her. Una wrote to her brother and told him she meant to see Alger secretly, whether her husband had forbidden it or not.

Her letter had an unexpected consequence because it arrived at a time when Eugene was afloat on a sea of troubles of his own. The shipping business which occupied him was in a desperate financial position, and he was painfully aware that he might have to raise a substantial amount of cash. In an emergency he had no better place to turn than Russel, and if his sister endangered her marriage by her foolish infatuation, that door might be closed forever. He did not care whom his sister slept with as long as it was not with someone who might endanger a loan.

Eugene set down his feelings in a blunt and uncompromising letter, demanding that Una remain faithful to her husband at least until times were better. She promised and would have kept it if she had not had a second, despairing note from Alger, who thought her silence meant she did not want to see him and sent her a letter of farewell, whether to the earth or to Paris she could not tell. It was too much for Una. Stopping only long enough to record in her diary that she meant "to see Horatio before he goes, no matter what the cost," she hurried to Alger's apartment, where a tender reconciliation took place.

Her appearance revived Alger as two corps of doctors could not have done. He even survived the shock when, eagerly discussing his great opus, *Tomorrow,* with her, she gently pointed out that Dickens had anticipated him in *A Tale of Two Cities.* Alger had, indeed, read the book and realized now that subconsciously he must have borrowed its plot. Una had rescued him from plagiarism, but she could not save him from his obsession with the Great Idea. He insisted that the title was still magnificent; he would simply think of some other plot to go with it, and now that Una had returned to him, he could do it.

The visit upset Una more than she would let him see. She went home and wrote perceptively in her diary: "I have met men whose faith in an idea has made them disgustingly wealthy and others whose faith in a party has carried them to high places in politics. Yet never have I met a man with such faith in himself as Horatio Alger, and with such ridiculous little cause. His naïveté makes me sorry for him. He seems to have been born an orphan and never since to have had a parent."

By now, however, it was more than faith with Horatio; it was the beginnings of paranoia. He sat alone in his room, except when Una could get away to visit him, and tried to organize his chaotic thoughts. He read *The Three Musketeeers* and considered writing a juvenile version of it. He dreamed a thousand plots to fit his title, *Tomorrow,* and discarded all of them. The dreams grew wilder. He visioned a vast history of the world in three volumes, titled *Yesterday, Today* and *Tomorrow,* but rejected that idea too because he was appalled by its magnitude. In any case, his masterwork must be a novel, he was convinced.

The gray, wheezing winter came to an end and it was spring. In the burgeoning glory of a Paris April, Horatio at last went so far as to write for the first time a part of the masterpiece he would call *Tomorrow.* It was only a first chapter, but it was a beginning and he hastily conveyed the news to Una, who could not help being excited too. Perhaps she had been too quick to judge him. Perhaps everything he had suffered and the long winter of preparation had given him the inspiration to realize his dream. She hurried to his apartment as soon as she could slip away, and there she read the first chapter, after which Alger feverishly outlined what would follow. Una read and listened with growing dismay. She went home and wrote candidly in her diary: "I spent the afternoon with Horatio and saw the opening paragraphs of his *Tomorrow.* May the Lord spare the man from a knowledge of his own incapacity!"

She knew it was useless to try to reason with him; all her gentle tenderness could not save him now. He was transported, carried away by his dream, and nothing could stand in his way.

The shadows of unreality were gathering about him even in the bright spring sunlight. Oddly enough, it was not *Tomorrow* he was really writing. As his pen raced onward, the manuscript developed into a book much like all the others, even to the length —70,000 words—and when he was through he called it *Struggling Upward.*

By this time Una was convinced that her lover was already mad. There was something in his eyes as he talked about his work that frightened her. She stopped seeing him, terrified of what he might do next in his manic transport. He bombarded her with a steady stream of hysterical messages: "See me, for God Almighty's sake!" "What have I done? Tell me, for Christ's sake!" Beside herself with fear, Una appealed to Eugene to save her before Alger invaded her house, and before her husband discovered what was going on.

Eugene responded gallantly; his own interests were still at stake. He called on Alger and found him half-alive, only the fanatic glitter in his eyes testifying to the destroying fire within him. Confronted with this melancholy spectacle, Eugene could not carry out his resolve to make Horatio understand that everything was and must be over with Una. Instead he resorted to a lame deception and told Alger that she was dying.

The reaction was an explosion. Horatio was rampant, ready to defy God and Russel and go to Una at once and snatch her back from the grave which had already claimed Patience and Wing, the only other humans he had ever loved. It was all Eugene could do to calm him. He told Alger that he would only make Una's condition worse by such behavior. He could do most for her at this juncture, Eugene declared, by leaving her strictly alone and giving her a chance to get well without giving her any more cause for anxiety. When she was well, they would meet again. Then he went away, and when Una had heard her brother's report, she went to the theater.

While he was waiting, anxious and tormented, Alger turned again to the elusive *Tomorrow* and found it still tantalizingly close to his disturbed consciousness. He struggled upward toward it as a drowning man reaches toward the surface. Still it eluded him. The Great Idea, the idea that would make him immortal, began to take on what seemed to him a physical shape, dancing before his eyes. He tried to capture it, stumbling about his room. Then, suddenly, the disintegration was complete.

The police, called by alarmed neighbors, found him screaming and beating at the walls. Then the final indignity. He was carried away, kicking and screaming, shouting that he must capture his Idea. They took him to a hospital and would have put him in a ward, but a man who had been in the crowd gathered in the street to watch Horatio's inglorious exit had followed and insisted that he be placed in a private room and given the best of care, for which the man said he would be glad to pay. The hospital authorities supposed he must be a relative, but he was only another of Horatio's incredible coincidences—a former bootblack resident of the Newsboys' Lodging House who had happened to pass by. Alger had once been kind enough to buy him the tools of his trade and give him a start up the ladder. It was an incident straight from an Alger book.

CHAPTER 10

For long weeks Horatio lay ill of mind and body in a Paris hospital. He wrote a long letter to his mother, who had been dead for many years. He coughed and shook with his fever. Eventually he recovered enough to be discharged, and without even a good-bye to Una, as far as anyone knows, he sailed back to New York, his mind cleared but his body still far from well.

Alger described his own homecoming: "I went right up from

the ship to the lodging house. When Charlie saw me he almost cried. He realized at once, apparently, how ill and weak I was. He was the only man whose questions I would have answered but he asked none. He put me in a carriage and drove me to his home. I felt somehow happy in the thought of his friendship and I said a prayer for him before I fell asleep."

Of this reunion, O'Connor himself wrote later: "I did not recognize him. I could not at first believe it was him. I said to myself this cannot be Horatio Alger. He was thin as a rail and pale as a sheet, all hollow in his cheeks. His eyes seemed to have got bigger and brighter and gave him a funny wild look. It seemed then he was dying. I knew it was Alger for certain when I heard him speak. His voice—that did not change. Well, I took him home with me and put him to bed."

He did much more. O'Connor asked no questions, but, as he always had, accepted Horatio on faith and took care of him as faithfully as though Alger were a son or a brother, giving him his own room and paying for his medical care and other expenses. Horatio had exhausted the little wealth he had accumulated.

It was a long siege. He was not out of danger for a long time, and sometimes he lapsed into a delirium in which he was once more pursuing the elusive Idea, the Great Book. From what he could understand of the obsession which still gripped his friend, O'Connor had no doubt that the dream would one day be realized, for in his mind there existed no doubt that Horatio was one of the great writers of the world. His simple faith in Alger approached idolatry. He read from Horatio's works to the assembled urchins as though they were Scripture.

Prepared to die at any moment, Alger amused himself composing epitaphs for himself as he lay endless days in bed; it was his childish method of getting even more worried sympathy and attention from O'Connor. His epitaphs, sadly, were no better than his books, from a literary standpoint.

"Here lies the body of Horatio Alger, Jr. Well, what of it?" he wrote.

"Here lies a good fellow who spent his life while he had it." Sometimes he did them in his customary bad verse:

> "Beneath this soil a Yankee lies,
> A Yankee very crankee.
> Move not his bones or he'll turn stones,
> And leap to life to spank 'ee."

Long after he recovered, when he was unwittingly near his actual death, Horatio composed the epitaph which remained his favorite, combining as it did several titles of books he had written which he liked best: "Six feet underground reposes Horatio Alger, *Helping Himself* to a part of the earth, not *Digging for Gold* or *In Search of Treasure,* but *Struggling Upward* and *Bound to Rise* at last *In a New World* where it shall be said he is *Risen from the Ranks.*"

This was a variation of another Alger pastime, writing autographs in verse using his book titles, of which this is a splendid example:

> "*Strive and Succeed,* the world's temptations flee—
> Be *Brave and Bold,* and *Strong and Steady* be.
> Go *Slow and Sure,* and prosper then you must—
> With *Fame and Fortune,* while you *Try and Trust.*"

O'Connor simply would not let Horatio die. When it appeared, three weeks after his return, that he had no better than an even chance to live, the superintendent assembled two hundred of his charges, and knelt with them while he prayed: "Good God, restore him to health. Take not away Horatio Alger." He neglected everything else to take care of his friend, and eventually he was rewarded by watching Horatio's slow, painful recovery, a process which took two years before he could call himself wholly restored.

Long before that time, he was well enough to start writing

again, and by the time he was entirely recovered, he was beginning to turn out books with a speed and in a quantity he had not exhibited before. O'Connor hovered over him like a mother hen, protecting him from his ever growing public and trying to preserve him from the people who were tempted to separate him from his increasing wealth. Alger was so well protected in these last years, seen by so few people, that it was even questioned seriously whether he existed. Alger, like Mark Twain, had to issue a statement declaring that he lived and flourished. He did not do it with Twain's good humor; Horatio was indignant.

Nevertheless a mythology grew about him, fostered and disseminated by the boys of the Lodging House, who loved him as much as ever and told tales about him wherever they went in the city. They were devoted to him. When the Spanish-American War broke out not long before his death, a boy whom Alger had once tutored at the House, now grown up and successful, remarked that "Mr. Alger could raise a regiment of boys in New York alone who would fight for him to the death."

O'Connor did his best, but he could not protect Horatio entirely from himself. He was ready to give his money or his time or his name to anybody who asked for them, if it seemed to him that the cause was worthy, and there were few he thought were unworthy. He lent his name constantly to dubious promotion schemes for charitable enterprises, and as constantly O'Connor saw to it that it was removed. He was nearly involved in a slick stock promotion scheme centered on a publication to be called the *American Boys' Weekly*, of which he would have been the editor and innocent front man. Thc promoter went to prison.

Since he could not always keep his eye on Horatio, O'Connor urged his friend to acquire a secretary, and after considerable hesitation, Horatio hired Frank A. Hoppe, who was only twenty-six and a former newsboy at the House, now a young man of such slight constitution that he could not take a job requiring any physical effort.

It was not altogether a happy arrangement. Alger was disturbed because Hoppe read his mail, which the secretary considered part of his job and Horatio thought of as spying. Considering the self-righteous way he wrote about hard employers in his books, Alger often gave poor Hoppe a rather bad time. Whenever he finished a book he was customarily in a bad humor, and then, as Hoppe wrote later, "it was wise to stay clear of him. He had a wonderful power for making life miserable." Once Alger got the idea that his books must have pictures, and he was in a rage to think they had not been illustrated before. "Good Lord! What I had to listen to about illustrations!" Hoppe recalled.

The secretary was not bemused by his employer's fame. He regarded Alger with candid eyes, writing of him: "I don't believe anything short of physical incapacity could have stopped Alger from writing juveniles. They had become a habit with him, quite as much as eating and sleeping. His time had to be occupied and he was accustomed to keeping busy with one manuscript or another. Whether he felt good or bad, he wrote. In my years of association with him I do not recall any expression of pleasure or satisfaction coming from him in connection with his work. Still he could no sooner have discarded it than he could have discarded his skin and taken on another."

Always Alger tried to push beyond the frustrating limits set by his stories. He wanted to express his ideas and opinions directly, which led him to write long prefaces, sometimes as long as three thousand words. This practice only led to angry disputes with his publishers, who eliminated them as fast as he wrote them. In that era of publishing, an author had few rights. A publisher could alter a manuscript as he chose, and Alger's chose to eliminate his prefaces. Once he threatened to sue the firm of J. R. Anderson and H. S. Allen, who had published his *Abraham Lincoln, the Backwoods Boy,* in 1883, because they did not print a preface, the longest he had ever written, which nearly equaled the text. To avoid the threatened suit, Anderson and Allen brought out the second edition with the original preface cut down to normal length. Alger was not pleased, but he dropped the suit.

Most often in these prefaces Horatio seemed compelled to explain the mechanics of his writing, as though he were trying to convince himself as well as others that he really was a writer. He told about the origin of his plots, how he conceived his characters, and his methods of research, in which he emphasized constantly the authenticity of his material.

O'Connor never failed to support Alger in his quarrels with the publishers. As far as O'Connor was concerned, Alger could do no wrong. He went so far in his idolatry as to propose seriously that Horatio would make a splendid President. Introducing his friend to the assembled boys in a special convocation he had called to explain to them the issues in the election of 1888, especially civil service, he declared: "You will now have the pleasure of listening to a man who is, in my humble opinion, as great as the two candidates who are running for office today. Though it is not something which he seeks, the office of President of the United States for Horatio Alger is not beyond the realm of possibility."

Probably the only person in the room who took this statement seriously, besides O'Connor, was Alger himself. He had never thought of it before, but as he considered it later, the conviction grew in him that O'Connor was right. Certainly the most incongruous of all Alger's many dreams was the vision he now entertained of the Presidency. It was characteristic of him that his thoughts centered on what a magnificent thing it would be to have his Great Book written by the President of the United States. It was purest fantasy. He never had any serious intention of running for office.

Alger was grateful to O'Connor for his endorsement, nonetheless. He was closer now in his relationship to the superintendent than he had ever been. In the morning, O'Connor stopped for him at the lodgings Horatio had acquired when he was well again and the two men walked down to the House, where Alger worked and talked all day. At night they walked home again, or else they would eat together first and then proceed to one home or another for an evening of conversation which often lasted until early morning. O'Connor was the only human being who could have listened at all, let alone with never-failing enthusiasm, to Alger's endless plans and dreams and theorizings about everything under the sun. When they passed an evening during which Alger worked and his friend sat smoking quietly nearby, it would end with O'Connor's reading what Horatio had written. The author could always be certain of the most warming praise. O'Connor never criticized.

Horatio had a brief enthusiasm for the piano. He bought one so that O'Connor could play it, and thought for a while of learning the instrument himself. But like his other enthusiasms, it died for lack of nourishment.

As it had from the beginning, his mind turned restlessly from one thing to another, seeking whatever it was that Horatio wanted so desperately all his life. He never quite knew, but the searching never stopped. For a time it seemed to him that the removal of religion from life after Wing's death was the cause of his emptiness, and now that this event was so far in the past, partially blotted out by the experience with Una, he turned tentatively toward religion again. He could not go back to the faith of his father, but he found himself receptive to the new idea of Christian Science, which was just then gaining popularity. He tried it for six months, and then it went the way of other enthusiasms. Horatio returned to the old gods after all; he had never really had the courage to break with them.

It was fortunate for him that he had rediscovered religion, because he shortly had need of it. One day O'Connor left work early, saying he had a headache and intended to go home and sleep it off, after which he would come over that evening to see Alger. When he had not appeared by ten o'clock, Horatio was alarmed and went to call on his friend, whom he found still dressed, lying on the bed and feeling too ill to go out. At Horatio's urging, he undressed and went to bed and lay there quietly while Alger read to him from the manuscript pages he had brought along, work he had done earlier in the evening on his new book, *Adrift in New York*. While he read, O'Connor fell asleep and Alger left him quietly. Returning in the morning when his friend failed to appear for their daily walk to the office, he found O'Connor dead.

In the face of this grief, Horatio's usual prolixity deserted him. He spent the night before the funeral writing a lengthy eulogy, but when he stood up the next day before the thousand boys who had gathered for the funeral from every corner of the city, he threw away his oration and said simply: "Charles O'Connor was the best friend that man or boy could have. God was good in giving him to us. No one can say how much he meant to us. Everywhere boys know the man Charles O'Connor was. He was the best friend I have ever known. He was the kindest and the least selfish. I loved him—all of us loved him. God will find a place for him close to His throne."

It was the most sincere, and the truest, utterance Alger ever made. But now he was alone in the world and he had only his writing to sustain him. He worked at it constantly, producing as many as seven books in his most productive year, 1888. Horatio was now at the height of his influence, and it was considerable; there was scarcely a literate family in the United States which did not know about him. His readers numbered such unlikely fans as John Drew and Pat Rooney and Christy Mathewson. That supreme egotist and great editor, Edward W. Bok, was growing up on a steady diet of Alger books. "They can laugh all they like at Alger now," Bok wrote years later, "but he pulled his weight in the world when he was with us." The literati were reading and discussing Henry James and William Dean Howells, but the country was reading Alger, and his audience was not entirely children by any means.

His publishers, whom he was helping to make rich, had a

naturally high opinion of him, but A. K. Loring, his first publisher, also had some perception about the reasons for Horatio's popularity. "Alger is the dominating figure of the new era," he wrote. "In his books he has captured the spirit of reborn America. The turmoil of city streets is in them. You can hear the rattle of pails on the farms. Above all you can hear the cry of triumph of the oppressed over the oppressor. Of no country but the United States could such stories be written and accounted true. Here, where there is no caste, they happen every day. What Alger has done is to portray the soul—the ambitious soul—of the country. He is outstanding today because he is the first to record lives with which we are all familiar. In centuries to come he will be outstanding because he was the first to record, in the fiction form, the narratives of every-day life."

Loring's may have been a wildly inaccurate estimate in some respects, but there was truth in it too, a truth which another of his publishers recognized. "To a greater extent than any other man he knows that men want to read about themselves," Frank A. Munsey wrote of Alger. "No one has been able to approach him in ability to depict the life of the downtrodden. He has a grip on his readers which no one will be able to loosen. . . ."

Munsey asserted with conviction that it was not unlikely Horatio would "go down in literary history as the greatest literary figure of his time," a prophecy he was later moved to modify considerably, when he was convinced that the man who had made so much money for him was only a curiosity of the times. "His style is crude and he lacks depth of imagination," Munsey noted correctly.

Alger himself had no illusions about his immortality. The poor opinion he had of his work was a better estimate than any his admirers made. "Times will change," he predicted. "Horse-cars will disappear. Boys no longer will black boots in the street. What I am describing will seem fantastic to coming generations. . . . Nobody will read them, even assuming they are well done. I should have let go. How many times I wanted to! Writing in the same vein becomes a habit, like sleeping on the right side. Try to sleep on the left side and the main purpose is defeated—one stays awake."

As his troubled life drew to a moody close, Alger was full of these pessimistic views of himself, most of them sadly accurate. "I suppose I should have married," he mused. "A man cannot go tramping over the earth forever, alone. He must plant roots which will spring to life—bring forth blossoms and comfort him."

After O'Connor's death, Horatio could not help feeling he had nowhere to go. The Lodging House had been the center of his world, and now it seemed full of strangers. There were new boys whom he did not know, lodgers who had arrived during the year following O'Connor's funeral, a period during which Alger virtually disappeared from view and never went near the House. The new superintendent, Theodore Heig, was friendly enough but Horatio conceived the erroneous notion that he was not wanted at the House any more. He met his old friends among the boys outside the building, and talked with them at dinner or in his room about starting another house as a rival. Heig heard of this proposal and went out of his way to assure Alger that he was welcome to resume his old style of life at the House.

Horatio was grateful for that, and tried to do it, but new boys were coming along rapidly and the old friends were gone. More and more he felt himself a stranger in the House. Nor could Heig possibly replace O'Connor, as no one could. Aimlessly, Alger drifted up to Cambridge from time to time, rehearsing painful memories of Patience Stires and mooning about Harvard with belated affection for the place. He wanted the University to recognize him as an author, but it disdained him. Instead it recalled him as the smallest boy in the class of 1852 and, because his name began with *A*, as the first student to have his name inscribed in the first yearbook. Horatio wept to think of it.

He tried to interest himself in the moral reforms of the day—child labor in factories, Anthony Comstock's assaults on sin—but he could not summon the old quick enthusiasms. The truth was that Horatio Alger was a man grown suddenly old, and consciously waiting to die, although the prospect frightened him. More and more his thoughts turned to his old New England home. He heard frequently from his sister Olive, now Mrs. Amos Cheney, who lived in South Natick and begged him to come there and end his days with her.

He decided to do it. On the day the United States declared war against Spain, April 23, 1898, he left the hysteria of the city forever. There was so much excitement at the Lodging House that his departure was scarcely noticed, except for one small boy who held the door open for him.

Horatio settled down to a quiet life in South Natick. Sometimes he walked along the banks of the Charles, or sat with the other loungers in the lobby of Bailey's Hotel. He visited local landmarks and thought about the rich history all around him. Gradually his health failed. He had a steady, racking cough. On occasion when he was out walking, an attack of it would cause him so much pain that he had to sit down on the ground and wait until someone could help him home. The doctor at last told him he must stay indoors. Alger took the doctor's advice, and he also took every patent medicine he thought might help him. Nothing, however, could delay his rapid deterioration.

In his sister's house he had a room of his own which he tried to make as nearly as possible like the one he had known in New York, which he had re-created wherever he happened to live. He had his familiar carpet sent up from the city, and placed his Shakespeare bust on the fireplace mantel. Beside his bed was a desk, full of paper and pencils which he did not touch. For a time he had his books lined up on shelves in his room, but he took to rereading them, and the gulf between what he had wanted to accomplish and what he had done was so depressingly apparent to him, that he could not stand to contemplate those dozens of titles staring down at him. He had the books removed; if he could, he said, he intended to forget them.

He had a few visitors, old friends of the family, but it was apparent to Olive that he wanted to be alone, as he had been so much in his lifetime, and she respected his wish. Frank Hoppe came up from New York to see him, expecting to do no more than pay his respects. He was doubtful whether Alger would even want to see him, but Horatio greeted him with something of his old enthusiasm and urged him to stay for several days. Hoppe was astounded when his former employer asked if he wouldn't like to come to work again. Alger told him he expected to get back to work soon but thought he was too weak to get anything done without an assistant. Hoppe gave him an equivocal answer and went back to New York, knowing in his heart he would never see Alger alive again.

The fact was that while Horatio lay coughing and gasping for breath, clutching at his side where he felt his heart might burst, he was planning to write The Book before he died. He lived only to possess once more enough strength to get out what he was still certain was inside him.

Hoppe brought back news of Horatio's condition, and Superintendent Heig thereupon performed a most thoughtful act. He wrote out a resolution extolling Alger's life and work, particularly at the House, got 149 residents to sign it, and took it to South Natick himself, where he presented it to Alger. There, in a touching few hours at the dying man's bedside, Heig did more to ease Horatio's passing than anyone else could have done.

There was, first of all, the resolution. Alger was profoundly moved as he read it. Then, as the two men talked, Horatio mourned that he was leaving no boy of his own behind him and Heig had the grace to remind him that he had more sons than any other man—hundreds and hundreds of the street urchins who had known him at the House and who peopled his books. Strangely, it was a new idea to Horatio and it became a deeply satisfying consolation to him in his last hours.

On a hot July day, the eighteenth, in 1899, as the century he had celebrated drew to a close, Horatio Alger, Jr., lay dying. His last act was to reach feebly for the paper and pencils beside his bed. There was a book, a great book, he must write before he died, he explained to sister Olive.

"You've written enough, Horatio," Olive said practically, and tucked him in again.

A few hours later he was dead.

PART THREE

ALGER THE WRITER

CHAPTER 1

WHILE Alger's supposed last works were still being published posthumously, actually the work of Stratemeyer-Winfield, reaction against him was setting in. The new American century that was beginning had gone beyond Horatio's simple tales. There was new naturalism in the nation's literature, and a change in children's books as well. The moral tales of the nineteenth century were being replaced by stories nearer to reality. It was fortunate Horatio did not live to observe this reaction. The swelling paperback figures which carried his sales figures to new heights would not have consoled him.

The reaction centered in schools and libraries, institutions which had long regarded Alger with suspicion as a subverter of taste in the young. Teachers now openly condemned his books, and they were removed from the shelves of both school and public libraries. As early as August, 1907, the Worcester public library board ruled that no Alger book could be circulated from its shelves, and this action was widely imitated in various parts of the country. Paradoxically, the more Alger was roundly condemned by educators and librarians, the more his posthumous sales increased.

This kind of pressure was bound to have an effect, and, after four or five years of it, sales and popularity alike began to fall off. Before his death he had been a best-seller at $1.25, and in the paperback boom early in the new century, he sold in much larger figures at ten cents. By the time the First World War began, however, production costs forced the price to fifteen cents, and at that price the decline began in earnest. When the Sunday schools, which had once bought Alger books by the hundred thousands, nearly stopped buying at all, the publishing business understood that the Alger era had ended.

Today there appears to be a faint revival of interest in Horatio's books, not as moral tales or as reading for the young, but as nostalgic reminders of a city, of a century in which life, in retrospect, seems more happy and secure. Yet, in contemplating a 1945 anthology of four Alger books to which he had been asked to contribute an introduction, Russel Crouse could not refrain from labeling them "a collection of literary museum pieces." They were, he continued, devoid of literary style, reflecting truth no more accurately than a Coney Island mirror, humorless, of unsound construction and untrue characterization.

Crouse thought the secret of Alger's appeal was in the homage his books paid to success. He suspected that more than one boy, after reading Horatio's books, "set out to be a richer if not a better man." Any sort of achievement appealed to Alger, Crouse noted. "He even admired city aldermen."

But if Alger was as bad as that, one might ask, why publish an anthology of his work in mid-twentieth century, containing *Struggling Upward*, *Ragged Dick*, *Phil, the Fiddler*, and *Jed, the Poorhouse Boy*. The answer, perhaps, was supplied two years later by Frank Luther Mott, in his survey of best-sellers, *Golden Multitudes*.

"To criticize Alger today," Dr. Mott wrote, "is to challenge the widespread and loyal Order of Old Fellows Who Read Alger When They Were Boys. They are apt to forget their author's banality, his typed characters, his bad writing, and his copybook moralities, and to remember only their boyish response to his getting-ahead thesis and their breathless interest in his rapid story-telling. Alger's name has become a by-word for the boy's success story, and that is no mean fame."

By 1953, too, there had been at least a partial revision of the attitude toward Alger which had been held for so many years by experts in children's literature. The multiple authors (Cornelia Meigs, Anne Thaxter Eaton, Elizabeth Nesbitt and Ruth Hill Viguers) of *A Critical History of Children's Literature*, published in 1953, concluded that Alger might not have been quite as bad as everyone had supposed:

"Artificial as his plots are, Alger had a genuineness of sympathy with his heroes, a naïve confidence in the unfailing power of thrift, cheerfulness and industry, which enlist a reader's willingness to see one more working out of the same old formula . . . Alger's heroes are not only universally successful, but they are always so cheery as they go whistling through their adverse circumstances and misadventures that it is a pleasure to see them arrive at the deserved reward."

Herbert Mayes, as Alger's first biographer, summed it up: "All of Horatio Alger's heroes started poor and ended up well-to-do. All of them were in search of money. Everybody could understand their motives. Therein is the main reason for Alger's literary leadership for thirty years . . . Alger's heroes never slew dragons. But they lifted mortgages."

It is often supposed that Alger was too obtuse to be aware of the deficiencies in his books, and was therefore unable to make them better, but his life discloses, as the preceding pages have shown, that he was more aware than anyone else of his failures. He was particularly conscious of his stylistic lacks, and he did his pathetic best to overcome them. He tried memorizing pages from books he knew were good and saying them over to himself in the hope that somehow he would acquire style by osmosis, or by mere proximity. He regarded Henry James as the finest writer alive, but fortunately made no attempt to imitate him. The imagination reels at the idea of an Alger book in the style of James, or for that matter, vice versa.

There is no denying that, along with his other faults, Alger was one of the most careless writers ever to drive a publisher to frenzy. Not only did he write with awesome speed, but at the height of his productivity, he often worked on two books simultaneously with the result that his characters became incongruously mixed. Thus, as Mayes points out, Luke Larkin appears suddenly in *Luke Walton.* They are, however, hardly distinguishable from each other. When his publishers got Chapter XIII of *Hector's Inheritance,* they were astounded to discover that Grant Thornton had been imported from *Helping Himself* to thrash a bully.

When a publisher did not hear from Horatio for some time, bad news was likely to follow. "Please destroy all manuscript on hand for *The Highest Rung,*" he wrote to one, "as I have decided not to go ahead with it. I am forwarding you instead opening chapters of *Frank and Fearless.*" He thought nothing of treating publishers cavalierly, even contemptuously, but he was instantly enraged if they made a mistake or, in his opinion, treated him badly. They knew how to get what they wanted out of him, however, and it was usually the delivery of a manuscript in a period of time which would be considered nearly impossible today. When J. R. Anderson & Co., for instance, urged him to complete his boys' life of Garfield, *From Canal Boy to President,* in a hurry so that it could be published in the same year as Garfield's death, he delivered it in thirteen days.

Always conscious of Alger's speed and habitual carelessness, the publishers went beyond the usual copy editing, which the editors performed themselves in those days, to prevent disasters. What they did not find, the readers were certain to discover. Boys were not always tolerant of a character like the hunter in *Tom Thatcher's Fortune* who saved the hero's life with a rifle in one chapter and appeared in the next one with the same weapon transformed to a revolver.

In the same book occurred what is probably the most famous of Alger's errors. A garrulous old character named Lycurgus B. Spooner, M.D., is telling the hero about being scalped by the Indians and then continuing on his way to new adventures.

"How was it you did not die?" Tom asks, ignoring the fact that scalping would not necessarily be fatal.

"The confounded redskins thought I was dead," Spooner says, "and left me lying on the prairie. But I was not so far gone as they supposed. After a while I came to and a party of travelers coming up took care of me. I recovered after a time and tried to make up for my loss by a wig."

"And how do you get along without a scalp?" the hunter, Peter Brush, inquires.

"Don't miss it," says Spooner. "I used to have headaches, but now I never have 'em."

Alger's working methods were as elemental as his stories. He made a rough outline of a proposed book, setting down the names of his characters, what they did for a living, and noting the circumstances of how they were to meet. Then he made himself a pot of black coffee and sat down to work with his pencils and cheap paper. When he rose from the table again, ten hours might have passed. In periods when he was particularly conscious of his mission as a writer, and imagining himself a Bohemian, he would put on a smock before he wrote and carefully disarray his hair, admiring the effect in a mirror.

When he got down to work Alger seemed incapable of writing narrative exposition in the usual manner of fiction when he was connecting his long passages of stilted dialogue. These connections were likely to be factual descriptions, or direct addresses to the reader, as though the author stood aside from his tale except in dialogue. The style of Alger's books, indeed, is reportorial, like his methods of research. Although he would have hated the idea, Horatio could have been an excellent reporter for any New York newspaper of his day. Here, for example, is Mark the Match Boy's introduction to the Newsboys' Lodging House, in which O'Connor appears as a real character:

The down-town Newsboys' Lodging House was at that time located at the corner of Fulton and Nassau Streets. It occupied the fifth and sixth stories of the building then known as the "Sun" building, owned by Moses S. Beach, the publisher of that journal. In the year 1868 circumstances rendered it expedient to remove the

Lodge to a building in Park Place. It is to be hoped that at some day not far distant the Children's Aid Society, who carry on this beneficent institution, will be able to erect a building of their own in some eligible locality, which can be permanently devoted to a purpose so praiseworthy.

Ben and Mark soon reached the entrance to the Lodge on Fulton Street. They ascended several flights of narrow stairs till they reached the top story. Then, opening a door at the left, they found themselves in the main room of the Lodge. It was a low-studded room of considerable dimensions, amply supplied with windows, looking out on Fulton and Nassau Streets. At the side nearest the door was a low platform, separated from the rest of the room by a railing. On this platform were a table and two or three chairs. This was the place for the superintendent, and for gentlemen who from time to time address the boys.

The superintendent at that time was Mr. Charles O'Connor, who still retains the office. Probably no one could be found better adapted to the difficult task of managing the class of boys who avail themselves of the good offices of the Newsboys' Home. His mild yet firm manner, and more than all the conviction that he is their friend, and feels a hearty interest in their welfare, secure a degree of decorum and good behavior which could hardly be anticipated. Oaths and vulgar speech, however common in the street, are rarely heard here, or if heard, meet with instant rebuke.

There follows a long conversation between O'Connor and Mark, of a kind Alger had heard many times when a new boy came to the House. At the end of it, the superintendent invites Mark to make use of the institution's bank, which Alger describes with his customary moral touches:

He pointed to a table beside the railing on the outside. The top of it was pierced with narrow slits, each having a number attached. Each compartment was assigned to any boy who desired it, and his daily earnings were dropped in at the end of the day. Once a month the bank was opened, and the depositor was at liberty to withdraw his savings if he desired it. This is an excellent arrangement, as it has a tendency to teach frugal habits to the young patrons of the Lodge. Extravagance is one of their besetting sins. Many average a dollar and over as daily earnings, yet are always ragged and out at elbows, and often are unsupplied with the small price of a night's lodging at the Home. The money is squandered on gambling, cigars, and theatre-going, while the same sum would make them comfortable and independent of charity. The disposition to save is generally the first encouraging symptom in a street boy, and shows that he has really a desire to rise above his circumstances, and gain a respectable position in the world.

Considering such flat descriptive narrative coupled with the unbelievable dialogue, it is difficult, superficially, to see what kept Alger's audience reading his books. The answer is to be found in a closer examination of the books themselves, which even now exert a fascination a sophisticated reader believes impossible until he finds himself, unbelieving and aware, but nevertheless absorbed in Alger's storytelling. An analytical look at Alger's work will disclose some of the reasons.

CHAPTER 2

The seeds of Alger's success were well planted in his first book, *Bertha's Christmas Vision*, subtitled *An Autumn Sheaf*, which was published in Boston by Brown, Bazin and Co., of 94 Washington Street, in 1856. The author had copyrighted it the year before in the clerk's office of the District Court of the District of Massachusetts. On the book's title page, Bertha, a fair-haired child, is shown asleep in bed, attended by three rather militant-looking angels.

This first effort is a rare book today, ensconced among far

more literary treasures in the New York Public Library, and sought by a few collectors, either of Alger or Americana. It is not the hardest to find of Alger's books, but as the antiquarians say, it is not easy to come by.

In dedicating the book "To My Mother," Horatio discloses in retrospect how much closer to Olive he felt than the known facts of his life would indicate, and to anyone familiar with that life, this dedication is revealing of the basic overwhelming sentimentality which pervaded everything he wrote and did.

"As I turn over the pages of this my first book," he begins, "and mark here and there a name which use has made familiar, I feel the more, that, but for your sympathy and encouragement, much would still remain unwritten. With me you have sorrowed over the untimely death of 'Little Charlie.' 'Bertha,' with her precious gifts,—whereof so many stand in need,—has grown to you and me not a child of fancy, but a living presence. 'Little Floy,' and the 'Child of the Street,' will recall, to your mind as to mine, the touching lines of Mrs. Browning:—

'Do ye hear the children weeping, O my brothers!
  Ere the sorrow comes with years?
They are leaning their young heads against their mothers;
  And *that* cannot stop their tears.
The young lambs are bleating in the meadows;
  The young birds are chirping in the nest;
The young fawns are playing with the shadows;
  The young flowers are blowing toward the west:
But the young, young children, O my brothers!
  They are weeping bitterly,—
They are weeping in the playtime of the others,
  In the country of the free.

. . . .

They look up with their pale and sunken faces,
  And their looks are sad to see;
For the man's hoary anguish draws and presses
  Down the cheeks of infancy.'

"To you, then, I dedicate this book,—which is partly yours, in spirit, if not in deed,—confident, that, whatever may be its shortcomings in the eyes of others, it will find a kindly welcome at your hands."

The twenty stories and poems which follow contain the essential formulas which never varied in Alger's subsequent work. He heard the children weeping, far more constantly than Elizabeth Barrett Browning. The title story is a short, unbelievably weak tale, barely more than a sketch, beginning with classic simplicity: "It was the night before Christmas." Bertha, who is not a poor child, unlike Alger's other youngsters, goes to sleep and is visited first by Santa Claus, then by three angels, representing Faith, Hope and Charity. The angels speak to Bertha in a verse style no more elevated than Alger provides for mere mortals. What they say, in effect, is that faith, hope and charity are good things, and the story closes: "So it was that little Bertha, attended by the three sisters, walked peacefully and happily through life. . . . Would that we all might be blessed with Bertha's Christmas vision!"

The first story in the book, however, which is titled "Little Floy; or, How a Miser Was Reclaimed," is in the authentic Alger pattern. It concerns a miser, Martin Kendrick, whose mean outlook on life is vaguely attributed to the fact that his daughter Florence ran away and married a young man against his wishes. On a cold winter night—Alger's winters are always bitter—a thin, shivering girl knocks on his door. She is ten years old, a little younger than most of Horatio's young people, and her name is Little Floy, a homeless child wandering the streets.

Against his better judgment, Martin Kendrick admits her to get warm, after which, Scrooge though he is, he cannot put her out again and permits her to stay the night. Thus, in a manner reminiscent of the way Alger attached himself to households, Little Floy becomes a part of the miser's barren home. Against his grudging will, she makes a cheerful place of it, brightening its appearance and baking bread for him. Busy as she is about the house, Floy begs for more work to keep her busy, and the old man brings her home some shirts to sew for a nearby sweat-shop. Naturally, she returns whatever money she makes to her benefactor.

Slowly, the reader sees, Floy is drawing the miser back into the world again, but the conversion is not complete until Martin is seriously ill and Floy nurses him to health. As he convalesces, the miser's transformation becomes complete, and when he recovers, he takes the unprecedented step of taking Floy to a store and buying some good clothes to replace her rags.

By this time, several months having elapsed, Martin gets around to asking the girl her real name. It is Florence Eastman, she says. He repeats the name, "starting back in uncontrollable agitation."

"Who was your mother? Tell me quick!" he implores.

A modern generation of readers would not need to be told that Floy's mother is Martin Kendrick's long-lost daughter, but it came as a revelation to Alger's young readers. Her mother and father are both dead, Floy says. The author appears to be conscious suddenly that it may strike his audience as odd that Floy has never asked the miser's name. Quite probably the idea did not occur to Alger until that moment.

"I have often wondered what it was, but never liked to ask you," Floy says, the epitome of shyness.

"Then," said he, in an agitated tone, "you shall know now. I am Martin Kendrick, your GRANDFATHER!"

After this speech, Alger closes his story in the same way he later concludes more than a hundred books—with a brief summary of the later years of his characters, so that the reader will have spelled out for him the rewards of virtue. In this case the summary takes no more than four sentences because "Little Floy" is only a short story, a quick trial flight, but the essence of all the other endings is there.

"Every day," Alger concludes, "Martin Kendrick became more alive to the claims of affection. His miserly habits gave way, and he became more considerate in his dealings with his tenants. The old house, in which he lived so many years, was torn down; and he bought a neat cottage just out of the city, where he and Floy live happily together. Floy, who has been sent to school, exhibits uncommon talent, and is fitting for the station she will soon assume as the heiress of her grandfather."

If this story has familiar overtones to present-day readers, they need only substitute "Little Orphan Annie" for Floy. The formula itself has its roots in the widely popular morality novels of pre-Civil War days (as far as its American origins are concerned), and it was to be repeated later in tales like *Mrs. Wiggs of the Cabbage Patch* and the *Pollyanna* stories.

There are other choice nuggets embedded in *Bertha's Christmas Vision.* One is a short story called "The Veiled Mirror," a shameless paraphrase of Dickens's *A Christmas Carol,* which had been published a dozen years before Alger wrote his piece. It is not impossible that the parallel was the same kind of unconscious plagiarism which led Horatio to believe he had invented a magnificent new story in the plot of *Tomorrow.* He had no Una to point out his error in this earlier attempt. Nor was it the only time Alger borrowed from Dickens, consciously or unconsciously. They were working in the same vineyard, after all, but Alger was employing a toothpick where Dickens used a shovel.

"The Veiled Mirror" reproduces the *Christmas Carol* in miniature. It opens with Mr. Hathaway, Alger's Scrooge, adding up his year's profits which, Horatio notes with his usual exactness, have come to $5,000. A stranger appears and asks him what he is doing with his money. "Have you thought to give of your abundance to those who are needy,—to promote your own happiness by advancing that of others?" the Stranger inquires.

Here the Dickens echo becomes deafening. "But there are almshouses and benevolent societies," Hathaway growls. "There cannot be much misery that escapes their notice."

"You shall judge for yourself," the Stranger tells him, and produces from under his cloak a mirror with a veil over it. Much as the three spirits did with Scrooge, the Stranger then shows Mr. Hathaway scenes of poverty and desperation in the mirror. Bob Cratchit appears faithfully in one scene as Frank Durell, Hathaway's clerk, who is seen reading a letter from his mother, telling him of a note for fifty dollars left by his dead father which is due immediately. She, of course, is penniless.

Hathaway awakes as from a dream. The Stranger is gone and he hears the chime of New Year's bells. (Alger had the grace to advance the time of his story by a week.) He hurries out into the street, immediately befriends a little girl he finds wandering there, and then hurries on to such other good deeds as sending a friend's son to college, and raising Durell's salary from five hundred dollars a year to seven hundred dollars, with a hundred-dollar advance to pay the note. ("Before you dot another 'i,' Frank Durell," Alger almost says.)

The longest story in *Bertha's Christmas Vision* is "Lost and Found" which, even more than "Little Floy," foreshadows Alger's later full-length narratives. Nearly all the familiar elements are in it, except that the chief protagonist is once more a girl. It would be eight years before Alger discovered boys as heroes.

Helen, the heroine of "Lost and Found," is older than Little Floy. She is, in fact, the same age as many of Alger's later boy heroes, between twelve and fourteen as the story begins. Helen lives with her uncle in the Five Points neighborhood, one of the worst in old New York—a spot near Chatham Square where five streets converged, and where there was concentrated for years more human misery and degeneration than in any other part of the city. Alger opens his tale with a description of the Five Points, a device he often used. It is a description which does not begin to do justice to the real nature of the place, but it is graphic enough to enchant a reader living in the hinterlands, who at once has his vision of the wicked city confirmed.

Helen's uncle sees an advertisement in the *Tribune* seeking a young girl to act as nursemaid and companion for two young children, the progeny of a rich merchant named Gregory. When he sees that name, Helen's uncle does what every Alger character does if he is surprised. He "starts." Then he tells Helen she must take the job because Gregory once cheated him out of a large sum of money, and he sees now an opportunity to get some of it back. All Helen has to do is to gain the trust of the household, fix the location of "a large amount of valuable plate," and open the front door for him some dark night so he can get it out.

"But would that not be robbery?" Helen asks, with consummate innocence.

The uncle makes an elemental attempt at rationalization. He was cheated, he tells Helen, and this is the only way he can be repaid. "Helen was no casuist," Alger observes solemnly, but she is afraid of her uncle, who confirms her fear at once by demanding, "Helen Armstrong, unless you promise me faithfully to perform the part I have assigned you, I will bind you out to Brady Tim, the grocer." Brady Tim, Horatio tells his readers in a mysterious characterization, is "a repulsive character and kept a grocery of the lowest kind." There is no doubt about what he would do to a bound girl: "Helen often heard him beating his children." Terrified, she agrees.

With her uncle dressed in a whiskered disguise as her grandfather, Helen is taken by him to the country home of the intended victim, P. H. Gregory, who lives in "a tasteful brown cottage" a few miles distant from the city. He calls it his "summer retreat." It is now June, Alger adds hastily.

Upset though she is by the deception, Helen is pleased to be in the country amid such luxury, after the squalor of the Five Points. She finds the children, a boy of six and a girl of eight, delightful. To Mrs. Gregory, a typically Algeresque calm and regal matron, Helen looks familiar. "Something there was in her expression that seemed to strike the chords of memory, but Mrs. Gregory dismissed it as only a chance resemblance."

Having given the plot away to any experienced Algerphile, Horatio goes on with it. The uncle reappears soon in his grandfather disguise to find out whether Helen has found out where Gregory hides his "plate." She has found it, since it is in plain sight, and her uncle tells her he will be back on Friday night to get it, according to plan. Once more Helen asks, opening her wide and innocent eyes, "But Uncle, wouldn't that be robbery?" The uncle wastes no more time in trying to make a casuist of Helen. She had better be ready at the door on Friday night, he says, or Brady Tim will have a new girl. In this conversation, thinking he is soon to be rid of the child entirely, the uncle discloses that he is not really related to her. Echoing now both Dickens and Dumas, it appears that Helen was kidnaped when she was a child by a woman, presumably Armstrong's dead wife, who made her beg on the streets.

Stricken by this knowledge and distraught by her role in the coming robbery, Helen is in bed with a galloping psychosomatic illness by Friday. Questioning her sympathetically, Mrs. Gregory finds out about the imimnent crime, and learns of Helen's distress in discovering that she now does not know who she is. The end is not difficult to foresee. It needs only one of Alger's favorite devices. Abruptly Mrs. Gregory sees for the first time an ivory ring Helen has always worn, and there can be no other ring like it. Helen is Mrs. Gregory's long-lost daughter.

When the uncle arrives that night for his plate, he is met by Mr. Gregory, but in a splendid display of magnanimity, the merchant lets him go if he promises to take the first ship to California.

There are other items in Horatio's first book, including a poem with the remarkable title, "The First Tree Planted by an Ornamental Tree Society," and a sketch prophetically called, "The Child of the Street," but the examples recounted are the prizes.

Whether Alger's second book, published the following year, was a forty-five page poem, *Nothing to Do: A Tilt at Our Best Society,* is open to question, but there is so much in it that seems pure Alger that one is almost inclined to believe the bibliographers who ascribe it to him. Frank Gruber, the authority in this matter, regards it as doubtful, however, basing his doubts on the existence of two other "Nothing" titles in his collection, both published in the same year, 1857, as the supposed Alger volume, which was put out anonymously by James French & Co. in Boston. One is *Nothing to Do: By a Lady*, from the house of Wiley & Halstead, different from the French publication in some respects but similar in others, including the frontispiece. The third "Nothing" book is *Nothing to Eat: Not by the Author of Nothing to Wear*, which was the original poem by William A. Butler, the starting point of this cycle of parodies. *Nothing to Eat*, published by Dick & Fitzgerald, is nearly identical in format, printing and binding with the Wiley & Halstead book, Gruber points out.

There is another reason to doubt that Alger wrote *Nothing to Do*. It is substantially better than any poem which is unquestionably his own. A brief comparison will make this plain, and at the same time underline the Algeresque qualities of the narrative piece, lending support to the theory that if Alger wrote it, the others are imitations in the bald manner of those pre-copyright days.

This is the beginning of the *Nothing to Do* ascribed to Alger:

"Augustus Fitz-Herbert, as all are aware,
  Having crossed the Atlantic, and got a moustache on,
Likewise being son of a known millionaire,
  Stands of course on the very top round of the fashion.
Being taught to consider himself, from his birth,
  As one of the privileged ones of the earth,
He cherishes deep and fitting disdain
  For those who don't live in the Fifth Avenue,
As entirely unworthy the notice or thought
  Of the heir of two millions and nothing to do.
He calls them *canaille,* which I'm credibly told,
  Is the only French word which he caught when away;
And though, in my case, if I might be so bold,

I should scarce say it paid one for half a year's stay.
The heir of two millions and nothing to do,
Who lives in a palace in Fifth Avenue,
As a matter of course, is not fitting comparison
For the heir of an inkstand and something to do,
Who lodges upstairs, in the house of Miss Harrison.

"In this model republic, the land of the free—
So our orators call it, and why should not we?—
'Tis refreshing to know that without pedigree
A man may still climb to the top of the tree;
That questions of family, rank, and high birth,
All bow to the query, How much is he worth?
That John Smith, plebeian, who forty years since
Walked Broadway barefooted, now rides as a prince;
Having managed, though not overburdened with wit,
But rather by chance and a fortunate hit,
To take a high place on Society's rounds;
His claims being based on pence, shillings and pounds.
I admit there's a certain republican merit
In making the fortune which others inherit;
But why should John Smith so completely ignore
The bridge which has brought him triumphantly o'er,
And turn with disgust from the opposite shore?"

Further on in the long poem, the author imparts a few lines of philosophy which are verse translations of an idea Alger expressed dozens of times in his books. If he did not write them in *Nothing to Do*, he could have. They read:

"For, though men have made money, and will do again,
There was never a case known where money made men;
And if Jones be a man in what constitutes manhood,
He's a far better match than young Frederic Stanwood,
Though the one be a clerk, and the other the heir
Of the house next M'Flimsey's, on Madison Square.

If one is deficient in wealth, we may find
The other quite bankrupt in morals and mind."

The poem ends on a further Algeresque note:

"Have you ever (forgive the bold impropriety)
Reckoned up your outstanding account with society,
Or consider how far, should your life close to-morrow,
You would merit her real and genuine sorrow?
If, in dying, the world be no wiser or better
For your having lived there, then you are her debtor;
And if, as Faith, Reason, and Scripture all show,
God rewards us in heaven for the good done below,
I pray you, take heed, idle worldling, lest you
With that better world should have nothing to do."

Turn now to an authentic piece of Alger poetry, a collection titled *Grand'ther Baldwin's Thanksgiving*, published by Loring eighteen years later, in 1875. In the title poem, Alger shows himself much under the influence of Henry Wadsworth Longfellow, who had already corrupted a substantial number of popular poets so that they could produce nothing but endless imitations of the nineteenth-century's master popular poet. The poem begins:

"Underneath protecting branches, from the highway just aloof,
Stands the house of Grand'ther Baldwin, with its gently sloping roof."

Three other couplets are enough to give the flavor of this poem, which is long enough to be narrative but scarcely qualifies since the story it tells is so slight. With a slight stumble in the meter, Alger proclaims:

"For the boys may hold high revel, and the girls

must have their way
That's the law at Grand'ther Baldwin's upon each
Thanksgiving Day."

At last, when the dinner comes, the poet greets it:

But the dinner—ah! the dinner—words are feeble
to portray
What a culinary triumph is achieved Thanksgiving
Day!

. . . .

Fairly groans the board with dainties, but the
turkey rules the roast,
Aldermanic at the outset, at the last a fleshless
ghost."

The poem ends with a long grace from Grand'ther, after which:

"His simple words in silence died; a moment's
hush, and then
From all the listening hearts there rose a solemn-
voiced Amen!"

The other poems in the volume are of varying meters, but their quality is the same. The essential mediocrity of Alger's mind illuminates them all, and sometimes the rhyme structure is strained to the point of hilarity, as in this verse from "Phoebe's Wooing":

Phoebe! Phoebe! Where is the chit?
When I want her most she's out of the way
Child, you're running a long account
Up, to be squared on Judgment Day.

In the section titled "Miscellaneous Poems," there is a small fruit of his rainy, disheartened stay in London, called "In the

Church at Stratford-on-Avon," although there is no record that Alger ever stood there. It begins:

"One autumn day when hedges yet were green
  And thick-branched trees diffused a leafy gleam,
Hard by where Avon rolls its silvery tide,
  I stood in silent thought by Shakspeare's tomb."

It did not matter to Horatio that he had never viewed a place. He could write about it with as much fervor and lack of grace as the others. In another "miscellaneous" poem, the reader finds him contemplating "Mrs. Browning's Grave at Florence":

"Florence wears an added grace,
  All her earlier honors crowning;
Dante's birthplace, Art's fair home,
  Holds the dust of Barrett Browning."

His Civil War poetry is as near to passion as he is able to achieve. This is the ending of "King Cotton":

"God speed the time when the guilty king
  Shall be hauled down from his blood-stained throne;
And the palace of Wrong shall crumble to dust,
  With its boasted corner-stone.

"A temple of freedom shall rise instead,
  On the desecrated site;
And within its shelter alike shall stand
  The black and the white."

There are four "Harvard Odes" in the collection, and with these Horatio achieved a tearful reverence he never surpassed. The first of these, "Fair Harvard, Dear Guide of Our Youth's Golden Days," is a fair sample of the others. It begins:

"Fair Harvard, dear guide of our youth's golden days;
At thy name all our hearts own a thrill;
We turn from life's highways, its business, its cares,
We are boys in thy tutelage still."

The titles, at least, of the other three odes deserve preservation. They are: "As We Meet in Thy Name, Alma Mater, Tonight"; "Fair Harvard, the Months Have Accomplished Their Round"; and "There's a Fountain of Fable, Whose Magical Power."

Alger would compose an ode at the drop of an invitation. This collection contains not only the Harvard quartet, but one "For the Consecration of a Cemetery," two "Occasional Odes," and his "Bi-Centennial Ode," which was sung at the bicentennial celebration of the incorporation of Marlborough, Massachusetts, on June 13, 1860.

Grand'ther Baldwin's Thanksgiving contains most of Alger's poetry which he considered important enough to publish, including "John Maynard," the most successful, which brought him into the clutches of the San Francisco ladies. To make further comment on his verse would be to labor an obvious point. In any case, *Bertha's Christmas Vision,* whose poetry was fully as bad as the collection quoted here, was only a minor preparation for Alger's work as was *Nothing to Do,* if, indeed, he wrote it. By 1864, in the heat of the war and his near escape from it, he was ready to write his first full-length novel.

CHAPTER 3

The ingredients of Horatio Alger's success are present in his first novel, *Frank's Campaign; or, What Boys Can Do on the Farm for the Camp.* Its plot is overlaid on a background of factual material, and while it does not derive from the rags-to-riches formula, it describes, or intends to describe, a young boy's triumph over difficulties through virtue. Alger dedicates it to "Charles Edward Paine, in Memory of Pleasant Hours Passed Together at Naples and Sorrento"—a friend and places of which there appear to be no record in Alger's travels, although undoubtedly it was a side excursion from Paris on his first trip there.

For this initial venture, Alger wrote one of his inevitable prefaces, briefer than the others. Whether its brevity was the result of his early timidity, or the ruthless editorial pencil his publishers wielded freely later on, it is impossible to say. In any case, it is typical, including Alger's own brand of heavy humor. The preface reads:

> The great struggle in which we are now engaged for the integrity of the Republic has imposed new duties and new responsibilities upon all classes of the people. This little volume is intended to show how boys can be of most effectual service in assisting to put down the Rebellion. Care has been taken to make the pictures given of camplife accurate and authentic. The description of the Battle of Fredericsburg [*sic*] is derived mainly from the graphic account given by Capt. Noyes, in his valuable work, "The Bivouac and The Battlefield."
>
> I trust that those of my young friends who may find themselves unexpectedly figuring in the story, will pardon the liberty which I have taken with their names. I should have been glad to make them all officers of the Rossville Guards, but it unfortunately happens that in every military organization the privates must greatly outnumber the officers. I am aware that Artemas Ward, the illustrious showman, raised a company composed entirely of brigadier-generals. I doubt, however, whether this arrangement would work well in the Army, though it is quite possible that we have some brigadier-generals who might profitably be promoted to privates.

Then Alger adds, hopefully: "Should *Frank's Campaign* have the good fortune to find favor among the class for whom it is written, it will be followed by other volumes devoted to boy-life."

Alger almost invariably began a story in one of two ways, either with a stretch of dialogue in which neither character was identified for a page or two, or else with a factual description of a place, invariably a real place, where the story was to start. *Frank's Campaign* begins with a description of a village green which is probably Revere, with overtones of Cambridge, where he had experienced personally a good many of the incidents described in the book as he drilled his home guard in the early days of the war. Titled "The War Meeting," Alger's first chapter starts:

> The Town Hall in Rossville stands on a moderate elevation overlooking the principal street. It is generally open only when a meeting has been called by the Selectmen to transact town business, or occasionally in the evening when a lecture on Temperance or a political address is to be delivered. Rossville is not large enough to sustain a course of lyceum lectures, and the towns-people are obliged to depend for intellectual nutriment upon such chance occasions as these. The majority of the inhabitants being engaged in agricultural pursuits, the population is somewhat scattered, and the houses, with the exception of a few grouped around the stores, stand at respectable distances, each encamped in a farm of its own.
>
> On Wednesday afternoon toward the close of September, 1862, a group of men and boys might have been seen standing on the steps and in the entry of the Town Hall. Why they had met will best appear from a large placard, which had been posted up on barns and fences and inside the village stores and post-office. It ran as follows. . . .

Here Alger reproduces an exact Civil War poster, labeled "War Meeting!" of a kind used to call townspeople together for a discussion of measures to supply a community's draft quota. This is followed by a careful reportorial description of the Rossville meeting, obviously a real one that Alger must have attended, in which the citizens discuss "the recent call and the general management of the war with that spirit of independent criticism which so eminently characterizes the little democracies which make up our New England States."

Like so many such convocations in the little democracies, the Rossville meeting turns into a factional contest between opposing elements in the town. In this case, naturally, the division is between the prowar and the antiwar camps, and, as naturally, Alger personifies this struggle between good and evil in the persons of an upright, patriotic farmer named Frost and the town's richest man, Squire Haynes. After an argument between these protagonists, the meeting sides with Frost and votes to pay $150 to each man in Rossville who is willing to enlist. Four men sign up at once.

The scene changes now to Rossville Academy, where Farmer Frost's son Frank is hard at work studying Latin so he can go on to college. As the author describes him, he is the epitome of Alger heroes: "Frank Frost is at this time in his sixteenth year. He is about the medium size, compactly made, and the healthful color in his cheeks is good evidence that he is not pursuing his studies at the expense of his health. He has dark chestnut hair, with a slight wave, and is altogether a fine-looking boy."

By contrast, at the desk behind Frank, sits Squire Haynes's son, John. He has "a thin face, very black hair, is tall of his age, and already beginning to feel himself a young man. His manner is full of pretension. He never forgets that his father is the richest man in town, and can afford to give him advantages superior to those possessed by his school-fellows. He has a moderate share of ability, but is disinclined to work hard. His affectation of superiority makes him as unpopular among his school-fellows as Frank is popular."

Squire Haynes, in the manner of all good nineteenth-century villains, has Frank's father, and therefore Frank himself, in his power by virtue of an $800 mortgage he holds on the Frost farm. The farmer is compelled to save every penny he can to liquidate it, consequently his son's chances of going on to college are dim.

Alger underlines the difference between Frank and John, which is also the difference between good and evil, by having Frank win the prize in the school essay contest, which John thinks should have been his. Even the titles of their essays are intended to characterize them. Frank's prizewinner is "The Duties of Boys in the Present National Crisis." John's is "The Military Genius of Napoleon." The prize so hotly contested is an edition of Whittier's poems in blue and gold binding.

When he hears the news that Frank has won, John behaves in accepted Alger fashion, that is, he "turned pale, and then red, with anger and vexation. He scowled darkly. . . ." More than that, however, he goes to his father and complains about the injustice of the contest decision. Squire Haynes soothes him by giving him $30 instead of the $25 he had previously promised him if he won, and promises to buy him a copy of Whittier bound in calf the next time he gets up to Boston. Well satisfied, John declares, "I wouldn't change places with Frank Frost now for all his prize."

" 'I should think not, indeed,' said the Squire pompously. 'Your position as the son of a poor farmer wouldn't be quite as high as it it now.'

"As he spoke he glanced complacently at the handsome furniture which surrounded him, the choice engravings which hung on the walls, and the full-length mirror in which his figure was reflected. 'Ten years from now Frank Frost will be only a common laborer on his father's farm—that is,' he added significantly, 'if his father manages to keep it; while you, I hope, will be winning distinction at the bar.' "

This scene of upper-class smugness in the Haynes mansion is immediately contrasted with the simple, wholesome manner of life on the Frost farm, where Frank lives with his two younger sisters, Alice, twelve, and Maggie, ten, and his little seven-year-old brother Charlie—Alger's favorite name for little brothers.

Frank's father is depicted as a man who has seen different, if not better, days. At the beginning of his unlikely career, as Alger depicts it, he was an artist for whom the world was not ready, and so he turned incongruously to farming. But he has carried some of his former cultured way of life with him. He subscribes to *Harper's*, both the weekly and the monthly; a weekly agricultural paper, a daily paper, and a child's magazine. His neighbors regard this literary activity as sinful extravagance and a little queer; they, apparently, never read anything, an accurate description of a good part of the rural population before the Civil War.

The War Meeting described in the first chapter has precipitated a crisis in the Frost household. Mr. Frost believes he is duty bound to enlist, but how can he leave the farm? Frank manfully offers to run it for him while he is gone, and his father agrees that this is the way it must be.

When the news of Farmer Frost's enlistment reaches the Haynes mansion, both father and son are annoyed. (It should be noted that the Squire's wife is dead, and Alger uses this as a rather halfhearted explanation of John's villainy, noting that the boy has never had a mother's love to guide him.) The Squire regards the enlistment as an act of ostentatious patriotism, on behalf of a cause with which he is not in sympathy. He also thinks Frost is a fool to place his farm in the hands of a young boy. As for John, he is against the Frost family on general principles, but he is still rankled by Frank's victory. This is evident by the joy with which he greets his father's announcement that he means to call in the mortgage the following July.

"I want to see Frank Frost's proud spirit humbled," John declares, with admirable candor.

At this point Alger introduces what is by far his most painful character, obviously inspired by Harriet Beecher Stowe's Topsy. Alger had read *Uncle Tom's Cabin* with intense admiration, and evidently believed that Topsy was an excellent comic device to lighten an otherwise tragic story. He needed no such device for

Frank's Campaign, but he must have been carried away by the emotions of the time and sought to characterize the Negro and his plight through the trials of a small boy named Little Pomp, the son of Chloe, an escaped slave from Virginia who takes in washing for a living.

The result is at once a stereotype and a caricature of the stereotype. Little Pomp is described as "a bright little fellow, as black as the ace of spades, and possessing to the full the mercurial temperament of the Southern negro. Full of fun and drollery, he attracted plenty of attention when he came into the village, and earned many a penny from the boys by his plantation songs and dances."

Chloe has a disabling accident and Frank takes in Little Pomp for a time, to help around the farm. The child speaks in the Uncle Tom dialect, which Alger tortures more than Mrs. Stowe did, and for the remainder of the book he appears in irrelevant episodes (except for one) as comic relief. He is constantly playing practical jokes, especially on an elderly spinster of the town, and his intermittent warfare with her runs like a subplot through the book.

Little Pomp becomes briefly useful when he plays a joke on John one day. John is not amused. He ties the boy to a tree and is about to whip him when Frank appears on the scene and stops him. The affair is none of his business, John says hotly.

" 'I think it's some of my business,' said Frank, coolly, 'when I find you playing the part of a Southern overseer. You are not in Richmond, John Haynes, and you'll get into trouble if you undertake to act as if you were.' "

This was the kind of scene, common to popular literature of the day, which Alger's Northern abolitionist audience found highly satisfying, and it is also helpful as a plot mechanism to develop the feud between John and Frank Frost.

But Alger is such a careless plotter that he lets the episode peter out in incongruity. The boys have a brief tussle in which John is pinned to the ground in helpless rage. When Frank lets him go, John slinks away, muttering to himself, "If he doesn't rue this day, my name isn't John Haynes." His revenge is unique. He makes an unsuccessful attempt to raid the Frost pigpen, and the incident ends.

At this point Alger introduces another element which was to become a favorite device with him: the mysterious stranger. Frank meets, by chance, a young man named Henry Morton who is stopping at the local hotel. The boys like each other at once, and since it develops that Henry is looking for a place to live in the neighborhood, Frank takes him to the farm, where he becomes a boarder. Henry is obviously cultivated. When his belongings arrive from New York, they contain many books and pictures which he installs in his room. Alger intimates in these and other ways that Henry is rich, but his mission in Rossville remains purposefully unexplained.

The story wanders onward at a sluggish pace which Alger soon learned to improve, when he had more practice and better materials to aid him. There is a chapter on Thanksgiving at the farm, a holiday Alger never misses an opportunity to describe in his books; he appears to prefer it to Christmas. Another chapter is devoted to the reading of a long letter from Frank's father, who has been wounded at the battle of Fredericksburg, which is described with the considerable help of Captain Noyes's "valuable work" acknowledged in the preface.

Now Alger draws on his wartime Cambridge experience and has Frank organize a military company among the Rossville boys, with Henry Morton as drillmaster. There is much detail about the company, drawn from life. Frank is elected captain, and John Haynes, who naturally expected to get the job, is not even chosen as a junior officer, whereupon he quits the company after the humiliation of seeing eight other officers elected over him.

The activities of the drill company are interspersed with episodes involving Little Pomp and his endless jokes, and another long letter from Henry Frost, describing life at the front. John contrives to stay in the framework of the plot by nearly drowning when his sailboat capsizes. Henry Morton rescues him.

The mystery about Henry is beginning to clear as the story

moves haphazardly to its climax. He discloses to the Frosts that he does, indeed, have money, as they and the reader have suspected, but he would have a good deal more if a rascally lawyer had not once defrauded his father. His mission in Rossville is to find the lawyer, whom he believes is Squire Haynes.

It is now July and Frank goes to the Squire seeking a renewal of the mortgage, which is due in ten days. Haynes artfully leads him to believe that he intends to renew it, meanwhile planning to foreclose on the due date, so that Frank will not have time to get up the money.

On the fateful day, the Squire is ready to spring his trap but Morton has anticipated him at the last moment. As Frank prepares to leave for the Squire's office, Morton appears. He has been absent for several days on a trip to New York, and has now returned, bringing an old man with him. Learning of the situation, he lends Frank the $400 he will need to pay off the mortgage, and together they go to the Squire to pay it. There, in Haynes's office, Henry reveals himself as Richard Waring, a name which of course causes the Squire to start, and demands restitution of the money entrusted to Haynes by his father twelve years before. He produces the missing witness to this transaction, James Travers, who is the old man he brought back from New York.

The Squire's downfall is complete. By making restitution, he is stripped of half his property. He is compelled to sell his fine house and move to Philadelphia, where, apparently, he carries on as before in a reduced state. John fails to get into college, and even worse, says Alger, "shows a disposition to be extravagant." Obviously no good can be expected of him.

Morton—or Waring, as he must now be called—buys the Squire's house in Rossville and prepares to settle down, offering to send Frank to college when the war is over. Even Little Pomp gives up his troublesome ways and does better in school. Frank remains a captain of the guard at home, while his father is made a captain in the field.

"As for our young hero, Frank," Alger concludes, "there can be no doubt that in his unselfish patriotism and steady discharge of duty, he is giving promise of a useful and noble manhood. His campaign is not yet finished, but we have seen enough of him to feel sure that while it continues, he will ever remain true to honor and duty."

One question remains for the doubtful modern reader: What is it that "Boys Can Do on the Farm for the Camps?" Take in small Negro problem children? Frustrate bullies? Organize drill teams? Become father substitutes? Running the farm seems to be the self-evident answer, but Frank's management of the place is never described, and in fact he would have lost it entirely if it had not been for the fortunate accident of Henry Morton's appearance with the $400 and the subsequent discomfiting of the Squire.

Alger evidently thought it was quite enough to depict Frank Frost as a patriotic boy who upheld virtue at home while his father did so on the battlefield. As his subsequent ragged heroes made the jump from poverty to substance by accident rather than virtue, so Frank's success is attributable to Henry Morton's timely appearance rather than his own patriotism. If his readers noticed this discrepancy, it never appeared in the sales figures. *Frank's Campaign* was not a runaway seller but its modest success encouraged Horatio to carry out his promise in the preface to write "other volumes devoted to boy-life."

CHAPTER 4

With *Frank's Campaign* successfully behind him, Alger was encouraged by A. K. Loring, his Boston publisher, to try again, and *Paul Prescott's Charge,* published in 1865, was the result. It was an inconsiderable effort, no doubt because it was written during Horatio's ministerial period in Brewster, when he was more uncertain than usual what to do with his life. But in 1866, removed to New York, he was ready to devote all his time to writing and in that year produced two books which are among his least known, but in several ways have a particular fascination for the explorer of Alger's life and works.

The first of these remains the most obscure. It is *Helen Ford,* his only full-length book in which a girl is the protagonist. One of his longest efforts, it embodies the essential elements of the Alger formula and also indirectly casts light on Horatio's peculiarly tangled personality.

To begin it, Alger uses his standard descriptive opening:

"Not many minutes from Broadway, situated on one of the cross-streets of the great thoroughfare, is a large building not especially inviting in its aspect, used as a lodging and boarding-house. It is very far from fashionable, since, with hardly an exception, those who avail themselves of its accommodations belong to the great class who are compelled to earn their bread before they eat it."

Among the inhabitants of the house are Alphonso Eustace, "a dashing young clerk"; Mademoiselle Fanchette, "the fashionable *modiste*"; and Martha Grey, "the pale seamstress." These and other denizens are presided over by Mother Morton. She is "a stout, bustling woman, of considerable business capacity; one of those restless characters to whom nothing is so irksome as want of occupation, and who are never more in their element than when they have a world of business on their hands, with little time to do it in. A widow, having with characteristic dispatch, hustled her husband out of the world in less than four years from her wedding-day."

Having thus expressed some of his hostility toward women with far more freedom than he usually exhibits, Alger quickly retreats. He explains that Mrs. Morton is called "Mother" because she is "of ample proportions," and because she is also "a good soul" when sickness or misfortune overtakes one of her boarders.

To Mother Morton's one day comes Helen Ford, a girl of fourteen, and her father, Robert, who is said to be forty but behaves as though he were that much older. In his anxiety to convey the idea that Mr. Ford is the apotheosis of the idealistic inventor with his head in the clouds, Alger makes him out to be close to idiocy. It is no wonder that little Helen treats him with the possessiveness and solicitude of a devoted mother.

Mother Morton shows them the only room she has available. This is the first time Alger describes a New York lodging-house room, of a kind with which he has just become acquainted, and he depicts it with depressing exactness, as he will from that time onward. The room is at the top of four flights of stairs, twelve feet square, scantily provided with furniture, "relieved" by two windows. Surveying this bleak prospect, Helen says cheerfully, "Just what we want, isn't it, Papa? See how bright and pleasant it is." Alger scarcely needs to point out that Helen is "accustomed to look on the bright side of things."

The negotiations are conducted entirely by Helen. Mr. Ford is dreamy and abstracted, scarcely seeming to know what is going on as Helen agrees to take the room for $1.75. Mother Morton expresses a vague and carefully veiled doubt about the morality of a grown man and a fourteen-year-old girl living in such cramped quarters, but it is no more than a suggestion because Helen's purity is of such unquestioned substance and her father is so totally unworldly that no one could possibly doubt either of them.

Pure or not, Helen is a spanking fourteen, as Alger shows in an incident the following morning, although he carefully shrouds her charms in the utmost respectability. She has risen with the dawn, cleaned the room and gone shopping, bringing home (Alger tells us, with his customary exactness) two loaves of bread, a pail full of milk and a half-pound of butter. When the other boarders see her for the first time, returning from this errand, "her cheeks were flushed with exercise, her eyes sparkled with a pleasant light, and her rare beauty, despite her plain attire, appeared to unusual advantage."

"Hey, what have we here?" says Alphonso Eustace, the dashing young clerk, when he sees her.

He makes a few brash remarks to her, as he would to any attractive young girl, but Helen rebuffs him with an ironclad innocence which would have discouraged Don Juan.

Her father is already busy inventing. Alger, who, of course, had no idea what an inventor actually did, depicts him as usually staring into space, thinking in large and abstract terms, although he has brought a small model of his invention to the room. It is, the modern reader discovers with astonishment, a prototype of the airplane. Ford describes it himself, in his grand and sweeping manner: "Borne aloft by the appliances which I shall furnish, man will emulate the proud flight of the eagle. He will skim over land and sea, and in his airy flight look down upon the monuments of human skill and industry flitting before him, like the shifting scenes of a panorama."

One would like to think that Alger had anticipated the Wright brothers in inventive imagination, but he makes it clear that he shares the opinion of the rest of the world that Robert Ford is a harmless eccentric. Certainly the inventor is out of key with the practical world in which boys rise from rags to riches. Alger sums him up condescendingly as "an amiable man, but strikingly deficient in those practical traits which usually mark our countrymen and command success even under the most unpromising circumstances. . . . No man of a well balanced mind would have labored with such sanguine expectations of success on a project so uncertain as the invention of a flying machine." So much for Horatio as prophet.

Ford's dependence on Helen is complete. He is so lost in his dreams that when the two go out for a walk, he, "plunged into his usual abstraction, would more than once have been run over by some passing vehicle but for her guardianship."

As the story moves along, Alger shifts awkwardly back and forth between the past and present tenses, but it is plain that he is learning more about writing. In spite of frequent pauses for irrelevant detail, the story moves much more rapidly than either of the first two books. But Alger cannot resist any opportunity to describe life in New York, which he was then discovering for himself. Often Helen and her father, after tea, walk up Broadway, where "life in all its varieties, from pampered wealth to squalid poverty, too often the fruit of a mis-spent life, jostled each other upon the sidewalk, or in the street." Horatio cannot stop moralizing.

To make ends meet, since her father is incapable of holding a job, Helen takes sewing from what Alger describes graphically as "a slop shop." As she goes back and forth between shop and home, her father sometimes accompanies her, and one day as they are resting in transit on the west side of Central Park, having wandered somewhat afield, a handsome carriage rolls by with an older and a younger man sitting in it.

Observing Helen and her father, the older man starts. It must be "Robert, my long-lost son," he says. But the younger one hastily assures him this cannot be; after all, they have proof that the missing son died in Chicago two years ago, having left home fifteen years before. The old man subsides, and both fall silent as the carriage rolls along, but "we are privileged to read what is concealed from all else," Alger confides.

It is, of course, the young man who has something to conceal. "Here is a new danger to be guarded against, just at the most critical time, too," his dark thoughts run. "Shall I never attain the object of my wishes? Shall I never be paid for the years in which I have danced attendance upon my uncle? I *must* succeed by whatever means. He cannot last much longer."

In keeping these thoughts unspoken, Lewis Rand is not only maintaining an obviously practical secrecy. He is demonstrating that Alger has advanced somewhat over the popular literature before the war, when such soliloquies were likely to be uttered aloud, in an aside, as they were in the theater for a long time afterward.

As the villain, Lewis obviously needs more of an introduction and Alger stops the story to give him one. His father is dead and he has grown up since the age of five with his uncle, the older man in the carriage, who had broken off with his son because the boy had married beneath him, "an awkward country girl," as Alger describes her, "without cultivation or refinement." Lewis hopes for the inheritance, but he knows his uncle has left everything to the son, if he can be found. It seems impossible today that any reader would fail to grasp that Robert Rand is, indeed, the "long-lost son," but Alger clearly expected his audience to be at least in temporary suspense and there is ample reason to believe they were.

There is no doubt in Lewis Rand's mind, however, that the son is at large, and the old man's recognition was correct. He knows he must make a desperate move, and he does so in a scene which must have seemed chillingly sinister at the time. He steals a copy of the will and takes it to the humble dwelling of Jacob Wynne, a "copyist," as Alger calls him. Lewis has once saved this man from a conviction for forgery, and using that fact as blackmail, although it is hardly necessary, considering Jacob's low character, he compels the copyist to forge a new will on the spot, leaving everything to him. While he is doing it, and as Lewis waits impatiently, there is another spectator of this scene —Wynne's wife, Margaret, supposedly asleep, but in reality spying from behind a door.

Armed with the new will, Lewis goes to see an unscrupulous lawyer, Richard Sharp. Alger did not like lawyers, and they often appeared as villains in his stories. Sharp is given the full benefit of Alger's waspishness in this respect. He is described as one of those "needy adventurers, well versed in the arts of pettifogging and chicanery, and willing for a consideration, to throw over the most discreditable proceedings the mantle of the law, thus perverting, to the injury of the public, that which was intended for its principal safeguard." Sharp inhabits "an exceedingly dirty little office not far from Wall Street."

Lewis Rand's business with Sharp is to obtain the lawyer's help in getting Ford (or Rand) out of town, a proposition to which he readily agrees when he understands the reason and sees a prospect of sequestering a portion of Lewis's inheritance, when the heir apparent gets it. By one of Alger's convenient coincidences, Sharp sees Helen and her father on the street next day, recognizes them at once from young Rand's description, and follows them home to see where they live.

Having advanced that portion of the plot as far as he can for the moment, Alger drops it entirely and goes back to Helen. She has become friendly with Martha Grey, the seamstress, who is her only friend in the house. Eustace is too forward; Mademoiselle Fanchette, an aging charmer, is jealous of her and snipes at her with snide remarks. But Martha is more like Helen's own sweet, innocent character, and they are friends.

Helen is invited one afternoon to go to the theater with Martha and the seamstress's flashy cousin. It is a Wednesday matinee, already an institution for ladies, and it is Helen's first visit to the theater, where she is enchanted by the entertainment, particularly the vocal soloists between the acts, in the custom of the time. Chatting with Martha next day in the seamstress's room about her new experience, she offers to sing a song from the show which Martha especially liked. It appears, to Martha's surprise, that Helen has a voice of "remarkable richness and power . . . of extraordinary flexibility and compass, whose natural power had evidently been improved by cultivation." She is, in a word, talented. Encouraged by Martha's applause, she sings "Home, Sweet Home" as an encore, which reduces the homeless Martha to tears.

Immediately after this scene, Alger demonstrates that he has not yet overcome his earlier bad habits. He writes a chapter describing how Helen, her father and Martha go to church one Sunday at Trinity, inserted apparently only to underline Helen's saintly character, which scarcely needs it, and to provide him with an opportunity to describe another part of New York, which he does at length, giving his readers a guidebook description of Trinity Church, the churchyard and the surrounding neighborhood.

But the plot picks up again when lawyer Sharp pays a call, talks his way into the Ford's room to interview them on a flimsy pretext, and so verifies their identity, which he reports to Lewis Rand at once.

Meanwhile, Helen is contemplating a new career. It is hard to get along with only the income from her sewing and, encouraged by her experience with Martha, she goes back to the theater to see if she can get a job singing between acts. Here Alger adds the theatrical to the list of his other cliché categories. Helen is rebuffed by an impatient manager, but as she turns away in tears, a messenger appears with the news that "Miss DeForrest is indisposed and will not be able to sing that evening." The manager calls Helen back and gives her an audition at once.

Hopefully, drying her tears, Helen sings "The Widow Machree" and "Comin' Thro' the Rye," completely charming the manager. Even the actors, rehearsing their next production (apparently it is a repertory theater) gather about the office door to hear her, and the whole scene is certain to remind the contemporary reader of almost any Warner Brothers musical comedy of the thirties.

Needless to say, she gets the job, at six dollars a week. There is only one problem. Helen dares not tell her father she has gone on the stage to earn money to keep their home, because presumably he would rather see her dead than sunk so low. Deceiving him proves easy, however. That night she leaves the house on a fictitious errand which Ford, busy inventing in his usual foggy state, never questions.

Hurrying to the theater, Helen opens to an audience of two

thousand people, among whom are Mlle. Fanchette, with Eustace, he agog and she raspy with jealousy, sneering at Helen throughout her performance. But the modiste is no judge of talent. The audience loves Helen. Her "Comin' Thro' the Rye" leaves them sodden with happiness. A "hard-featured Scotchman" in a front seat wipes a tear from his eye, because her singing reminds him of "a flower that had once bloomed in his home, but had faded early—transplanted to the gardens of Paradise."

While Helen is bringing down the house, Sharp is making another call on Ford, alone and helpless without his daughter. He flatters the inventor about his flying machine, pretends to be interested in investing in it, and offers to lend Ford $200, without interest or security, to help speed the perfection of his invention. Ford signs the note at once, so overjoyed he does not even notice it is made out for $300 instead of $200, although Sharp gives him only the smaller amount.

Soon after, Ford discovers his daughter's new career by accident when he passes by the theater one day with her and sees her name so prominently displayed on the billboard outside that even he cannot miss it. Surprisingly, he makes no objection, although when he learns that she has gone on the stage to make money for them, he tells her grandly that he has just acquired $200 and their worries are virtually over. This is the first time Helen has heard about the loan, and she tries unsuccessfully to make him give the money back. Ford assures her earnestly that it is all he needs to perfect his machine, that Sharp is an honest gentleman, and there is nothing to worry about.

Now love, or what passes for it in an Alger novel, enters Helen's life. She meets the young man in the opposite apartment. He is of "middle height" (Alger never had a tall hero; he himself was short) and he has a face "whose boyish bloom had hardly given place to the more mature expression of manhood." His name is Herbert Coleman, an artist, a farmer's son who has come to the city to seek his fortune.

At this juncture Alger writes an extraordinary scene in which he mixes all the elements of his work in an indescribable stew. It is an episode in which Helen and her father decide to give themselves a treat one day and go to Staten Island on the steamboat, where they expect to enjoy the pleasures of the amusement park which flourished in those days not far from where the ferry slips are today. Horatio describes the trip across the Bay in detail, with his usual meticulous, guidebook attention to detail, but he is lost when he tries to convey the flavor of the amusement park. To him a merry-go-round is "a wooden enclosure, where wooden horses, each bearing a rider, were revolving under the impulse of machinery."

By coincidence, several characters in the drama are visiting the amusement park that day. Jacob Wynne, the copyist, is there with a girl who is not his wife, but they are followed by Margaret Wynne, who thus far in the book has made a career of spying. When Jacob leaves his friend for a moment, Margaret, heavily swathed in veils, takes his arm, leads him aside and reveals herself. Jacob starts, of course, but he seems prepared to brazen it out. Margaret demands to know who the other girl is. "I have a right to know," she says. With a sneer, he implies that this is not the case, and Margaret cries, aghast, "My God, what do you mean?" Profanity was permitted Alger characters in moments of exceptional stress.

Jacob proves to be as villainous as his friend Rand. Still sneering, he tells Margaret that they were married by a fake priest, who had donned the robes only for the ceremony, or as Jacob puts it more tellingly, "The priest who performed the ceremony was so only for that occasion." Margaret, staggered by this knowledge, mutters that she has only one thing to live for now —"Revenge!" She disappears, and Alger describes her distraught progress back from Staten Island through a terrible storm to some remote rural spot near New York where her mother lives. She arrives drenched, hysterical and ill. By this time Alger has forgotten completely about Helen and her father. What happened to them on Staten Island remains undisclosed, as well as how *they* got home through the storm. But Margaret is safely tucked away for a few chapters. She lies in her mother's house for weeks, near death.

Meanwhile, Helen is accosted one night as she walks home from the theater by a young patron whose name is Albert Grover. He is one of those rich young bounders whom Alger so emphatically despises, and he arrogantly thrusts his attentions, which are clearly far from honorable, upon poor Helen who scarcely knows what to say except "No!" At that moment "a manly voice" says "leave this young lady alone." It can be no other than Herbert Coleman—"the opposite lodger"—as Horatio calls him. He chides Helen for walking home alone at night, and she tells him that Martha Grey had been walking home with her every night until recently when the seamstress, who is exhausted from her work, had found it too much for her.

"Let me look upon you as my sister," says Herbert, and volunteers to be her brotherly escort every night. They become intimate at once: he will call her Helen; she will call him Herbert.

Grover, who is persistent as well as rich, makes another attempt upon Helen's honor next night, but this time he finds Herbert at her side. "You may as well give it up," the opposite lodger advises him. "Henceforth this young lady will have an escort able and willing to chastise all who are disposed to offer her annoyance." Grover slinks away, discouraged by this barrage of rhetoric.

Meanwhile, in Rand Senior's "palace-like structure fronting on Fifth Avenue," the old man is dying. He instructs Lewis to draw up an advertisement for the newspapers, in a last effort to find out whether his son is living. Lewis promises piously to carry out his instructions, but of course has no intention of doing so. Instead, he tells Sharp to foreclose on Robert Ford's note, in the hope that this will force the Fords to leave town before the dying Rand can somehow find his son.

Sharp carries out his assignment by a peculiarly dastardly ruse. Calling on Ford, he tells the inventor that he has raised money on the note but asserts that in doing so he has stipulated expressly Ford should not be called on for it. Then he sends around an unscrupulous colleague to represent himself as the other lender, who declares that his circumstances have changed and he must call in the note at once. Ford, of course, cannot pay and the conspirator says he will seize the model of the inventor's flying machine in satisfaction.

A financial crisis confronts the Fords. Helen's father has $120 remaining from the original loan, which he had thought was only $200 and has now discovered from the conspirator's demand was hiked to $300. In sum, he needs $180, and even though the theater manager has doubled Helen's salary, they are a long way from being able to raise this amount.

Meanwhile, Sharp has been having some shrewd second thoughts about the situation. From his conversations with Lewis Rand he now knows the whole story, and it occurs to him that he might do better in the end by double-crossing Rand and bringing father and son together, since the inventor is certainly an easier man to handle than Rand. Besides, he has come to have a certain fondness for Ford, which is difficult for the reader to believe but necessary for Alger to establish for purposes of his plot.

Sharp calls on the Fords and finds both of them home. Helen hospitably invites him to dinner, and during the course of the meal, Ford confesses what Helen has never known but Sharp has known all the time—that his real name is Rand. In that case, Sharp says, he should know his father is dying, and he gives Ford-Rand the Fifth Avenue address.

Having lost his vagueness momentarily, Robert hurries to his father's house, where he confronts Lewis standing at the foot of the stairs to bar his way. Brushing his cousin aside, the inventor rushes to the bedside and there is a classic scene of forgiveness as the old man dies.

When the will is produced to be read, it is the one Lewis had

Jacob Wynne forge, leaving everything to him. To protect himself in the somewhat embarrassing circumstances, Lewis offers his cousin a small farm in Pennsylvania, thinking it will quiet him and get him out of the way. Impractical though he is, the inventor sees through this fraud and pride compels him to reject it. He angrily denounces Lewis, who "turns red and white by turns," but recovering from this colorful display, he "laughs sardonically," and when he is alone again, gives himself up to "the intoxicating dream of power which his wealth would give him."

While these events have been occurring, poor Margaret Wynne has been languishing for six weeks in her mother's house. She has nearly recovered from her flight through the storm, but she is still weak and is still in a confused state of mind about Jacob, unable to believe he is not really her husband. Bored with her convalescence, she asks her mother for a paper to read. As she puts it in her elegantly direct way, "I get tired looking at the cat." The mother is not given to reading, but looking about the house, she finds a newspaper which has come wrapped around a package.

Seizing on this as better than nothing, Margaret opens the paper and at once sees old Mr. Rand's death notice. The scene she witnessed from behind the door the night the will was forged comes back to her. Jacob must now have consummated the other part of the bargain he made that night, she reflects. Lewis had promised him a thousand dollars more when his uncle died. If Jacob is a thousand dollars richer, then Margaret means to see him.

Weak as she is, Margaret struggles into her clothes and leaves the house while her mother is out, getting a ride into the city on a farmer's cart. As she wanders up Broadway, Alger helpfully provides her with a coincidence. She sees Jacob, fashionably dressed, passing by with a girl on his arm. Half-fainting from shock at the sight, as well as from her weakened condition, Margaret falls on the steps of a fashionable store. Horatio injects one of his notes of social commentary by having an officious clerk about to kick her off the steps when Helen, returning from the theater, coincidentally passes by and intervenes. Observing that Margaret is weak and ill, Helen takes her home and puts her up temporarily with Martha Grey.

From Martha, as she recovers again, Margaret learns who Helen and her father are, because the seamstress has learned the whole story of Lewis Rand's perfidy from her friend. But Margaret, who now holds the key to exposing the fraud, perversely will not tell what she knows until she has seen Jacob again and finds out definitely whether it is true they were never married. What bearing this has on the matter, Alger does not tell his readers.

Returning to her former home, Margaret finds Jacob there, counting his money. He has just reached $700. Margaret is not interested in the money, only her marital status, and she begs Jacob to say that what he told her on Staten Island isn't true. But he regards "the anxious face before him with the triumph that a low mind always feels when it has by any means gained an ascendancy over a stronger one."

Margaret leaves in despair, and faints again on the street. The convenient passerby this time is Lawyer Sharp, who cannot help looking for business no matter where it appears. He takes her to his office. When he tells her he is a lawyer, she tells him everything she knows about Jacob. Seeing an opportunity to further his own interests, Sharp has Jacob arrested and taken to the Tombs. But Margaret proves to be one of those women who cannot forsake a man no matter how often he does her wrong. When Sharp tells her what he has done, and aware that she alone is responsible, she is assailed by doubt and remorse. She still loves Jacob, she decides, and goes to prison to see him. When she sees him in a cell, her remorse is so great that she offers not to bear witness against him, and so free him. A transformation has taken place in Jacob. The experience of being thrown into the Tombs, coupled with his wife's generous offer, is too much for his weakly evil character. He admits that their marriage was genuine after all.

That is all Margaret needs to hear. She will never testify against Jacob now, she tells Sharp. The lawyer finds this news only momentarily frustrating. Knowledge of the forged will *does* give him power over Lewis, he realizes. He goes to Lewis, pretending to represent Robert, and asserts that his client has told him he will settle for half the estate. Lewis laughs at the idea, whereupon Sharp discloses his knowledge of the forgery.

Once more Lewis's sallow face is engulfed in a brilliant display. He "goes white and red by turns," but Sharp relentlessly compels him to sign an agreement turning over half his estate.

Meanwhile, back at the boardinghouse, all is not well. Poor Martha faints from overwork, and Herbert appears to have changed toward Helen. She scarcely sees him any more, although he still calls her "my little sister" when they meet. Finally he confesses that poverty is driving him to the wall. His uncle Zebina (Alger always gives his rural characters stereotype names) has made what he apparently thinks is a generous offer to come back home and work in his country store for $55 a month. Herbert can scarcely bring himself to think of giving up art for life in a country store, and Helen is no help. "The offer seems kindly meant," she says.

At this critical point, Sharp appears with the good news that half the inventor's estate has been restored to him. In repayment for what he has done to secure it, Sharp modestly offers to manage it. The estate will, he says, exceed $500,000; the Fords are rich.

As a freshly minted heiress, Helen's first act is to buy a picture from Herbert for $150 to keep him in the city. To save her friend's pride, she employs Sharp as the nominal buyer. Overjoyed, Herbert turns down Uncle Zebina's offer.

Part of the estate proves to be a house on Twenty-third Street, to which Helen and her father now move. Martha goes with them as a companion; no longer will she be compelled to expend her eyes and her strength on making clothes. Helen gives up her theatrical career so that her father will have company in the evening, but, before she leaves, she gives a benefit performance on her last night for an ill fellow performer who has been a dancer between the acts.

Alger has left so many stray ends of plot untied that it takes him longer than usual to conclude his story in an epilogue. Four years have passed. Helen is getting an education from private tutors, because her father is still so dependent on her that he cannot send her away to school. Meanwhile, he has given Herbert $5,000 to go abroad and pursue his art studies, disguising the gift as a commission to copy some Italian masterpieces for him, a practice common at the time. Herbert is in Italy now, studying and copying, but he and Helen correspond. "They have tacitly dropped the old designation of brother and sister," the reader learns with some relief, and "Knowing what we do of their feelings toward each other, we need not be surprised if they are bound some day by a nearer tie."

As for Robert Ford, or Rand, he has given up inventing, leaving his flying machine to the future ministrations of the Wright brothers. He spends his time in his magnificent new library, pottering about harmlessly among his books. Sharp serves as his business manager with "ability and fidelity," the reader is bemused to learn. Alger apparently anticipates this reaction. He notes, somewhat apologetically, that the lawyer is not entirely rid of his "idiosyncracies," as Horatio is now pleased to call villainy, but these are "now of a harmless nature." That is, he no longer runs up bills which he is unable to liquidate, and he has ceased to exercise his professional sharpness on the newsboys and cheat them out of the price of a paper.

One of his remaining idiosyncracies, it turns out, has been to propose marriage to Martha. But Alger realizes this would be too much for even the most trusting of his readers. Sharp cannot be permitted too great a reward for his villainy, so Martha must refuse him. But why? Horatio is equal to that one. "She has," he says piously, "never recovered from an early disappointment, which, without robbing her of happiness, has made it impossible for her to love again."

Still, the question of Sharp continues to bother Alger. He cannot let him go with this simple rebuff, and in the hurried prose at the end, one can almost see him looking around for a way out. He finds it. Sharp is trying to persuade a wealthy widow to marry him, which seems a delightful prospect except that she has a foul temper. But that is not enough, and Alger knows it. Despairingly, he frankly admits "qualms of conscience" about permitting Sharp such prosperity, and concludes weakly that he thinks "poetical justice" will be done through his prospective unfortunate marriage.

At least there is no trouble with Jacob Wynne. He has reformed completely, and Robert has given him a good deal of copying business of a more legitimate kind. He and Margaret are happy at last. Only Lewis remains, and for him there is no hope, although as a result of what can only be described as Sharp's stupidity, he is still a rich man, in possession of half an estate he has no right to whatever. Alger realizes this contradiction, too, but he has a moral answer ready. Lewis, he says, is a bitter man, living amid the fleshpots of Europe. He is what will later be called a poor little rich boy. "Happiness must be earned; it can never be bought," Horatio remarks sententiously.

"And so, reader, farewell!" Alger concludes regretfully. "What remains in store for Helen Ford, whether of joy or of sorrow, it is not mine to read. Let us hope that her life may brighten continually till its close; that her years, whether few or many, may be made happy by the consciousness of duty well performed; that she may dispense liberally unto others of the good gifts with which God has crowned her, and make her life a benefaction to humanity!"

Comparing this book with *Frank's Campaign*, written only two years before, it is easy to see that, bad as *Helen Ford* may be, Alger has learned much. He has, in fact, gained so much confidence with "Helen" that he feels himself ready to try an adult novel.

CHAPTER 5

It is difficult to understand why Alger thought he was writing an adult novel when he composed *Timothy Crump's Ward,* which he subtitled *A Story of American Life.* By comparison, *Helen Ford,* which he meant as a story for young people, is rich in plot and characterization. There is nothing in *Timothy* to distinguish it from dozens of other Alger products intended solely for the young people's market. The style is identical; in length it is somewhat shorter. When it later appeared, rewritten, as *Jack's Ward,* there was no discernible difference except for a slight change in plot. The writing and tone were the same, as indeed they are in all Alger books.

Nevertheless, *Timothy* is worth a brief examination because it throws additional light on Alger as a writer, coming as it does in the same year, almost in the same creative breath, as *Helen.* In this pathetic, often laughable, attempt to write an adult novel, Alger demonstrates with depressing clarity why his Great Dream could never come true.

The demonstration begins with the opening, in which Alger attempts to get away from the formula he had already established for himself by trying to create an atmosphere rather than simply describing something real from his experience. But he is only three paragraphs into his story before he lapses into his usual literal method. Here is the beginning of Chapter One, which, as he says, "Introduces The Crumps":

It was drawing towards the close of the last day of the year. A few hours more, and 1836 would be no more.

It was a cold day. There was no snow on the ground, but it was frozen into stiff ridges, making it uncomfortable to walk upon. The sun had been out all day, but there was little heat or comfort in its bright, but frosty beams.

The winter is a hard season for the poor. It multiplies their necessities, while, in general, it limits their means and opportunities of earning. The winter of 1836–37 was far from being an exception to this rule. It was worse than usual, on account of the general stagnation of business.

In a humble tenement, located on what was then the outskirts of New York, though to-day a granite warehouse stands on the spot, lived Timothy Crump, an industrious cooper. His family consisted of a wife and one child, a boy of twelve, whose baptismal name was John, though invariably addressed, by his companions, as Jack.

There was another member of the household who would be highly offended if she were not introduced, in due form, to the reader. This was Miss Rachel Crump, maiden sister of Uncle Tim, as he was usually designated.

In the next paragraph, which describes Rachel Crump, Alger makes his first flight toward what he conceives of as an adult novel. Rachel is a stereotype, like Little Pomp, Eustace, Uncle Zebina and the others, but in apostrophizing her in the vein of the popular romantic novels of the Civil War era, Horatio thought he was writing on a higher plane than children would understand or appreciate. He continues:

Miss Rachel was not much like her brother, for while the latter was a good-hearted, cheerful, easy man, who was inclined to view the world in its sunniest aspect, Rachel was cynical, and given to misanthropy. Poor Rachel, let us not be too hard upon thy infirmities. Could we lift the veil that hides the secrets of that virgin heart, it might be, perchance, that we should find a hidden cause, far back in the days when thy cheeks were rounder and thine eyes brighter, and thine aspect not quite so frosty. Ah, faithless Harry Fletcher! thou hadst some hand in that peevishness and repining which make Rachel Crump, and all about her, uncomfortable. Lured away by a prettier face, you left her to pass through life, unblessed by that love which every female heart craves, and for which no kindred love will compensate. It was your faithlessness that left her to walk, with repining spirit, the flinty path of the old maid.

Descending from this cloud, Alger describes the remainder of the Crump family and, by now well into the book, tells the reader of the situation they find themselves in on New Year's Eve. They are about to be evicted for nonpayment of rent next day. A knock on the door does not bring a happy coincidental arrival of help from some expected or unexpected quarter, as in other Alger novels, but another cliché—a basket on the doorstep with a one-year-old baby girl in it. An accompanying note says the child's guardians "find it expedient to entrust it to others to be brought up." To take care of her, the letter goes on, $300 has been deposited in a specified bank, and a similar deposit will be made every year as long as the child is with the Crumps. "All attempts to fathom whatever of mystery may attach to this affair," the note ends mysteriously, "will prove useless."

Except for Rachel, whose every speech is a gloomy comment, the Crumps are delighted with the unexpected bundle. But then the Crumps are one of the most determinedly cheerful families in all literature, we learn at once. Imminent eviction, no prospects, a baby to take care of—these melancholy circumstances only inspire them to a serene, confident outlook, to which Rachel's comments are a woeful Greek chorus.

At least the arrival of the baby with her $300 deposit is enough to save them from eviction. With rigid honesty, however, they determine that the money must be spent almost entirely on the child, not on themselves. Meanwhile, they must look elsewhere for their further salvation. Had they known it, they would have needed to look no further than Alger's talent for coincidence.

One night as Timothy is returning home after a fruitless search for work, he sees a man being robbed on the street and frightens off the thug. The intended victim has reason to be particularly grateful; he is carrying $1,500 in cash. After warmly shaking Timothy's hand as a first installment, he asks him to call at his office in Wall Street the next day.

Anyone not a devoted Alger reader might be surprised at this businessman's idea of gratitude when Timothy appears, although in the context of the times it may have been generous of him to have offered Timothy a job as porter in his office, and as a bonus, an envelope containing $100 to be given to his wife. Alger does not explain why the envelope is to be given to Mrs. Crump, but the older readers for whom the book was intended understood well enough, if they read it. An employer did not entrust extra money to an employee, unless it was someone he knew well; the supposition was that he would drink it up before he got home. Timothy's benefactor need not have worried.

After this incident, there is an eight-year lapse of time. When we see the Crumps again, little Ida, the foundling, has grown up to that precocious stage which characterizes Alger's preadolescents. The Crumps have given her good clothes and sent her to private school out of the annual deposit. They have kept none of the money for themselves. Ida has become one of the family. They think of her as their own child.

A knock on the door brings a disturbance to this domestic Eden. The caller is a woman who says she is a nurse, bearing a letter which purports to be from Ida's real mother. Mrs. Crump, reading the letter, learns from it that the child still cannot be claimed, but the mother has taken rooms in the neighborhood nearby and wants to see her daughter secretly. The nurse is to bring her there on a visit, and will return her.

Mrs. Crump's response to this startling turn of events is to ask a question which apparently has been disturbing her for eight years. "Was—is Ida the child of shame?" she inquires. "No," the nurse answers shortly, and Ida is saved from disgrace.

The Crumps are not ready to let their foster child go so easily. Timothy does not trust the nurse, who says her name is Mrs. Hardwicke, and the whole family, particularly Rachel, is disquieted by the idea of letting Ida go away with a stranger. They invite Mrs. Hardwicke to spend the night, promising to let her take the girl in the morning.

In reality, of course, Mrs. Hardwicke intends to kidnap Ida, which she does the next morning with ridiculous ease, while the Crumps look on doubtfully. Ida, who has assumed her foster family's cheerful outlook, does not realize she is being kidnaped until she finds herself on a train and learns its destination is Philadelphia. Here Alger plants an awkward device by introducing a boy Ida knows who happens to be selling apples on the train that day.

Once in Philadelphia, Mrs. Hardwicke takes Ida to the mean tenement where she lives with her evil, drunken husband, Dick. There the nurse drops her disguise, produces a pistol, and assures the terrified Ida that she will be killed if she attempts to escape, or even if she succeeds in escaping.

A few days later, Peg, as Mrs. Hardwicke is familiarly called, takes Ida out to shop. She sends the child into a baker's store to pass a counterfeit dollar for a loaf of bread, over Ida's horrified protests.

Here Alger introduces the second coincidence in a book which is not only unusually replete with them but contains, near the end, one of his surpassing efforts in this category. The baker who is the recipient of Ida's bad dollar is no other than Timothy Crump's brother, Abel. Either Timothy is an exceptionally bad correspondent or the mail from New York to Philadelphia has been delayed, because Abel knows nothing of Ida. Nor, it seems at the moment, does he know a bad dollar when he sees one, since Ida gets her bread.

After nearly a week has gone by, the Crumps in their slow-witted way begin to wonder what is keeping Ida. When the boy who saw her on the train stops by and lets this knowledge slip out in an idle comment, they approach as near to alarm as they are capable, and Jack Crump, by this time a boy of twenty and apparently somewhat thick between the ears, sets off for Philadelphia to find Ida.

Ida, meanwhile, is not confined. Peg takes her out occasionally, usually to pass counterfeit money for merchandise. On one of these expeditions she is approached by a young artist who is so attracted by her beauty that he persuades Peg to let him go home with them and sketch her.

Jack, arriving in Philadelphia, goes at once to see Abel, and there he learns that Ida has come into the store because the baker recognizes her from Jack's description. Then he sees Mrs. Hardwicke in the street, by coincidence. With any other but a Crump, the story would have ended at this point, but Peg easily lures him to a house operated by a man who is involved with the counterfeit money ring, and there he is led unsuspecting into a room and locked in, after which Peg leaves. His jailer gives Jack some old magazines to relieve his boredom, and in one of them he finds a story called "The Adventures of Baron Trenck," who tells how he escaped from a European dungeon. Deciding to emulate the baron, Jack cuts his way through the door with a knife and escapes.

Peg, reasonably believing herself safe from the trivial annoyance of Jack's pursuit, has gone to see John Somerville, a dissipated clubman. It is Somerville, we learn, who employed her eight years before to put Ida on the Crumps' doorstep. Now she tries to blackmail him for $1,000, telling him she has the child and will give it back to the mother. The conversation reveals that the mother rejected Somerville and married his cousin, and when the cousin died after a few years of marriage, Somerville was rejected again when he renewed his proposal. Furious, he hired Peg and her husband to kidnap the child and leave it with a family. Somerville now believes Peg means it when she says she will disclose the whole plot to Ida's mother, and he promises to give her the money next afternoon.

With this scheme successfully under way, Peg returns to see how her captive, Jack, is faring and discovers he has fled. At that moment the doorbell rings. It is Jack with the police, who promptly arrest both Peg and Foley, the gang member who was Jack's jailer. Peg resolutely refuses to tell where Ida is before she is taken away, but as Jack wanders off again, Alger leads him into a maze of coincidences, the first of which occurs when he sees the young artist's painting of Ida in a store window.

While he is inquiring from the proprietor where Ida might be, a lady shopping in the store also sees the picture. She starts, and inquires of the proprietor who the girl in the portrait is; it is someone she knows, she thinks. Jack steps forward and introduces himself. They exchange stories and the lady proves to be Ida's long-lost mother, Mrs. Clifton, who invites him to ride home with her in her carriage. The carriage and her house establish that Mrs. Clifton is rich, and that Ida is an heiress, if she can be found.

It is not until Mrs. Clifton and Jack have been sitting in her house talking for some time that it occurs to either of them they could have asked the proprietor of the store where the artist lives, and through him find Ida. They hurry back to the store, get this information, and rush off to the artist's studio. Helpfully, he goes with them, points out Peg's house, and goes in to see if she is there. He returns to say that Ida has been carried away by a gentleman only an hour before.

The gentleman was John Somerville, who has decided to take Ida home with him and forestall Peg, not knowing his blackmailer is already in prison. Ida, it may be added, takes her sudden change of circumstances with Crump-like serenity; nothing has really disturbed her, not even the confinement with Peg. Now, when Somerville tells her he must leave her for a little while, she tries to amuse herself by reading but is quickly bored by this occupation and wanders to the window, looking out on busy Fifth Avenue. There she sees a carriage passing slowly, "on account of a press of carriages," and in it she recognizes Jack, who is sitting beside Mrs. Clifton. They are returning from their trip to Peg's house. The traffic is moving very slowly. Ida has time to run out of the house and up to the carriage before it goes by. Jack pulls her in, and Mrs. Clifton cries out, "My child, my child!" and clasps Ida, who is no more astonished by this turn of events than a Crump should be.

Jack explains the situation and Ida "hardly knows whether to feel glad or sorry." As they talk, Ida remarks "What will the gentleman say?" meaning Somerville, and sure enough, at that moment she looks out the carriage window and exclaims, "Why, there he is now." John Somerville is indeed passing by. Alger has planted this coincidence only so that Mrs. Clifton can see who is responsible for Ida's most recent abduction.

Now Jack and Ida ride with Mrs. Clifton to her home, where a message awaits her. It is from Peg, in jail, asking to see her. Mrs. Clifton goes and takes Ida with her, and the little girl astounds her former captor by declaring she is sorry to see Peg in such circumstances.

"I can't help it," says the child, her face beaming with a divine compassion; "it must be so sad to be shut up here, and not be able to go out into the bright sunshine. I do pity you." Then Ida forgives her as well.

This is too much for Peg, as it may well be for later readers. "There have been times when I thought I should like to lead a better life," Peg says.

Then she discloses to Mrs. Clifton the whole story of the original kidnaping, telling how John Somerville put her up to it. But how could she do such a thing, Mrs. Clifton asks, and for her pains gets a stern lesson in social philosophy.

"Madame, you are rich," Peg says. "You have always had whatever wealth could procure. How can you understand the temptations of the poor? When want and hunger stare us in the face, we have not the strength to resist that you have in your luxurious homes."

"Pardon me," Mrs. Clifton murmurs, and promises to help Peg reform.

When they come back from the jail, Mrs. Clifton finds Somerville waiting for her. He is a persistent lover. Having failed by every other means, he now tries to blackmail Mrs. Clifton into marrying him, promising to return Ida to her if she says yes, not knowing the child is in the house at that moment. Alger is as careless with his time lapses as he is with other details, but the reader gathers that all the events just described, beginning with Jack's initial discovery of Peg in the street, have happened on the same day.

Mrs. Clifton waits until Somerville has made his base proposition, then she scornfully reveals the true situation and tells him she now knows the entire sordid business. He is a beaten man. "John Somerville rose and left the room. His grand scheme had failed."

Meanwhile, back at the Crump house, there is hysterical anxiety. "I am beginning to feel anxious about Jack," says Mrs. Crump. "It's almost a week since we heard from him. I'm afraid he's got into some trouble."

But at that very moment a coach pulls up to the door, a "handsome carriage" drawn by "two elegant bays." It is Ida and Jack and Mrs. Clifton, who now plays the role of Lady Bountiful usually enacted by a successful character at the end of an Alger book. The Crumps must move to Philadelphia, she says, so they can be near Ida. She will get Timothy a job there. Ida's gift to the family, through Mrs. Clifton, is "a neat brick house in a quiet street."

A brief epilogue, shorter than most Alger conclusions, provides the usual rosy future for all the characters. Tim soon has his own business. Jack becomes a thriving young merchant. Ordinarily he could be expected to marry Ida, but the age difference is too much for Alger, and in any event he shrinks from their close relationship, even though blood was not involved. Ida, he says, grows ever lovelier. "If she does not marry well and happily, it will not be for want of opportunity." Even Aunt Rachel comes home one day with "a short man, stout and freckled," whom she introduces as "my consort." She adds characteristically, "I don't expect to live long, and it won't make much difference."

In Alger's fictional world there is hope for everyone. Peg, with Dick conveniently dead, finds through Mrs. Clifton "a position in which her energy and administrative ability," a mysterious phrase, "found fitting exercise, and she leads a laborious and useful life, in a community where her antecedents are not known."

Thus Alger's "adult" novel ends. Its comparative failure is explained easily. There is no boy protagonist following the Alger path which he had yet to mark out plainly, and its plot is not romantic enough for the kind of popular novel people were reading at the time. Romance of the most extravagant variety was the essence of best-selling fiction after the Civil War, and Alger was simply incapable of writing it. He shrank from portraying adult love except in the noblest, most respectable terms, and he could not bring himself to depict the violence which poured blood through the tales of the period. He could only write variations on his formula, of which *Helen Ford* had been one and *Timothy Crump* another. *Helen* was the better seller simply because it was a better story.

But the preliminary excursions were over. After he discovered the Newsboys' Lodging House, Alger went back to the basic ingredients he had begun to put together tentatively in *Frank's Campaign,* and with the inexhaustible factual stories of his little friends to fuel his shallow imagination, he began to turn out in 1868 the stories which followed one after the other until he died. There was one book between *Timothy* and *Ragged Dick.* It was *Charlie Codman's Cruise,* representing A. K. Loring's attempt to keep his profitable new property writing while he settled himself in New York. It was a feeble and unprofitable attempt, but neither Alger nor Loring was alarmed by its failure, which again was only comparative. The newsboys were waiting to be mined.

CHAPTER 6

While he was working on *Charlie Codman's Cruise* in 1867, Alger was also writing *Ragged Dick; or, Street Life in New York with the Boot-blacks* as a serial in Adams's magazine, *Student and Schoolmate*. Its success was instantaneous. For the first time Alger was reaching directly the boy audience whose hero he would soon become, and they recognized at once what he had to give them. Loring and Adams saw it too; in *Ragged Dick* they knew they had struck gold. As it was being published in 1868, Alger was already hard at work on its successor, *Fame and Fortune,* which was serialized in *Student and Schoolmate* during 1868 while *Dick* was selling furiously in book form.

It is hard to agree with those critics who assert that *Ragged Dick* is Alger's best book. True, it has certain virtues which the others do not possess. Dick has more dimension than the other Alger heroes, who quickly became indistinguishable from one another. Where the others are saturated in virtue, Dick begins with some bad qualities, like swearing, smoking, gambling and a love for the theater, all of which he rapidly overcomes. He is more real than the other, later heroes, perhaps, because Alger had just discovered the Newsboys' Lodging House. He was still excited about his discovery, and Dick was unquestionably drawn from life.

Except for the delineation of Dick, however, who stands out

above the other heroes, his story is markedly below the plot level of the books which came after. *Ragged Dick,* indeed, scarcely has a plot at all by comparison with Alger's later productions. In a book of 295 pages, the plot does not begin to move until page 129. Nearly half the volume is devoted to a tour of New York City, conveying something of Alger's excitement about his new home, but it is more guidebook than novel, although Horatio attempts a few incidents, as if becoming aware intermittently that he was, after all, writing a story.

The book has more of Alger's literal quality than any of the others, apparently by design, as Alger makes clear in a somewhat apologetic preface. "*Ragged Dick,*" he says, "is the first volume of a series intended to illustrate the life and experiences of the friendless and vagrant children who are now numbered by thousands in New York and other cities." He continues:

> Several characters in the story are sketched from life. The necessary information has been gathered mainly from personal observation and conversations with the boys themselves. The author is indebted also to the excellent Superintendent of the Newsboys' Lodging House in Fulton St., for some facts of which he has been able to make use. Some anachronisms may be noted. Wherever they occur, they have been admitted, as aiding in the development of the story, and will probably be considered as of little importance in an unpretending volume, which does not aspire to strict historical accuracy.
>
> The author hopes that, while the volumes in this series may prove interesting as stories, they may also have the effect of enlisting the sympathies of his readers in behalf of the unfortunate children whose life is described, and of leading them to cooperate with the praiseworthy efforts now making by the Children's Aid Society and other organizations to ameliorate their condition.

It is, in brief, to be as much tract as story, and that is how it turns out.

As the book opens, Dick is being wakened by a porter who

works for a Spruce Street business firm. It is seven o'clock and he has overslept because he had been to the Old Bowery Theatre the night before, on money saved from shoeshines. Hearing of Dick's extravagance, the porter implies that some boys get money from stealing, but Dick is indignant. He wouldn't steal. "Oh, I'm a rough customer," he says, "but I wouldn't steal. It's mean."

He has been sleeping in a wooden box half filled with straw. When he rises from it and pulls himself together, Alger describes him as having torn pants two sizes too large, a vest with all but two buttons gone, a shirt looking as though it had been worn a month, and a coat too long for him, "dating back, if one might judge from its general appearance, to a remote antiquity." His hands and face are dirty.

"But in spite of his dirt and rags," Alger is quick to comment, "there was something about Dick that was attractive. It was easy to see that if he had been clean and well dressed he would have been decidedly good-looking. Some of his companions were sly, and their faces inspired distrust; but Dick had a frank, straightforward manner that made him a favorite."

Here Alger performs his unprecedented and never repeated depiction of a hero as something less than perfect. "Our ragged hero wasn't a model boy in all respects," he admits frankly. "I am afraid he swore sometimes, and now and then he played tricks upon unsophisticated boys from the country, or gave a wrong direction to honest old gentlemen unused to the city. A clergyman in search of the Cooper Institute he once directed to the Tombs Prison, and, following him unobserved, was highly delighted when the unsuspicious stranger walked up the steps of the great stone building on Centre Street, and tried to obtain admission."

Dick was also, Alger continues relentlessly, "careless of his earnings," and he had "formed the habit of smoking," although he was "rather fastidious about his cigars, and wouldn't smoke the cheapest." Alger adds flatly: "No boy of fourteen can smoke without being affected injuriously. Men are frequently injured by smoking, and boys always." Later generations ridiculed this advice, but Alger has the last laugh.

Worse than swearing and smoking, Alger goes on in his pursuit of truth, drawing upon his intimate knowledge of newsboy life, Dick lost money at a notorious gambling house on Baxter Street, where "juvenile gangsters" also drank "a vile mixture of liquor at two cents a glass."

Boys who considered themselves at least partly sunk in sin were delighted to find that a young man could rise above his ignoble self if he had the good qualities of Ragged Dick. Nevertheless, Alger was fearful they might think he was condoning vice. "I have mentioned Dick's faults and defects," he says solemnly, stepping forth in his role of author, "because I want it understood, to begin with, that I don't consider him a model boy. But there were some good points about him nevertheless. He was above doing anything mean or dishonorable. He would not steal, or cheat, or impose upon younger boys, but was frank and straight-forward, manly and self-reliant. His nature was a noble one, and had saved him from all mean faults. I hope my young readers will like him, as I do, without being blind to his faults. Perhaps, although he was only a bootblack, they may find something in him to imitate."

Having introduced Dick at length, Alger starts him on his day. Leaving his wooden box on Spruce Street, he goes to a cheap restaurant for breakfast. A cheap restaurant in those days, the modern reader learns with nostalgia, sold Dick coffee for five cents, and for ten cents more he got a plate of beefsteak with a plate of bread thrown in.

Filled with this nineteenth-century equivalent of orange juice, cereal and toast, Dick strolls out to work, which is shining shoes for ten cents a job. He has a small piece of luck early in the day. A customer gives him a $2 bill to change, and when Dick takes it into a nearby store, an unscrupulous clerk tries to swindle him out of it by claiming it is counterfeit. Dick refuses to be fooled.

He brings the customer in and the fraud is exposed, after which he is given fifty cents as a reward while the proprietor is busy punishing sin by firing the clerk.

"I'm in luck," Dick chortles, pocketing his fifty cents. "I guess I'll go to Barnum's tonight, and see the bearded lady, the eight-foot giant, the two-foot dwarf, and the other curiosities too numerous to mention."

Thus, with this unlikely speech, Alger characterizes his hero further and conveys more information about New York in one blow.

Earlier that morning Dick has had another encounter with a customer which Alger uses to introduce a character who will figure in the story later on, and at the same time to demonstrate the curious way his hero talks. The conversation is worth reproducing because it conveys so well the particular quality of this book.

"How much?" asked a gentleman on his way to his office.

"Ten cents," said Dick, dropping his box, and sinking upon his knees on the sidewalk, flourishing his brush with the air of one skilled in his profession.

"Ten cents! Isn't that a little steep?"

"Well, you know 'taint all clear profit," said Dick, who had already set to work. "There's the *blacking* costs something, and I have to get a new brush pretty often."

"And you have a large rent too," said the gentleman quizzically, with a glance at a large hole in Dick's coat.

"Yes, sir," said Dick, always ready to joke; "I have to pay such a big rent for my manshun up on Fifth Avenoo, that I can't afford to take less than ten cents a shine. I'll give you a bully shine, sir."

"Be quick about it, for I am in a hurry. So your house is on Fifth Avenue, is it?"

"It isn't anywhere else," said Dick, and Dick spoke the truth there.

"What tailor do you patronize?" asked the gentleman, surveying Dick's attire.

"Would you like to go to the same one?" asked Dick, shrewdly.

"Well, no; it strikes me that he didn't give you a very good fit."

"This coat once belonged to General Washington," said Dick comically. "He wore it all through the Revolution, and it got torn some, 'cause he fit so hard. When he died he told his widder to give it to some smart young feller that hadn't got none of his own; so she gave it to me. But if you'd like it, sir, to remember General Washington by, I'll let you have it reasonable."

"Thank you, but I wouldn't want to deprive you of it. And did your pants come from General Washington too?"

"No, they was a gift from Lewis Napoleon. Lewis had outgrown 'em and sent 'em to me,—he's bigger than me, and that's why they don't fit."

"It seems you have distinguished friends. Now, my lad, I suppose you would like your money."

"I shouldn't have any objection," said Dick.

"I believe," said the gentleman, examining his pocketbook, "I haven't got anything short of twenty-five cents. Have you got any change?"

"Not a cent," said Dick. "All my money's invested in the Erie Railroad."

"That's unfortunate."

"Shall I get the money changed, sir?"

"I can't wait. I've got to meet an appointment immediately. I'll hand you twenty-five cents, and you can leave the change at my office any time during the day."

"All right, sir, where is it?"

"No. 125 Fulton Street. Shall you remember?"

"Yes, sir. What name?"

"Greyson,—office on second floor."

"All right, sir; I'll bring it."

"I wonder whether the little scamp will prove honest," said Mr. Greyson to himself, as he walked away. "If he does, I'll give him my custom regularly. If he don't, as is most likely, I shan't mind the loss of fifteen cents."

This is a fair sample of Alger narrative, odd grammar and all. As Dick goes on about his morning's business, he overhears a conversation in front of the Astor House, in which a Mr. Whitney expresses regret that he cannot show his young nephew, Frank, around New York. Frank is about Dick's age, fourteen. Always alert for business, Dick volunteers to act as guide. Mr. Whitney thinks this "rather a novel proposal," but he notes that Dick "looks honest," and adds, "He has an open face, and I think can be depended upon."

With this he takes Dick to his room in the Astor and gives him a half-worn "neat gray suit" of Frank's from the boy's trunk; the nephew is on his way to boarding school. He also makes Dick wash, and the bootblack finds "the sensation of cleanliness . . . both new and pleasant." "He now looked quite handsome, and might readily have been taken for a young gentleman." Dick has even blacked his own boots.

Dick and Frank start out on their tour of the city, and the plot stops for chapter after chapter while Alger describes New York. To the young readers in the provinces who had never been there, the description must have seemed graphic and exciting. In retrospect, however, it is unfortunately true that Alger had little more real talent for this kind of descriptive writing than he had for creating believable adult fiction. His mind grasped only superficialities. The real New York escaped him, or else he could not express it.

The tour begins with an exposition of how difficult it is for pedestrians to get across Broadway in the heavy traffic. Once on the other side, the boys walk through City Hall Park, admire its buildings, and then trudge on to Chatham Street, with its merchants trying to pull in customers from the street by physical force if persuasion fails. The walk is interlarded constantly with Dick's characteristic comments. For example, he tells Frank that Baxter Street is the cheapest place for clothes.

"I suppose the Baxter Street tailors are fashionable," Frank jokes.

"In course [*sic*] they are," Dick says. "Me and Horace Greeley always go there for clothes. When Horace gets a new suit,

I always have one made just like it; but I can't go the white hat. It ain't becomin' to my style of beauty."

On Baxter Street, Dick buys a cap for seventy-five cents—further evidence of his extravagance—and they walk on to Broadway and Chambers Street, where A. T. Stewart's splendid department store on the corner is described. "It's the biggest store on Broadway," Dick says, but Alger supplies a footnote: "Mr. Stewart's Tenth Street store was not open at the time Dick spoke."

They walk up Broadway, Dick explaining as they go. He talks about the town's other shopping districts, and speaks lovingly of one of his favorite places, Barnum's Museum, which Alger footnotes: "Since destroyed by fire, and rebuilt farther up Broadway, and again burned down in February."

The city unfolds as they move uptown: the Old Bowery, New York Hospital, and No. 365 Broadway, at the corner of Franklin St., which is Taylor's Saloon—"Now the office of the Merchant's Union Express Co.," says Alger's footnote. Taylor's must not have been a saloon in the conventional sense, because Dick and Frank stop in it for an ice cream.

The title of the following chapter, as in some of the others, might have been taken directly from a guidebook: "Up Broadway to Madison Square." The St. Nicholas and Metropolitan hotels are described, also the Mercantile Library in the Clinton Hall Building, with its 50,000 volumes. "Now not far from 100,000," Alger is careful to add in his running footnotes. Then come Cooper Institute and the Bible House, which brings another revealing remark from Dick.

"Did you ever read the Bible?" Frank asks.

"No," said Dick; "I've heard it's a good book, but I never read one. I ain't much on readin'. It makes my head ache."

Then come Union Square and George Washington's statue, and facing the Square, the Fifth Avenue Hotel. "I once slept on the outside of it," Dick recalls. "They was very reasonable in their charges, and told me I might come again."

"Perhaps sometime you'll be able to sleep inside," Frank answers consolingly.

"I guess that'll be when Queen Victoria goes to the Five Points to live," Dick says ruefully. Alger interrupts him to observe chauvinistically that St. James's Palace is not as fine looking as the Fifth Avenue Hotel. He describes St. James's as a "very ugly looking brick structure, and appears much more like a factory than like the home of royalty."

The boys witness the "drop game" being played, with Dick as the intended victim, but he confounds the crook by passing him a counterfeit bill. By this time Frank is entirely fascinated with his new companion and Dick is relaxed enough to tell him his early history. It is a typical newsboy's story, one Alger must have heard in endless variations. His mother died when he was three, and his father went to sea and disappeared. The people his mother boarded with took care of him until he was seven, then the woman died, the husband went out West, and Dick was thrown on the street. He had started out to be a newsboy, but his sense of humor had undone him. Stuck with a bundle of unsold *Heralds* one morning, he had cried, "Great news! Queen Victoria assassinated!" and a gentleman had threatened to have him "took up." Here Alger was reporting a newsboy practice which began with the first newsboy who shouted on the streets and did not end until the disappearance of the last one. In Dick's case, he was compelled to go into the match business, but he had to burn the last of his matches to keep from freezing.

Frank's reaction to this melancholy recital is pure Alger. " 'You've seen hard times, Dick,' said Frank, compassionately."

As the boys talk and walk, Frank urges Dick to study and work and make something of himself, but warns he must "work in the right way."

"What's the right way?" Dick inquires.

When Frank replies, it is Alger speaking. "You began in the right way when you determined never to steal, or do anything mean or dishonorable, however strongly tempted to do so. That will make people have confidence in you when they come to know you. But, in order to succeed well, you must manage to get as good an education as you can. Until you do, you cannot get a position in an office or counting-room, even to run errands.

" 'That's so,' said Dick soberly. 'I never thought how awful ignorant I was till now.'

" 'That can be remedied with perseverance,' said Frank. 'A year will do a great deal for you.'

" 'I'll go to work and see what I can do,' said Dick, energetically."

The tour continues. On the Third Avenue and Harlem line of horsecars, there is an incident in which a woman has her purse stolen and blames Frank, then discovers it isn't stolen after all. Dick amuses the other passengers by the way he handles the irritable old lady.

Getting off the horsecars the boys walk over to look at Central Park, then in construction. It is described as "very rough and unfinished, no more than a rugged tract of land, very rocky in parts, with no houses of good appearance near it and only rude, temporary workmen's huts to be seen." Frank is disappointed. "My father's got a large pasture that is much nicer," he says.

They take the Sixth Avenue cars to go back downtown, getting off at the Astor House, but the tour continues as they walk to Wall Street, then to the Custom House, which Frank compares to the Parthenon. Dick has never heard of the Parthenon, nor of Athens, for that matter.

Near the Custom House they meet a boy from the country who has just been swindled, and as they are taking the Wall Street ferry to Brooklyn, they see on it the man who did the swindling. Dick recognizes him from the country boy's description and from having seen him before as one of the numerous small-time crooks who haunt Broadway and fleece visiting innocents. Dick threatens to expose him and gets the countryman's fifty dollars back. Returning across the river, they meet the hoodwinked boy—it is the book's first coincidence—and Dick gives his money back to the victim, whom Alger describes condescendingly as "Jonathan," employing his customary stereotype.

By the time they return to the Astor House, Frank and Dick are fast friends. Mr. Whitney is well pleased by Frank's account of their adventures, and delivers to Dick one of those sententious lectures which were to fill so many pages in later books.

"I hope, my lad," he says, "you will prosper and rise in the world. You know in this free country poverty in early life is no bar to a man's advancement."

As proof of this central Alger thesis, Whitney cites his own history, declaring that once he was "as poor as you," but rose because he was "lucky enough to invent a machine, which has brought me in a great deal of money."

Thus, in stating the thesis which was to make him famous, Alger unwittingly shows his own inner disbelief in it, on the same page. Whitney rose from rags to riches, not through virtue and hard work but because he was "lucky enough to invent a machine." Alger has Whitney add hastily that it was "a taste for reading and study" which put him in the way of success, but the damage has been done, and there is a hollow sound to Mr. Whitney's parting cliché-laden advice, "Save your money, my lad, buy books, and determine to be somebody, and you may yet fill an honorable position."

Dick bids good-bye to Frank and Whitney, who gives him five dollars for his day's work and attaches another piece of advice to it: "Sometime when you are a prosperous man, you can repay it in the form of aid to some poor boy, who is struggling upward as you are now."

"I will, sir," Dick says manfully.

The reader is now on page 129 and the plot begins to move at last. With the wealth he has acquired that day, Dick is able to hire a room on Mott Street; for a while, at least, he will not have to sleep in a packing box. Like most rooms occupied by Alger heroes, it is small, mean and dirty. As always, Horatio gives its exact dimensions and location: About ten feet square, on the third floor. It is even smaller than Helen Ford's, which the constant reader will remember was twelve feet square and four flights up.

Next day when he appears in Frank's hand-me-down neat gray suit, Dick is a boy so transformed that the other bootblacks observe him with wonder. One of them is Mickey Maguire from the Five Points, "a stout, redhaired, freckled-faced boy of fourteen. . . . This boy, by his boldness and recklessness, as well as by his personal strength, which was considerable, had acquired an ascendancy among his fellow professionals, and had a gang of subservient followers, whom he led on to acts of ruffianism, not unfrequently terminating in a month or two at Blackwell's 'Island.' " Mickey had served a term there which had made him "a little more cautious about an encounter with the 'copps,' as the members of the city police are, for some unknown reason, styled among the Five-Point boys." ("Cop" was a new slang word when Alger wrote *Ragged Dick.* He persistently spells it with two p's in all his books.)

Mickey picks a fight with Dick, who is "far from quarrelsome" but is "ready to defend himself on all occasions." On this occasion he is about to give Mickey Maguire a sound beating when a "copp" comes up and spoils the fun. The incident is inserted gratuitously, with no relation to the plot, apparently for no other purpose than to let Alger demonstrate his knowledge of New York's gangs of young hoodlums, who in reality made the rumbles of today seem like a harmless exercise.

Dick is becoming ambitious. He puts five dollars in a savings bank, and in doing so, for the first time signs his full name, Richard Hunter, on the account book. It is also the first time —on page 158—that Alger permits his readers to know the hero's full name. He has always been Ragged Dick before, and even refers to himself by that name.

He also acquires a tutor, meaning to repair his educational deficiencies. Alger's time sequence is as vague as usual, but one gathers it was only the day after his tour with Frank that he goes down to Fulton Street and pays back Mr. Greyson's fifteen cents—change from the quarter he could not break the day before. Greyson is so pleased with his honesty that he invites him to come to Sunday school at his church on the corner of Fifth Avenue and Twenty-first Street.

Another quick twist in the plot introduces Henry Fosdick, a homeless shoeshine boy whom Dick takes in as a roommate. Fosdick has a mysterious past. Obviously he has had a good education, but for some reason has not put it to use. He is not a success at shining shoes. Although he is only twelve, Alger notes, Fosdick "knew as much as many boys of fourteen." In exchange for sharing a room, he agrees to teach Dick reading and writing, and also instructs his new friend in how to say his prayers.

The two boys go to Greyson's church, where they meet his wife and his nine-year-old daughter, Ida, and are invited home afterward for Sunday dinner. Little Ida takes a noticeable fancy to Dick, and it appears that Alger has laid the groundwork for one of his long-range romances, but apparently he forgot about it, because Ida disappears, not to be seen again.

Sunday school now becomes a regular affair. On the way home from it the following week, Dick is attacked anew by Mickey Maguire, who fires a stone at him, runs away, and falls down and hurts himself. There is no explanation whatever for this episode. It is simply inserted with no relation to the plot.

Life has truly begun all over again for Dick. In the evening he studies and learns, and begins to speak in a strange mixture of his old patois and standard English. "I'll be satisfied when I know as much as you," he tells Fosdick, and then in the next breath remarks, "Then there ain't any end to learnin'."

The story becomes partly Henry Fosdick's at this point. Dick gives him his savings to buy clothes, in an exemplary display of generosity, and Fosdick, suitably arrayed, tries to get a job as errand boy in a store. Alger uses this incident to show how a poor boy can beat out a rich boy, Roswell Crawford, who is after the same job. Like his success stories, it is a false example. For poor Fosdick would have been thrown out unceremoniously because he is not able to bring any recommendations, except that by an Alger coincidence Mr. Greyson enters the shop to buy a hat at the moment of decision, and remains to vouch for his young friend's character. Since Greyson is an excellent customer, the proprietor hires Fosdick over the other applicants, including Roswell Crawford, who takes his defeat with the sneering bad grace of Alger's rich boys.

Nine months later, Fosdick is a success at the store. His salary has been raised from three dollars to five dollars a month. Dick is doing so well that he has managed to save $117. He studies regularly and has started to attend evening school.

Dick wants to give Tom Wilkins, a fellow bootblack, four dollars to save him and his mother from being evicted, but when he goes to get his bankbook, he discovers it has been stolen from his room. Suspicion falls on a fellow lodger, James Travis, "a bar-tender in a low groggery in Mulberry St." Dick is on hand when the bank opens next morning, explains his trouble and suspicions to an officer, and Travis indeed soon appears, attempting to pass himself off as Dick. He is nabbed by "a burly policeman" and is led away.

The story meanders on in this disconnected manner, every incident virtually complete in itself. Dick hears from Frank, who is at boarding school in Barnton, Connecticut, and in reply writes his first letter. He also looks around for a better job than shoeshining, but business is slow. Now, however, comes the lucky break, the accident which was to become a standard Alger device in the rags-to-riches formula.

One day Dick goes with Fosdick to Brooklyn on an errand for his employer. They take the South Ferry and are enjoying the voyage across the Bay when a man with two children comes on deck. The children, Alger notes in his usual meticulous fashion, are a boy, six, and a girl, eight. The boy leans over the rail and falls into the water. His father's reaction is typically Algeresque. " 'My child!' he exclaimed in anguish,—'who will save my child? A thousand—ten thousand dollars to anyone who will save him!' "

Long before this generous offer, Dick has plunged into the water and rescues the little fellow, quite naturally as he is about to sink "for the third and last time."

"My brave boy," says the father, "I owe you a debt I can never repay. But for your timely service I should now be plunged into an anguish which I cannot think of now without a shudder."

"It wasn't any trouble," Dick says modestly. "I can swim like a top."

Dick is taken to the father's home in Brooklyn and put to bed to dry out, and when he wakes, he is given a new suit of clothes immediately. James Rockwell, the nearly bereaved parent, seems to have forgotten about the ten thousand dollars he promised in an unguarded moment, but he does give Dick a job in his countinghouse on Pearl Street as a clerk, at a magnificent ten dollars a week. In a little less than twenty years, if he saves all his money, Dick will have earned his ten thousand dollars reward.

The disjointed tale comes to an end on this happy note. "Here ends the story of Ragged Dick," Alger writes. "As Fosdick said, he is Ragged Dick no longer. He has taken a step upward, and is determined to mount still higher. There are fresh adventures in store for him, and for others who have been introduced in these pages. Those who have felt interested in his early life will find his history continued in a new volume, forming the second of the series, to be called,—

FAME AND FORTUNE:
or,
The Progress of Richard Hunter"

Nor did Ragged Dick's story end with the promised second volume. A year later, in 1869, Alger was in full stride and wrote four published books, *Ralph Raymond's Heir* (using Arthur

Hamilton Gleason as a pseudonym), *Mark the Match Boy*, *Rough and Ready* (serialized in *Student and Schoolmate*), and *Luck and Pluck*.

Mark the Match Boy reintroduces Richard Hunter, whom Alger was reluctant to let go as his most profitable and successful character to date. He remained Horatio's favorite to the end.

The story of Mark begins with a chapter titled, "Richard Hunter at Home." It is one of Alger's dialogue beginnings, as follows:

"Fosdick," said Richard Hunter, "what was the name of that man who owed your father two thousand dollars, which he never paid him?"

"Hiram Bates," answered Fosdick, in some surprise. "What made you think of him?"

"I thought I remembered the name. He moved out West, didn't he?"

"So I heard at the time."

"Do you happen to remember where? Out West is a very large place."

"I do not know exactly, but I think it was Milwaukie." [*sic*]

"Indeed!" exclaimed Richard Hunter, in visible excitement. "Well, Fosdick, why don't you try to get the debt paid?"

"Of what use would it be? How do I know he is living in Milwaukie now? If I should write him a letter, there isn't much chance of my ever getting an answer."

"Call and see him."

"What, go out to Milwaukie on such a wild-goose chase as that? I can't think what you are driving at, Dick."

"Then I'll tell you, Fosdick. Hiram Bates is now in New York."

"How do you know?" asked Fosdick, with an expression of mingled amazement and incredulity.

"I'll show you."

Richard Hunter pointed to the list of hotel arrivals in the "Evening Express," which he held in his hand. Among the arrivals at the Astor House occurred the name of Hiram Bates, from Milwaukie.

"If I am not mistaken," he said, "that is the name of your father's debtor."

"I don't know but you are right," said Fosdick, thoughtfully.

After a little more of this stupefying conversation, Alger steps in to identify his characters:

While the boys,—for the elder of the two is but eighteen—are making preparations to go out, a few explanations may be required by the reader. Those who have read "Ragged Dick" and "Fame and Fortune,"—the preceding volumes in this series,—will understand that less than three years before Richard Hunter was an ignorant and ragged bootblack about the streets, and Fosdick, though possessing a better education, was in the same business. By a series of upward steps, partly due to good fortune, but largely to his own determination to improve, and hopeful energy, Dick had now become a book-keeper in the establishment of Rockwell & Cooper, on Pearl Street, and possessed the confidence and good wishes of the firm in a high degree. . . .

The room which they now occupied was situated in St. Mark's Place, which forms the eastern portion of Eighth Street. It was a front room on the third floor, and was handsomely furnished. There was a thick carpet, of tasteful figure, on the floor. Between the two front windows was a handsome bureau, surmounted by a large mirror. There was a comfortable sofa, chairs covered with hair-cloth, a centre-table covered with books, crimson curtains, which gave a warm and cosey look to the room when lighted up in the evening, and all the accessories of a well-furnished room which is used at the same time as parlor and chamber. This, with an excellent table, afforded a very agreeable home to the boys,—a home which, in these days, would cost considerably more, but for which, at the time of which I write, sixteen dollars was a fair price.

It may be thought that, considering how recently Richard Hunter had been a ragged bootblack, content to sleep in boxes and sheltered doorways, and live at the cheapest restaurants, he had become very luxurious in his tastes. Why did he not get a cheaper boarding-place, and save up the difference in price? No doubt this consideration will readily suggest itself to the minds of some of my young readers.

As Richard Hunter had a philosophy of his own on this subject, I may as well explain it here. He had observed that those young men who out of economy contented themselves with small and cheerless rooms, in which there was no provision for a fire, were driven in the evening to the streets, theatres, and hotels, for the comfort which they could not find at home. Here they felt obliged to spend money to an extent of which they probably were not themselves fully aware, and in the end wasted considerably more than the two or three dollars a week extra which would have provided them with a comfortable home. But this was not all. In the roamings spent outside many laid the foundations of wrong habits, which eventually led to ruin or shortened their lives. They lost all the chances of improvement which they might have secured by study at home in the long winter evenings, and which in the end might have qualified them for posts of higher responsibility, and with a larger compensation.

Richard Hunter was ambitious. He wanted to rise to an honorable place in the community, and he meant to earn it by hard study. So Fosdick and he were in the habit of spending a portion of every evening in improving reading or study. Occasionally he went to some place of amusement, but he enjoyed thoroughly the many evenings when, before a cheerful fire, with books in their hands, his room-mate and himself were adding to their stock of knowledge. The boys had for over a year taken lessons in French and mathematics, and were now able to read the French language with considerable ease.

After this extended exposition, which was in reality an argument with himself, an elaborate rationalization of Richard Hunter's brief life and works, Alger shows us that Ragged Dick hasn't really changed so much after all. A fellow lodger who thinks his way of life is rather queer, sneers, "Are you studying for a college professor?"

"I don't know," Dick replies "good-humoredly," exhibiting a flash of the old Ragged Dick, "but I'm open to proposals, as the oyster remarked. If you know any first-class institution that would like a dignified professor, of extensive acquirements, just mention me, will you?"

Mark the Match Boy's story is somewhat lost in this volume, so involved is Alger with characters from earlier books in the series. Fosdick comes into money, Richard advances his fortunes, and Roswell Crawford appears as a clerk in a store, doing his best to come to a bad end. Even Mickey Maguire appears, somewhat subdued and having risen not at all. Mr. O'Connor, the efficient superintendent, is there and the Lodging House itself, as has been noted earlier. Mark's simple story becomes merely an annex of Dick's, as he becomes Richard Hunter's ward. He turns out, of course, to be the long-lost grandson of Mr. Bates.

It will be observed that there are no girls to clutter the story. In this series, Alger has moved completely into the world of boys, and girls are nearly excluded except for little Ida's brief appearances in *Ragged Dick.* Richard Hunter, even at eighteen, does not appear to be aware that there is such a thing as another sex in the world. He is a completely sexless hero, reflecting the complete maleness of Alger's own world between his first flight from Paris and his meeting with Una in Peekskill.

There were three more books to come in the "Ragged Dick Series." *Rough and Ready; or, Life Among the New York Newsboys,* which appeared in the same year as *Mark,* was one of them. The other two appeared in the following year, 1870, as *Rufus and Rose; or, The Fortunes of Rough and Ready*, and *Ben, the Luggage Boy; or, Among the Wharves.*

In these sequels, Richard Hunter sinks out of sight as Alger tells his Ragged Dick and Mark the Match Boy stories over and over. He has no interest in Richard Hunter as a grown man, except as an example of success.

Aside from the psychological implications, there was no reason for him to be interested. In the "Ragged Dick Series" he perfected the formula he had discovered after several fumbling starts, although "discovered" may not be the word. It might be more accurate to say he stumbled into it, as he did into the episodes of his own life. In any case, *Ragged Dick* and its successors in the series had fairly launched him. The rest was easy.

CHAPTER 7

Alger's ventures into nonfiction came about as the result of a publishing idea in the house of J. R. Anderson & Co. After President Garfield was assassinated in 1881, several publishers prepared to rush into print with various kinds of volumes commemorating the dead statesman's life. Anderson hoped to be first by hiring a writer known for his speed, and at the same time he intended to take advantage of the ready-made market already created by Alger. Presumably Anderson also anticipated a good sale to the adult market as well.

In one respect the house chose well in selecting Alger. He produced the book for them in a record thirteen days, as has been noted, and his established audience did ensure a good if not sensational sale. As a book, however, if Anderson cared about that aspect of it, *From Canal Boy to President; or, The Boyhood and Manhood of James A. Garfield,* may well be the worst Alger ever wrote after his initial success. It is fictionalized biography—a biographical novel, we would call it today—but it lacks the skill which can make this kind of book a valid literary form. It reads exactly like what it is: a quick, jerry-built attempt to capitalize on the sensational death of a popular President. Alger dedicated it solemnly "To Harry and James Garfield, Whose Private Sorrow Is the Public Grief, This Memorial of Their Illustrious Father Is Inscribed with the Warmest Sympathy."

In his inevitable preface, Alger is more than usually apologetic, apparently having no illusions about what he has done.

> If I am asked (he says), why I add one more to the numerous lives of our dead President, I answer, in the words of the Hon. Chauncey M. Depew, because "our annals afford no such incentive to you as does his life, and it will become one of the Republic's household stories."
>
> I have conceived, therefore, that a biography, written with a view to interest young people in the facts of his great career, would be a praiseworthy undertaking. The biography of General Garfield, however imperfectly executed, can not but be profitable to the reader. In this story, which I have made as attractive as I am able, I make no claim to originality. I have made free use of such materials as came within my reach, including incidents and reminiscences made public during the last summer, and I trust I have succeeded, in a measure, in conveying a correct idea of a character whose nobility we have only learned to appreciate since death has snatched our leader from us.
>
> I take pleasure in acknowledging my obligations to two Lives of Garfield, one by Edmund Kirke, the other by Major J. M. Dundy. Such of my readers as desire a more extended account of the later life of General Garfield, I refer to these well-written and instructive works.

It must be said for Alger that he made contemporary history palatable to his boy readers. His life of Garfield is written like any other Alger tale, with imagined dialogue in large doses. Some of the chapter titles are reminiscent of his book titles: "John Jordan's Dangerous Journey," and "Garfield's Bold Strategy."

When Garfield is elected President, Alger observes, revealing more than he intended: "Had this been a story of the imagination, such as I have often written, I should not have dared to crown it with such an ending. In view of my hero's humble beginnings, I should expect to have it severely criticized as utterly incredible, but reality is oftentimes stranger than romance, and this is notably illustrated in Garfield's wonderful career."

Possibly in deference to the grief of Garfield's sons, to whom the book is dedicated, but more likely because sex appears never and violence seldom in an Alger book, Horatio skips over lightly the details of Garfield's assassination. He does not even name the assassin, referring to him as a "wretched political adventurer." Thus the history may have been palatable to his audience, but the view remains superficial.

The book is shamelessly padded at the end, where Alger reprints as a chapter the entire eulogy delivered by Chauncey Depew to the G.A.R., and as a last chapter, the complete eulogy delivered by B. A. Hinsdale, who succeeded Garfield as president of Hiram College.

Nevertheless, the volume was a success and Alger was encouraged from several sources to continue his "Boyhood and Manhood Series of Illustrious Americans." This time the choice of subject was Horatio's, and he chose Daniel Webster, a man he had admired all his life. As a boy he had been stirred by Webster's orations, and when the great man died during Alger's senior year at Harvard, it was as though a personal friend had gone.

Alger had memorized several of Webster's speeches, and he was fond of reciting them to the boys at the House. His favorite peroration was Webster's splendid secession speech, concluding: "Secession! Peaceable secession! Sir, your eyes and mine are never destined to see that miracle. The dismemberment of this vast country without convulsions! The breaking up of the fountains of the great deep without ruffling the surface! . . . Where is the line to be drawn? What States are to secede? What is to remain America? What am I to be? An American no longer? . . ."

From Farm Boy to Senator, Being the History of the Boyhood and Manhood of Daniel Webster, was a labor of love, which may account for the fact that it was Alger's longest book. For reasons which are not clear, Anderson was not the publisher. The story itself was an expanded and rewritten version of a serial Alger had written for *The New York Weekly* ten years before, refurbished to fit the new series Horatio had launched with Garfield. It was published in 1882 by J. S. Ogilvie & Co., a house which flourished for a time at 31 Rose Street in New York.

For once Alger's preface is neither perfunctory nor exhortatory, but reflects the genuine enthusiasm he brought to this work. He writes:

But thirty years have elapsed since the death of Daniel Webster, and there is already danger that, so far as young people are concerned, he will become an historic reminiscence. Schoolboys, who declaim the eloquent extracts from his speeches which are included in all the school speakers, are indeed able to form some idea of his great oratorical powers and the themes which called them forth; but I have found that young classical students, as a rule, know more of Cicero's life than of his. It seems to me eminently fitting that the leading incidents in the life of our great countryman, his struggles for an education, the steps by which he rose to professional and political distinction, should be made familiar to American boys. I have therefore essayed a "story biography" which I have tried to write in such a manner as to make it attractive to young people, who are apt to turn away from ordinary biographies, in the fear that they may prove dull.

I have not found my task an easy one. Webster's life is so crowded with great services and events, it is so interwoven with the history of the nation, that to give a fair idea of him in a volume of ordinary size is almost impossible. I have found it necessary to leave out some things, and to refer briefly to others, lest my book should expand to undue proportions. Let me acknowledge then, with the utmost frankness, that my work is incomplete, and necessarily so. This causes me less regret, because those whom I may be fortunate enough to interest in my subject will readily find all that they wish to know in the noble Life of Webster, by George Ticknor Curtis, the captivating Reminiscences, by Peter Harvey, the Private Correspondence, edited by Fletcher Webster, and the collection of

Mr. Webster's speeches, edited by Mr. Everett. They will also find interesting views of Mr. Webster's senatorial career in the Reminiscences of Congress, by Charles W. March.

If this unpretending volume shall contribute in any way to extend the study of Mr. Webster's life and works, I shall feel that my labor has been well bestowed.

But no amount of enthusiasm could improve Alger's work. Whatever he did, the result was the same. *From Farm Boy To Senator* begins with one of his dialogue openings, and the first chapter is titled "The Cotton Handkerchief," in the manner of his regular novels. Here is the way the book begins:

"Where are you going, Daniel?"
"To Mr. Hoyt's store."
"I'll go in with you. Where is 'Zekial this morning?"
"I left him at work on the farm."
"I suppose you will both be farmers when you grow up."
"I don't know," answered Daniel thoughtfully. "I don't think I shall like it, but there isn't anything else to do in Salisbury."
"You might keep a store and teach school like Master Hoyt."
"Perhaps so. I should like it better than farming."

Is this a conversation between one of Alger's young teen-age heroes and an adult, as it appears to be? Not at all. Alger continues: "Daniel was but eight years old, a boy of striking appearance, with black hair and eyes, and a swarthy complexion. He was of slender frame, and his large dark eyes, deep set beneath an overhanging brow, gave a singular appearance to the thin face of the delicate looking boy."

In the early part of the book, before Webster grows up and enters public life, Alger is able to invent long stretches of dialogue and to dramatize the boyhood scenes. Then, as time passes, there is less and less dialogue, more actual quotations from Webster's speeches, and straight narration, much of it paraphrased from the histories acknowledged in the introduction.

Horatio could not treat his subject as an adult because he was neither a historian nor a biographer and because he was, in this instance as in others, not capable of writing about adult lives, even when the material was factual.

Nevertheless, Alger made one more attempt at biographical fiction and added a third and final volume to his "Boyhood and Manhood" series with the publication in 1883 of *Abraham Lincoln, the Backwoods Boy; or, How a Young Rail-Splitter Became President.* Anderson was again the original publisher, but the book was so popular it went through several reprints by other houses, and after Alger's death, it became a profitable Street & Smith paperback title, with some slight revisions by an unknown hand.

This book has had the benefit of an examination by an Alger collector and Lincoln scholar, Jordan D. Fiore, who summarized his study in a paper published by the Illinois State Historical Society Journal, in its autumn, 1953, issue. Fiore at the time was assistant to the director of libraries and museums and instructor of bibliography in the College of Liberal Arts at Boston University.

He notes that the book, like so many of the others, "shows signs of having been written hastily and carelessly," although it seems to have made little difference whether Horatio took his time or not. As in his two previous efforts in the field, he used no primary sources, noting in his preface: "I can hardly hope at this late date to have contributed many new facts, or found much material." This is an astonishing statement considering the shelves of new material turned up by Lincoln scholars since 1883. Alger simply followed his usual method of consulting the standard studies of Lincoln which were then in print, and, as Fiore notes, he quoted generously, sometimes without use of quotation marks, and added several of the more popular Lincoln anecdotes, printing them at full value without qualification.

The opening portions of the book follow the pattern laid down in the two previous volumes. Alger uses imagined dialogue and fictionalization to reconstruct scenes of young Abe at home, at school, and in his first jobs. Anecdotes from other biographies are repeated nearly verbatim, and the well known events in Lincoln's early life are recounted in their popular versions.

As always, Horatio seasoned his narrative with moral observations at every possible point. Thus, in narrating Lincoln's rescue from drowning at seven, he writes: "God looks after the lives of His chosen instruments, and saves them for His work." Again, commenting on Abe's hard work and poverty in his youth, he notes: "But Abe is not to be pitied for the hardships of his lot. That is the way strong men are made."

Alger quotes with obvious approval Lincoln's famous letter in which he lectures his stepbrother, John D. Johnston: "Your thousand pretences for not getting along better are all nonsense. . . . *Go to work* is the only cure for your case." That was right out of the Alger lexicon, and Horatio could not help adding smugly:

> Nothing can be plainer, or more in accordance with common sense than this advice. Though it was written for the benefit of one person only, I feel that I am doing my young, or possibly some older, readers a service in transferring it to my pages, and commending them to heed it. . . . In this country, fortunately, there are few places where an industrious man can not get a living, if he is willing to accept such work as falls in his way. This willingness often turns the scale, and converts threatening ruin into prosperity and success.

The omissions Alger made in telling Lincoln's story were entirely characteristic. He never mentions such controversial issues as the legitimacy of Nancy Hanks, the romance with Ann Rutledge, or Lincoln's troubles with his wife. Nor does he hesitate to edit a Lincoln letter in the interests of morality. For example, Abe's letter to his stepbrother of January 12, 1851, about the impending death of Thomas Lincoln is quoted, including the statement that Abe cannot visit his father because

Mary is "sick-abed." But, as Fiore points out, Alger carefully omitted the further explanation: "It is a case of baby-sickness, and I suppose it is not dangerous." Pregnancy and childbirth are never mentioned in Alger's books, and he did not think it proper to mention that Mary was then carrying the third Lincoln child, William.

For every anecdote Alger borrowed from the several biographies available to him, he had a corresponding moralistic comment in his own familiar style. After telling the anecdote about Lincoln's error as a store clerk in making change, and how he rectified it, Alger remarks: "If I were a capitalist, I would be willing to lend money to such a young man without security."

He was selective in his anecdotes, choosing only the ones which could be used for positive moral comment, like the change story, illustrating Lincoln's honesty. He hammered every point home. The change story is followed by the one about Abe's miscalculation in weighing tea, and what he did to set it right. Alger steps in to observe: "I think my young readers will begin to see that the name so often given, in later times, to President Lincoln, of 'Honest Old Abe,' was well deserved. A man who begins by strict honesty in his youth is not likely to change as he grows older, and mercantile honesty is some guarantee of political honesty."

Again, commenting on how Lincoln was compelled by Josiah Crawford to work for three days in payment for a borrowed book damaged in a storm, Alger says he thinks the penalty was "only equitable, and I am glad to think that Abe was willing to act honorably in the matter." As Fiore observes, "Alger boys always took the honorable road, whatever the cost."

That is the way the Lincoln story develops in Alger's hands: favorable anecdote followed by moral comment, over and over. Everything is turned to this advantage, even Lincoln's adversities, which are only demonstrations, in Alger's eyes, of how God moves "in a mysterious way, His wonders to perform." Thus, venturing into political analysis, Alger sees virtue in the fact of

Lincoln's defeat for the Senate in 1858, reasoning that if he had been elected he might possibly have alienated enough Republicans by some erroneous, unspecified actions to prevent his nomination and election in 1860. If that had happened, he observes, "The nation would never have discovered the leader who, under Providence, led it out of the wilderness, and conducted it to peace and freedom."

Once Alger seems to feel that he may have overdone it, and protests without much conviction that he does not wish to "moralize over-much," although he has done nothing else. Then he recalls that "in the lives of all there are present disappointments that lead to ultimate success and prosperity," and he cites the youthful ambitions of Garfield and Washington to go to sea —ambitions which they were properly dissuaded from so that they might become successes in other fields. Alger even notes Oliver Cromwell's early decision to emigrate to America, which was frustrated, leaving him to remain "in his own country to control its destiny, and take a position at the head of affairs." The moral is obvious. "Remember this when your cherished plans are defeated," Alger charges his young readers. "There is a higher wisdom than ours that shapes and directs our lives."

Having acknowledged these and other distortions, Fiore arrives at a fair estimate of Alger as a Lincoln biographer. He remarks that "few Lincoln students profess to have read" Horatio's volume "and not one considers the book a good biography. But the work was not entirely without merit in its time. It had value as a portrait for young people in the 1880's, when Alger was perhaps more real to American boys than was Abraham Lincoln. In this book, one of the earlier studies designed for juvenile reading, the picture of Lincoln was a fair and adequate one, and contributed to the popular impression of him then held by the youth of America."

Nevertheless, for reasons which he never explained, Alger gave up his "Boyhood and Manhood" series after the Lincoln book. Probably it was because he found writing these worthy books about worthy men unexciting. He much preferred the newsboys' stories and the familiar formula for presenting them, in both of which he felt much more at home. They were less work and far more rewarding, in every way. True, he did hope to write a biography of Bryan, a man whom he admired intensely, and whose Cross of Gold speech he knew by heart but never dared recite to the boys because it was too partisan. He would have written the book, but he conceived the idea too late and died before he could get to it.

It may have been as well. Possibly there is truth in Mayes's observation that there was "some kinship between the extraordinary ambitions these two men had, and in their failures," but it would not have resulted in a book any different than the others, it seems safe to say. The outer limits of Horatio Alger's talents were marked by every volume he turned out. Nothing could have induced him to exceed them.

EPILOGUE

WE HAVE come to the end of our story, as Horatio himself might have written, but unfortunately there is no way to tie up the package neatly in the manner of an Alger epilogue. His characters moved on into the rosy glow of a happy, successful adult life, where Alger could not follow them. When his limited imagination failed him in this respect, as it sometimes did, he retreated to the safety of a favorite phrase, "It is not given to me to know."

Certainly it is not given to anyone to make a final estimate of Alger. There will be as many varying opinions about him as there are writers and critics who consider his work. Of these there is no overwhelming number. The fact that this volume is only the second Alger biography in nearly forty years is proof that those who survey and assess the American literary scene have not considered his work important enough to merit their serious attention. Literary critics scarcely mention him at all, nor do the literary historians. His muddled, strange life has not attracted a single scholar of prominence, as far as an extended study is concerned.

As we advance farther into the Space Age, it appears inevitable that Alger will continue to recede into the mists of a century which will seem ever more remote and improbable.

When the men still alive who remember reading his books as boys are dead, he will lose the last of his audience. A contemporary high school generation whose idols are J. D. Salinger and William Golding are not likely to find anything to detain them in Alger's work, if indeed they have ever heard of it. Horatio's curious life and his stilted, old-fashioned books are surely teetering on the brink of total oblivion. This volume may well be the last look at them.

What refuses to die is the idea his books represent, nor does the steady advance of society from laissez faire to the welfare state appear to be obliterating it. The "Horatio Alger story," "the Alger-like climb to success," "the Horatio Alger image"—these are phrases which recur again and again today in newspapers, magazines and books. The idea has strong survival power.

It survives because it symbolizes the individual's hope, his dream of rising above his circumstances to "be somebody," against the opposition of "they," meaning the Establishment. Rychard Fink, professor of philosophy at Newark (N.J.) State College, points this out in his introduction to a recent paperback collection of Alger books, which includes *Ragged Dick* and *Mark, the Match Boy*.

"There is evidence in over one hundred novels that Alger pleaded the case of the common man and doubted the morality of many of those who owned and managed society," Professor Fink observes. He cites Dale Carnegie, Norman Vincent Peale and the Lloyd C. Douglas school of fiction as Alger's contemporary successors, and remarks: "He helped make success a quasi-religious moral idea that leaves people who fail (whether in spelling or in something bigger) with the conviction they are unloved. He stands for trying harder, wanting more, and contributing to the community chest. The people who want to distribute Sears, Roebuck catalogs to Russians to persuade them of America's superiority are his disciples, too."

The persistence of the rags-to-riches idea in American popular thought suggests that perhaps some critics and historians have neglected Alger unwisely—the critics because he was popular, not literary, and the historians because they regard his influence as minimal. They may prove to be right in the end, but it is possible they have dismissed Alger too hastily as a reflector of something important in American life. *The Saturday Evening Post*, from 1900 to 1930, has been dismissed in the same way, and for the same reasons, yet no one can pretend to understand the American people without having examined what the *Post* printed and said during those three critical decades, when the magazine's great editor, George Horace Lorimer, was closer to the reality of America than any occupant of the White House, and much nearer than any of the critics who sneered at the *Post* as a middle-class, bourgeois publication.

"Any person who wants to know his country should get acquainted with Horatio Alger. It is dangerous to ignore a man whose ideas hang on so stubbornly," Professor Fink asserts, and he is right. As we have seen, it is impossible to take Alger's plots and characters seriously, and his own life can be viewed as nothing more than an implausible tragedy, played out in mingled pathos and bathetic comedy. The American Dream itself has been recast to fit the new organization of society.

Still, the idea persists. It may be dying, but it has lasted for a century and its vitality has survived two world wars which have made a profound change in American life. Rags to riches—the rise of the individual from obscurity to success—is not an idea which died with the nineteenth century. Reorganized, redirected, channeled it may be, but it remains, whatever its true validity, a vital part of the American character.

AN ALGER BIBLIOGRAPHY

The problem of compiling a complete and accurate bibliography of Horatio Alger's books is so formidable that it will probably never be done to everyone's satisfaction. By far the best in print is Frank Gruber's, published in *The Antiquarian Bookman* of November 13, 1948, at the conclusion of an article about the Alger books written from the collector's standpoint. As this writer and collector notes, not even the Library of Congress possesses a complete set of Alger first editions and a bibliography has never been compiled. Gruber's own checklist is the fruit of six years' collecting.

Other checklists exhibit the usual errors of duplicated titles. Some even carry titles which Alger meant to write and did not, or others, as Gruber says, which "never existed but sounded as though they *might* be Alger titles." The reprint publishers further complicated the problem by retitling some of the Alger books they published.

An independent investigation confirms the accuracy of Gruber's contention that there are only 106 genuine Alger books. Eleven others published under Alger's name were the work of Edward Stratemeyer, using the pseudonym of Arthur M. Winfield. They appeared posthumously under circumstances previously described. The Stratemeyer Algers and other late Algers are scarce but not rare books, as are first editions of *Ragged Dick*. Even harder to find, as Gruber notes, are the eight books published in paper wrappers by Burt's Boys' Home Library, and Munsey's Popular

Series for Boys and Girls. Only two Alger books are officially classified as rare: *Timothy Crump's Ward* and *Bertha's Christmas Vision.*

The list which follows is basically Gruber's, with whatever additions and corrections, none of them important, further investigation has disclosed. The 106 authentic Alger titles are listed first, in chronological order, followed by the spurious Stratemeyer titles and a few others of unknown origin which are not certified as authentic. Appended are three more which appeared in magazines but were never published in book form.

While the author believes the following list to be the most complete and accurate yet published, it is not guaranteed against error. The body of Alger's work still awaits the meticulous research of the professional bibliographer who believes his task is worth the effort.

1856—*Bertha's Christmas Vision*

1857—*Nothing to Do* Anonymous (James French & Co., Boston) A narrative poem.

1864—*Frank's Campaign; or, What Boys Can Do on the Farm for the Camp* (A. K. Loring, Boston) (Campaign Series)

1865—*Paul Prescott's Charge* (Loring) (Campaign Series)

1866—*Helen Ford* (Loring)

Timothy Crump's Ward Anonymous (Loring) Also published in paper wrappers, in Loring's Railway Companions series; later rewritten as *Jack's Ward,* under Alger's name.

1867—*Charlie Codman's Cruise* (Loring) (Campaign Series)

1868—*Ragged Dick; or, Street Life in New York with the Bootblacks* (Loring) Serialized in *Student and Schoolmate,* 1867 (Ragged Dick Series) *Fame and Fortune; or, The Progress of Richard Hunter* (Loring) Serialized in *Student and Schoolmate,* 1868 (Ragged Dick Series)

1869—*Ralph Raymond's Heir,* by Arthur Hamilton Gleason (pseudonym)

Mark the Match Boy; or, Richard Hunter's Ward (Loring) (Ragged Dick Series)

Rough and Ready; or, Life Among the New York Newsboys (Loring) Serialized in *Student and Schoolmate,* 1869 (Ragged Dick Series)

Luck and Pluck; or, John Oakley's Inheritance (Loring) (Luck and Pluck Series—First Series)

1870—*Rufus and Rose; or, The Fortunes of Rough and Ready* (Loring) Serialized in *Student and Schoolmate,* 1870 (Ragged Dick Series)

Sink or Swim; or, Harry Redmond's Resolve (Loring) Serialized in *Ballou's Monthly* (Luck and Pluck Series—First Series)

Ben, the Luggage Boy; or, Among the Wharves (Loring) (Ragged Dick Series)

1871—*Paul the Peddler; or, The Adventures of a Young Street Merchant* (Loring) Serialized in *Student and Schoolmate,* 1871 (Tattered Tom Series—First Series)

Strong and Steady; or, Paddle Your Own Canoe (Loring) Serialized in *Young Israel,* 1871 (Luck and Pluck Series—First Series)

Tattered Tom; or, The Story of a Street Arab (Loring) (Tattered Tom Series—First Series)

1872—*Slow and Sure; or, From the Sidewalk to the Shop* (Loring) Serialized in *Student and Schoolmate,* 1872 (Tattered Tom Series—First Series)

Strive and Succeed; or, The Progress of Walter Conrad (Loring) Serialized in *Young Israel,* 1872 (Luck and Pluck Series—First Series)

Phil the Fiddler; or, The Young Street Musician (Loring) (Tattered Tom Series—First Series)

1873—*Try and Trust; or, The Story of Abner Holden's Bound Boy* (Loring) Serialized in *The New York Weekly,* 1871 (Luck and Pluck Series—Second Series)

Bound to Rise; or, Up the Ladder (Loring) (Luck and Pluck Series—Second Series)

1874—*Risen from the Ranks; or, Harry Walton's Success* (Loring) Serialized in *Young Israel* (Luck and Pluck Series—Second Series)

Brave and Bold; or, The Story of a Factory Boy (Loring) Serialized in *The New York Weekly* (Brave and Bold Series)

Julius; or, The Street Boy out West (Loring) (Tattered Tom Series—Second Series)

1875—*Jack's Ward; or, The Boy Guardian* (Loring) Slightly rewritten version of *Timothy Crump's Ward* (Brave and Bold Series)

Herbert Carter's Legacy; or, The Inventor's Son (Loring) Serialized in *Young Israel,* 1875 (Luck and Pluck Series—Second Series)

The Young Outlaw; or, Adrift in the World (Loring) (Tattered Tom Series—Second Series)

Grand'ther Baldwin's Thanksgiving (Loring) Poems.

Seeking His Fortune, by Alger and Olive A. Cheney (his sister) (Loring) A collection of "dialogs" (one-act plays)

1876—*Sam's Chance; or, How He Improved It* (Loring) (Tattered Tom Series—Second Series)

Shifting for Himself; or, Gilbert Greyson's Fortune (Loring) (Brave and Bold Series)

1877—*Wait and Hope; or, Ben Bradford's Motto* (Loring) Serialized in *Young Israel,* 1877, as *Wait and Win* (Brave and Bold Series)

1878—*The Western Boy.* Reissued as *Tom the Bootblack; or, The Road to Success* (Ogilvie & Co., New York)

The Young Adventurer; or, Tom's Trip Across the Plains (Loring) Serialized in *Young Israel* (Pacific Series)

1879—*The District Telegraph Boy* (Loring) (Tattered Tom Series—Second Series)

The Young Miner; or, Tom Nelson in California (Loring) (Pacific Series)

1880—*Tony the Hero; or, A Brave Boy's Adventure with a Tramp* (Ogilvie & Co.) Reissued as *Tony the Tramp.* Serialized in *The New York Weekly,* 1878.

The Young Explorer; or, Among the Sierras (Loring) (Pacific Series)

1881—*From Canal Boy to President* (J. R. Anderson & Co.)

1882—*Ben's Nugget* (Porter & Coates) (Pacific Series)

From Farm Boy to Senator (Ogilvie) Serialized in *The New York Weekly,* 1872.

1883—*The Train Boy* (Carleton & Co.) Serialized in *The New York Weekly,* 1883.

Abraham Lincoln, the Backwoods Boy; or, How a Young

Rail-Splitter Became President (J. R. Anderson & H. S. Allen)

The Young Circus Rider (Porter & Coates) (Atlantic Series)

1884—*Dan the Detective* (G. W. Carleton & Co.) Reissued as *Dan, the Newsboy*. Serialized in *The New York Weekly*, 1880.

Do and Dare; or, A Brave Boy's Fight for a Fortune (Porter & Coates) Serialized in *Golden Argosy*, 1883.

1885—*Hector's Inheritance; or, The Boys of Smith Institute* (Porter & Coates) Serialized in *Golden Argosy*, 1883 (Atlantic Series)

1886—*Helping Himself; or, Grant Thornton's Ambition* (Porter & Coates) Serialized in *Golden Argosy*, 1884 (Atlantic Series)

1887—*Joe's Luck* (A. L. Burt Co.) Boys' Home Library No. 1 (paper wrappers) Serialized in *The New York Weekly*, 1878.

Frank Fowler (Burt) Reissued as *The Cash Boy*. Boys' Home Library No. 4 (paper wrappers) Serialized in *The New York Weekly*.

The Store Boy (Porter & Coates) Serialized in *Golden Argosy*, 1883 (Way to Success Series)

The Adventures of a New York Telegraph Boy; or, "Number 91," by Arthur Lee Putnam (pseudonym) Reissued as *Mark Mason's Victory; or, The Trials and Triumphs of a New York Telegraph Boy*. Munsey's Popular Series for Boys and Girls, No. 5. (paper wrappers) Serialized in *Golden Argosy*, 1886 (Appeared later, slightly rewritten, under two other titles; see *A.D.T. 79* entry in 1892)

1888—*Robert Coverdale's Triumph; or, On the Wave of Success* (Burt) Serialized in *Golden Argosy*, 1881. Reissued as *Robert Coverdale's Struggle*.

Tom Thatcher's Fortune (Burt) Boys' Home Library No. 11 (paper wrappers) Serialized in *The New York Weekly*, 1882.

Tom Temple's Career (Burt) Boys' Home Library No. 14 (paper wrappers) Serialized in *The New York Weekly*, 1879.

The Errand Boy; or, How Phil Brent Won Success (Burt) Boys' Home Library No. 14 (paper wrappers) Serialized in *The New York Weekly*, 1883.

Bob Burton; or, The Young Ranchman of Missouri (Porter

& Coates) Serialized in *Golden Argosy,* 1889 (Way to Success Series)

Tom Tracy; or, The Trials of a New York Newsboy, by Arthur Lee Putnam (pseudonym) Munsey's Popular Series for Boys and Girls, No. 10 (paper wrappers) Serialized in *Golden Argosy,* 1887.

The Young Acrobat of the Great North American Circus Munsey's Popular Series for Boys and Girls, No. 8 (paper wrappers)

1889—*Luke Walton; or, The Chicago Newsboy* (Porter & Coates) Serialized in *Golden Argosy,* 1887 (Way to Success Series)

Adrift in New York; or, Tom and Florence Braving the World (Porter & Coates)

1890—*Ned Newton,* by Arthur Lee Putnam (pseudonym) (U.S. Book Co.) Serialized in *Golden Argosy,* 1887.

Struggling Upward; or, Luke Larkin's Luck (Porter & Coates) Serialized in *Golden Argosy,* 1886 (Way to Success Series)

The Erie Train Boy (U.S. Book Co.) Serialized in *Golden Argosy,* 1890.

Mark Stanton, by Arthur Lee Putnam (pseudonym) Reissued as *Both Sides of the Continent; or, Mark Stanton* (U.S. Book Co.)

The Odds Against Him. Reissued as *Driven from Home; or, Carl Crawford's Experience* (Penn Publishing Co.) Serialized in *Golden Argosy,* 1889.

The $500 Check (U.S. Book Co.) Serialized in *Golden Argosy,* 1888.

1891—*Dean Dunham; or, The Waterford Museum* (U.S. Book Co.) Serialized in *Golden Argosy,* 1888.

A New York Boy, by Arthur Lee Putnam (pseudonym) (U.S. Book Co.) Serialized in *Golden Argosy,* 1888.

1892—*The Young Boatman.* Reissued as *Grit, the Young Boatman of Pine Point* (Penn Publishing Co.) Serialized in *The New York Weekly,* 1884.

Digging for Gold (Porter & Coates) Serialized in *Golden Argosy,* 1891.

A.D.T. 79, by Arthur Lee Putnam (pseudonym) Reissued

as *Mark Mason's Victory, and Trials and Triumphs of Mark Mason* (U.S. Book Co.) Serialized in *Golden Argosy*, 1892.

Tom Brace; Who He Was and How He Fared, by Arthur Lee Putnam (pseudonym) (U.S. Book Co.) Serialized in *Golden Argosy*, 1889.

Ralph Raymond's Heir (F. M. Lupton Co.) Published in 1869 as an adult novel under pseudonym Arthur Hamilton Gleason. Reissued, slightly rewritten, under Alger's name.

Walter Griffith; or, The Adventures of a Young Street Salesman, by Arthur Lee Putnam (pseudonym) Reissued as *Striving for Fortune* (U.S. Book Co.) Serialized in *Golden Argosy*, 1887.

1893—*Facing the World; or, The Haps and Mishaps of Harry Vane* (Porter & Coates) Serialized in *Golden Argosy*, 1885 (New World Series)

In a New World; or, Among the Gold Fields of Australia (Porter & Coates) Serialized in *Golden Argosy* (New World Series)

Ben Bruce; or, Scenes in the Life of a Bowery Newsboy, by Arthur Lee Putnam (pseudonym) (U.S. Book Co.) Serialized in *Golden Argosy*, 1892.

1894—*Only an Irish Boy; or, The Story of Andy Burke's Fortunes* (Porter & Coates) Serialized in *The New York Weekly*, 1874.

Victor Vane, the Young Secretary (Porter & Coates) Serialized in *Golden Argosy*, 1893.

1895—*Adrift in the City* (Porter & Coates) Serialized in *The New York Weekly* as *Oliver the Outcast*, 1887.

1896—*Frank Hunter's Peril* (H. T. Coates & Co.) Serialized in *The New York Weekly*, 1886.

The Young Salesman (H. T. Coates & Co.) Serialized in *The New York Weekly*, 1894.

1897—*Frank and Fearless; or, The Fortunes of Jasper Kent* (H. T. Coates & Co.) Serialized in *The New York Weekly*, 1885.

Walter Sherwood's Probation (H. T. Coates & Co.) Serialized in *Golden Argosy*, 1890.

1898—*A Boy's Fortune; or, The Strange Adventures of Ben Baker* (H. T. Coates & Co.) Serialized in *Good News*, 1893.

The Young Bank Messenger. Reissued as *A Cousin's Conspiracy* (H. T. Coates & Co.) Serialized in *Golden Argosy*, 1898.

1899—*Rupert's Ambition* (H. T. Coates & Co.) Serialized in *Golden Argosy*, 1893.

1900—*A Debt of Honor; or, The Story of Gerald Lane's Success in the Far West* (Burt) Serialized in *Golden Argosy*, 1891.

Jed the Poorhouse Boy (H. T. Coates & Co.) Serialized in *Golden Argosy*, 1892.

1901—*Lester's Luck* (H. T. Coates & Co.) Serialized in *Golden Argosy*, 1893.

Making His Mark (Penn Publishing Co.)

1902—*A Rolling Stone; or, The Adventures of a Wanderer*. Reissued as *Wren Winter's Triumph* (Thompson and Thomas) Serialized in *Golden Argosy*, 1894, under the Putnam pseudonym.

The World Before Him. Reissued as *Making His Way* (Penn Publishing Co.) Serialized in *Golden Days*, 1880.

Tom Turner's Legacy; or, The Story of How He Secured It. Serialized in *Golden Argosy*, 1890.

Andy Grant's Pluck (Coates) Serialized in *Golden Argosy*, 1895.

1903—*Bernard Brook's Adventures; or, The Story of a Brave Boy's Trials* (Burt) Serialized in *Golden Argosy*, 1893, as *A Bad Lot*, by Arthur Lee Putnam.

Forging Ahead. Reissued as *Andy Gordon* (Penn Publishing Co.) Serialized in *Golden Days*, 1881.

Chester Rand; or, The New Path to Fortune (Coates) Serialized in *Golden Argosy*, 1892.

1904—*Finding a Fortune*. Reissued as *The Tin Box* (Penn Publishing Co.) Serialized in *Golden Days*, 1882.

1905—*Mark Manning's Mission; or, The Story of a Shoe Factory Boy* (Burt)

1906—*The Young Musician; or, Fighting His Way* (Penn Publishing Co.) Serialized in *Golden Days*, 1881.

1907—*In Search of Treasure; or, The Story of Guy's Eventful Voyage* (Burt) Serialized in *Golden Argosy*, 1894.

Wait and Win; or, The Story of Jack Drummond's Pluck. Reissued as *Work and Win* (Burt) Serialized in *Golden Argosy* as *Work and Win,* 1884.

The following titles were those written by Stratemeyer, published under Alger's name:

1900—*Out for Business; or, Robert Frost's Strange Career* (Mershon Co.)
Falling in with Fortune; or, The Experiences of a Young Secretary (Mershon Co.)

1901—*Young Captain Jack; or, The Son of a Soldier* (Mershon Co.)
Nelson the Newsboy; or, Afloat in New York (Mershon Co.)

1904—*Jerry, The Backwoods Boy; or, The Parkhurst Treasure* (Mershon Co.)
Lost at Sea; or, Robert Roscoe's Strange Cruise (Mershon Co.)

1905—*From Farm to Fortune* (Stitt & Co.)
The Young Book Agent (Stitt & Co.)

1906—*Joe, the Hotel Boy; or, Winning Out by Pluck* (Cupples & Leon Co.)
Randy of the River; or, The Adventures of a Young Deckhand (Chatterton-Peck Co.)

1908—*Ben Logan's Triumph; or, The Boys of Boxwood Academy* (Cupples & Leon)

The following titles, issued under Alger's name by various publishers, cannot be authenticated as written by Alger, and are probably spurious:

Ben Barton's Battle
Cal Cooper's Triumph
Dean Dexter
Five Hundred Dollars (may be a reissue of *The $500 Check*)
Frank Starr's Purpose
Hobart, the Hired Boy
The Last Word
The Making of a Man
Ned Nestor's Plan
Plan and Prosper
Sandy Stone

Tom Turner
Toward the Top
The Young Entertainer
The Young Soldier

These are the three Alger book-length novels which ran as serials in magazines but were never published as books:

A Fancy of Hers, an adult girls' story, published complete in *Golden Argosy,* March, 1892.

Silas Snobden's Office Boy, serialized in *Golden Argosy,* 1889.

Cast Upon the Breakers, serialized in *Golden Argosy,* 1893.

INDEX